SAINTS

and

Servants of God

S. Catherine of Siena, patroness and exemplar of both S. Rose of Lima and Bl. Columba of Rieti. The photo is of a marble bust by Jacobo della Quercia based on a death mask of S. Catherine.

Saints and Servants of God

The Lives

of

S. Rose of Lima,

of

Blessed Colomba di Rieti,

and of

S. Juliana Falconieri

Originally published in London by Thomas Richardson and Son in 1863 as part of a series edited by Fr. Frederick Faber of the Oratory, this derivative edition has been re-typeset and enhanced with one hundred thirty-three images. By and large the sketches in her biography taken from Michael A. Fuentes, *Lima, Sketches of the Capital of Peru* are intended to be evocative of Lima as St. Rose would have known it. The persons depicted are therefore types rather than persons known to St. Rose.

The very many paintings devoted to her go a long way towards capturing her spiritual life and Heavenly destiny, but Lima was–per the sketches–a very earthy place, the place where she nevertheless became a great saint.

There is little art devoted to St. Colomba, and practically all dedicated to S. Juliana recalls the remarkable circumstance of her death. The Image Index has citations for the pictures not captioned.

These lives are taken from the Oratorian Lives of the Saints edited and probably translated by Frederick W. Faber. Lee M. Gilbert is the editor in 2020.

© 2021 by Arthur M. Gilbert and Son, Publishers. All rights reserved.

www.auldsnu.com

12051 SE 31st Pl, Ste 15
Milwaukie, OR 97222

ISBN: 978-0-578-79603-1
Library of Congress Control Number:

PRINTED IN THE UNITED STATES OF AMERICA

TO

THE NUNS OF ENGLAND,

WHO SHIELD THEIR COUNTRY BY THEIR PRAYERS,

AND BY THEIR MEEK AUSTERITIES

MAKE REPARATION FOR ITS SINS;

AND TO

THE SISTERS OF MERCY,

WHOSE CHARITY IS THEIR ENCLOSURE,

WHILE FOR THE LOVE OF THEIR HEAVENLY SPOUSE

IN HIS POOR AND SUFFERING MEMBERS

THEY DENY THEMSELVES

THE PEACE AND PROTECTION OF THE CLOISTER.

> Daughters of Mary ! in retreats obscure,
> Lost to man's thought and eye, amid the trees
> And unfrequented fields, on bended knees
> Sueing for England's pardon, lives so pure
> Mingle in heaven and God's approval share
> With that uncloistered love, whose willing feet
> Are borne through jeering crowd and gazing street
> To scenes of lonely want and pining care.
> For you the holy past is now unfurled,
> That with its bright examples you may feed
> The spirit of devotion. While the world
> Honours your goodness with its hatred, you,
> Still to your high and calm vocation true,
> May win fresh light and strength from what you read.
>
> Frederick W. Faber.

PREFACE

The Life of S. Rose is translated from the French of Father Jean Baptiste Feuillet, a Dominican friar, and Missionary Apostolic in the Antilles; the copy which has been followed is the third edition, published at Paris in 1671, the year of her canonization by Clement X. *The Life of the Blessed Colomba of Rieti*, also of the third Order of S. Dominic, is translated from an Italian quarto, published at Perugia in 1777, and compiled partly from the Processes and partly from the famous MS. of Father Sebastiano degli Angeli, a Dominican friar at Perugia, and the Saint's confessor. This MS. is preserved at S. Dominic's at Perugia, and a Latin translation of it has been given by Papebroch in the *Acta Sanctorum*, the fifth vol. of May. It should be observed that Father Sebastiano (whose date is 1512) cites the testimony of Colomba's first confessor at Rieti, Father Giacomo di Castello. The reader should also be warned that several stiff and unenglish expressions, which he will find in the Life of Blessed Colomba, belong to the proper and recognized terminology of Mystical Theology, and so have been left without change, and indeed in many cases they could only have been rendered by some very circuitous paraphrase. *The Life of S. Juliana Falconieri* is translated from the Italian of Francesco Lorenzini, who dedicated his little work to Clement XII. The book was printed at Rome, without any date on the title-page, but the date of the Imprimatur of the Master of the Sacred Palace is June 15, 1737.

English readers, who may not have been in the habit of reading the Lives of the Saints, and especially the authentic

Processes of the Congregation of Sacred Rites, may be a little startled with the Life of S. Rose. The visible intermingling of the natural and supernatural worlds, which seems to increase as the saints approach through the grace of God to their first innocence, may even offend where persons have been in the habit of paring and batting down the "unearthly," in order to evade objections and lighten the load of the controversialist, rather than of meditating with awe and thankfulness and deep self-abasement on the wonders of God in His saints, or of really sounding the depths of Christian philosophy, and mastering the principles and general laws which are discernible even in the supernatural regions of hagiology.

The habit of always thinking first how any tenet, or practice, or fact, is most conveniently presentable to an adversary, may soon, and almost imperceptibly, lead to profaneness, by introducing the spirit of rationalism into matters of faith; and to judge from the works of our greatest Catholic divines, it would appear that the deeper theologian a man is, the less does he give way to this studious desire of making difficulties easy at any cost short of denying what is positively de fide. They seem to handle truth religiously just in the way that God is pleased to give it us, rather than to see what they can make of it themselves by shaping it for controversy, and so by dint of skilful manipulation squeeze it through a difficulty. The question is, not "What will men say of this? How will this sound in controversy? Will not this be objected to by heretics?" but, "Is this true? Is this kind of thing approved by the Church? Then what good can I get out of it for my own soul? Ought not my views to be deeper than they are?" The judiciousness of publishing in England what are actually classical works of piety in Catholic countries is a further question, which the result alone will decide, and that possibly at no very distant date. All that need be said here is, that it has not been done in haste, in blindness, or in heedlessness, but after grave counsel and with high sanction.

If, then, anyone unaccustomed to the literature of Catholic countries, and with their ears unconsciously untuned by the daily dissonance of the errors and unbelief around them, should be startled by this volume, let him pause before he pronounces judgment. Persons, who have unfortunately more call to defend their religion than time to study it, fancy they gain a sort of mock strength, or at least pleasantly and triumphantly surprise an adversary, when they throw overboard to his mercy, as sailors throw meat to a shark, anything wonderful, as though it were necessarily superstitious. But in this way a man may make wild work of solemn things without knowing it, and he whets rather than stays the appetite of his opponent, who presently follows him up again with a new, and, indeed, in his case, an unanswerable charge of inconsistency. A Catholic, do what he will, cannot weed his religion of the supernatural; and to discriminate between the supernatural and the superstitious is a long work and a hard one, a work of study and of reverent meditation. O how hard it is, if men do not kneel to meditate, to hear a thing denied all round them every day, and yet maintain a joyous and unshaken faith therein!

In this one volume we have two Lives, both taken from the authentic Processes: one is of a holy woman of Central Italy in the fifteenth century; the other a South American in the seventeenth; and when the series gets on, and the reader finds men and women of different centuries, and vastly different characters, of the hills of Apulia and Calabria, from the plains of Lombardy and the stony forests of Umbria; from Spanish convents and French seminaries; from the dark streets of a Flemish town, the margin of a Dutch canal, or the ilex woods of Portugal; from the cities of Germany and Hungary, or the mines and river-sides of South America; popes and simple nuns, bishops and common beggars, the learned cardinal and the Capuchin lay-brother, the aged missionary and the boy in the Jesuit novitiate, the Roman princess and the poor bed-ridden Estatica, before the Reformation and after it—all presenting us with the same picture, the same supernatural actors, the same familiarity with good and evil spirits, the same daily colloquial intercourse with the unseen world, the same apparently grotesque anecdotes of miraculous control over nature—and the Lives narrating all this, translated from four or five different languages, and composed by grave theologians and doctors—the erudite Augustinian, the judicious Dominican, the good Franciscan full of simplicity and unction, the fluent Oratorian so eminent in devotional biography, the sound, calm, discriminating Jesuit, who, above all others, has learned how to exercise the constant caution of criticism without injuring his spiritual-mindedness—when all this is before him, crowned with the solemn and infallible decrees of canonization and beatification, it may seem to him then a serious question whether he himself is not out of harmony with the mind of the Church, whether his faith is not too feeble, and his distrust of God's wonders too over-weening and too bold, whether, in short, for the good of his own soul he may not have the principle of rationalism to unlearn, and the temper of faith, sound, reasonable, masculine, yet childlike faith, to broaden, to heighten, and to deepen in himself by the very contemplation of what may now be in some degree a scandal to him—namely, *Quam mirabilis est Deus in sanctis suis.*

In order to furnish to the reader the theological view of this important question, the more important now from the envenomed determination with which the enemy of souls has recently directed his assaults against Catholic hagiology, that portion of Benedict XIVth's grand work on the Canonization of Saints, which treats of heroic virtue and what constitutes its heroicity, raptures, visions, miracles, and the tests the Church employs in the investigation of them, as well as the principles by which her decisions are guided in the discernment of spirits and all that is mystical and preternatural, is now being translated from the Latin, and will be published either in the Series or uniform with it. The theological reputation of this great modern pope renders it unnecessary to say anything of the value of a work which is as indispensable to confessors and spiritual directors, as it is important for those who wish to obtain anything like a clear insight into Christian philosophy and its connexion with theology.

There is something very consoling in observing how the great Spirit of unbelief has of late years concentrated his energies against the Catholic Saints and their wonderful biographies. It is as though amid the darkness of his clouded intelligence that fallen Ruler had shrewdly divined the road which the Holy Spirit had gone in the guidance of the Church. The revived seriousness and activity which he saw all around him, the growing glory and lustre of Holy Church, the wonderful and almost unusual outpouring of miraculous powers, the solemn exhibitions of the mysterious and the preternatural in the valleys of the Tyrol and of Tuscany, as well as elsewhere, together with the honest abandonment of the old fortresses of historical falsehood, which fall to the ground temple and tower almost daily, and the reparation which the erudition of heretic scholars is continually making to the honour and purity of the Church, even in what are called her dark ages, might seem to have bred in him a grave suspicion that controversy was outworn and its day over, and that charges, which one writer took on tradition from another, and reiterated till he came to believe them himself, had ceased, which was after all the great point, to command the belief of others. He saw that the earnestness which men began to feel about their souls would make it necessary for him to change his point of attack and his method of operations: he directed his fury therefore against the virtues and marvels of the Catholic Saints. When a blind instinct, feeling for the truth in the dark, outside the communion of the One Fold, sought a refuge in the biographies of the Saxon and Norman worthies, who were once the glory of our poor country, that moment, although uncongenial doctrine and imitation of Catholic usage had managed to obtain just an adequate amount of querulous toleration, a very torrent of profane fury and infidel reviling was poured out upon hagiology; it was like an eruption: protestantism, stung and lacerated by the burning load attempted to be put upon it, writhed with fierce and vehement contortions, and flung forth its fire and lava, like Enceladus hopelessly disquieted beneath his incumbent Etna.

Since then, still unrelieved from his prophetic fear, the Enemy of souls has directed the brilliant but shallow and ungodly eloquence of irreligious reviews against the canonized servants of God, although neither sparkling sarcasm, nor wordy antithesis, nor patronising impertinence avail to hide the foolishness, the want of depth, and the absence of all grasp of philosophical principles or sound historical learning which these poor effusions show; neither is it at all improbable that volumes of the present Series may evoke from the same baffled spirit a more bitter invective still. But what then? Is it not a consolation for us in our work to see how the Evil One dreads it by his furious warfare, and points out and magnifies its importance by his very rage against it? Now, as before, the foolishness of the cross, the simplicity of the faith, the calm trustful dignity of the Church, and the untremulous voice of her infallible decrees will prevail: the noisy profaneness will spread knowledge without impairing faith; and the lowly obscure disciples of our Blessed Lord will not be robbed of their consolation through an idle and a craven fear of provoking a pointless taunt.

We must not, therefore, necessarily conclude that scandal is being given if a clamour is raised, or if the real latent infidelity of the clamour be clothed in the pomp of sober words or frightened piety. Piety is never frightened but where faith is weak, and although it would be wicked indeed to run so much as a risk of offending out of a mere spirit of wanton enterprise, it would be worse still to impair our heritage of truth, to withhold now what the Evil One himself is showing us is needed now, and to keep profaneness quiet at the expense of His honour who worketh wonders, and the honour of those to whom we look, not only as the instruments whereby He works His wonders, but also as our advocates with His bounty and His pity, living and acting around His Throne to-day. O in how many may not weak faith be strengthened, and by how many may not dangerous and unsound principles be abandoned, and from how many minds may not stray sympathies with heresy be weeded out, and how many hearts may there not be moved to higher things, to loftier aims, to more heavenly vocations, by this exhibition of the Saints of God! How many are there who by these very Lives have been already won from their tearful wanderings to their Shepherd's fold! and how many more may not God have predestined yet to come the same sweet road under the same gentle compulsion! And while the spirits of unbelief are being strangled by the power and the simplicity of these holy ones of God in hearts and consciences here and there, surely if we have faith in our exorcisms, we shall not be alarmed if they glare and cry and menace fearfully, remembering that when the King of Saints bade the dark spirit go forth from the harmless boy, he went forth "crying out and greatly tearing him, and he became as one dead;" and it is written that at the very sight of Jesus, "when he had seen Him, immediately the spirit troubled him, and being thrown upon the ground, he rolled about foaming." There is not a word of this which is not instructive allegory to those who see it spiritually verified around them now: the presence of Jesus is first a trouble, then a pain, but a loving and merciful exorcism at the last.

F. W. Faber.

St. Wilfrid's,

Feast of Our Lady of Redemption,

1847.

La Merced, a church that S. Rose frequented

CONTENTS

THE LIFE OF S. ROSE OF LIMA

PAGE

CHAPTER I.   1
    Her country, her birth, her inclinations, and the vow of virginity which she made at the age of five years

CHAPTER II.   8
    Her obedience, the respect she had for her parents, and the assistance she rendered them

CHAPTER III.   14
    S. Rose takes the habit of the Third Order of S. Dominic, in imitation of S. Catherine of Siena, whom she had taken for her model

CHAPTER IV.   21
    Her humility, her incomparable purity of heart, and other virtues

CHAPTER V.   27
    Her fasts, her disciplines, and the other austerities with which she macerated her body

CHAPTER VI.   37
    Of the sharp-pointed crown which she wore on her head, and of the hardness of her bed

CHAPTER VII.   46
    Of her solitude, and the hermitage which she had built in her father's garden, that she might live quite separated from men

CHAPTER VIII.   53
    Jesus Christ espouses the Blessed Rose in the presence of the ever Blessed Virgin

CONTENTS

CHAPTER IX.   59
Of the close union with God to which she attained by means of mental prayer

CHAPTER X.   65
She is tormented with interior pains to so frightful a degree, that she is examined by some divines, who declare her state to be from God

CHAPTER XI.   73
Of the familiar manner in which Jesus Christ, the Blessed Virgin, S. Catherine of Siena, and her Guardian Angel conversed with her; and of the victories which she gained over the devils who tempted her

CHAPTER XII.   83
Of her invincible patience under persecution, in sickness, and in her other sufferings

CHAPTER XIII.   89
Of her love for her Divine Spouse Jesus Christ, and of the miracle which she entreated Him to work to inflame the hearts of men with His Divine love

CHAPTER XIV.   98
Of her devotion towards the most Blessed Sacrament, in defence of which she once prepared herself to suffer martyrdom

CHAPTER XV.   105
Of her devotion to an image of our Blessed Lady, to the sign of the cross, and to her dear mistress S. Catherine of Siena

CHAPTER XVI.   114
Of her zeal for the salvation of souls, and her care in assisting the poor in their sickness and necessities

CHAPTER XVII.   125
Of her confidence in God, and of the protection she received from Him in her necessities

CHAPTER XVIII.   131
God makes known to S. Rose that a monastery of nuns will be built in Lima, under the name of S. Catherine of Siena, and reveals to her several other secrets

CHAPTER XIX.   137
Of her last illness and death

CHAPTER XX.   149
Of the honour which S. Rose received after death, and of the translation of her body, which took place some time afterwards

CHAPTER XXI   162
Of the revelations which several persons had of the glory of S. Rose

CHAPTER XXII.   167
    Of the miracles which Almighty God worked through the merits of S. Rose

    1. Of the conversions which the prayers of S. Rose obtained

    2. Two dead persons raised to life, and many miraculously cured by touching the body of S. Rose, and invoking her assistance in their infirmities

    3. After S. Rose's death many sick persons were restored to health, and several women assisted in their labour, by touching her veil or some part of her dress.

    4, Several persons afflicted with dysentery, quinsy, fever, frenzy, and other maladies have been miraculously cured by earth from the sepulchre of our Saint.

    5. Pictures of S. Rose applied to persons afflicted with leprosy, quinsy, gout, headache, and other infirmities, have been the means of restoring health to them

CHAPTER XXIII.   192
    Of the efforts made at Rome to obtain from the Pope her canonization

---

THE LIFE OF THE BLESSED COLOMBA OF RIETI

PART I. WHICH CONTAINS THE LIFE WHICH COLOMBA LED IN RIETI, HER NATIVE CITY, AND DURING THE TIME WHICH PRECEDED HER ARRIVAL IN PERUGIA.

CHAPTER I.   202
    Origin, birth, and infancy of Colomba. Extraordinary events which predict her future sanctity

CHAPTER II.   207
    Colomba's childhood and youth.—Her progress in virtue.—She makes a vow of virginity during a heavenly vision

CHAPTER III.   213
    Colomba Suffers much in keeping her vow.-—She refuses the

CONTENTS

marriage arranged by her parents.— She cuts off her hair.—She is beaten by the devil

CHAPTER IV.   221
Progress of Colomba in perfection.—Her languishing love for God and hunger after the Holy Communion are refreshed from heaven.—Visions and ecstasies which she enjoys in her father's house

CHAPTER V.   227
Colomba's spiritual hunger increases and is again miraculously assuaged.—Her extraordinary rapture.—She takes the habit of the Third Order

CHAPTER VI   232
Colomba's proceedings after taking the habit.—Her pilgrimage to Viterbo, to visit our Lady "of the Oak," and the miracles which took place

CHAPTER VII   239
Miracles wrought by Colomba in Rieti.—A mysterious vision which she has there, and her wonderful departure

CHAPTER VIII   243
Extraordinary journey of Colomba to Foligno, and several miracles wrought there

PART II. OF THE LIFE OF THE VIRGIN S. COLOMBA, WHICH CONTAINS THE ACTIONS SHE PERFORMED IN PERUGIA.

CHAPTER I   249
Honourable reception given to Colomba by the Perugians.—The city opposes her departure, and the inhabitants resolve to erect a monastery for her.—Colomba makes her solemn profession

CHAPTER II   254
Of the foundation and erection of the new monastery, dedicated by Colomba to S. Catherine of Siena.—The number of sisters is multiplied.— Rule given by Colomba to the new monastery.—Prophecies and miracles wrought by our Saint

CHAPTER III   262
Suffering love of Colomba.—She takes upon her self the scourge of the plague to deliver the city of Perugia.—Persecutions and grievous calumnies endured by our Saint.—Her first public ecstasy

CHAPTER IV   269
The life and spirit of Colomba are, by an order from Rome,

made the subject of secret research, and formally examined.—The love of Colomba now appears, aspiring to the possession of God. —Her spirit of prophecy.—She foretells the time of her death

CHAPTER V — 274
Colomba's love incessantly tends towards Almighty God.—Wonderful events which occurred during the time Alexander VI remained in Perugia

CHAPTER VI — 280
Various miracles wrought by Colomba.—Prophecies, revelations, and an ecstasy which she has in public

CHAPTER VII — 286
Colomba accepts the post of prioress through obedience.—Great calumnies and persecutions which are patiently endured by our Saint.—Her self-abasement and humility

CHAPTER VIII — 292
Constant and courageous love of Colomba.—The orders from Rome which gave her pain are rescinded.—She obtains a new confessor.—She is again warned by heaven of the time of her death

CHAPTER IX — 296
Unitive love of Colomba, which is at the same time ardent and inflamed.—She prepares herself for death. - She receives a celestial gift.—Wonderful ecstasy.—Miraculous communion

CHAPTER X. — 300
Transforming love of Colomba—Her last sickness—Heavenly visions.—Her last instructions and happy passage

CHAPTER XI. — 307
Solemn obsequies rendered to Colomba.—Miracles which took place, and her burial

CHAPTER XII. — 310
Blessed Colomba appears to several persons, and revelations of her glory are made in different places. —Veneration is immediately shown to her sepulchre, and continued

CHAPTER XIII. — 317
Of the translation of the body and holy relics of the Blessed Colomba

CHAPTER XIV. — 326
Spirit of B. Colomba, drawn from the virtues she practiced

CONTENTS

THE LIFE OF S. JULIANA FALCONIERI

CHAPTER I. Which serves as a preface to the Life	335
CHAPTER II. Birth of S. Juliana, and her manner of life till the age of fourteen	347
CHAPTER III. Of S. Juliana's life, from her fourteenth year to her death	350
CHAPTER IV. Of S. Juliana's happy death	367
CHAPTER V. Of the miracles and graces granted by God, through the intercession of S. Juliana	375
CHAPTER VI The last chapter, which serves as an epilogue	387
A Devout Exercise in Honour of S. Juliana Falconieri	394
Image Index	402

An harquebusier

Publishers Note Regarding the Life of S. Rose.

To give the reader some further context for St. Rose's life, she was the daughter of a retired harquebusier in the Spanish Imperial Army, M Gaspar de Flores de la Puente, who was born about 1530 in Extremadura Spain, from which area came also Pizarro, Cortes and de Soto. On May 1st, 1577, he married Maria de Oliva Herrera (1559-1637) in the Sagrario in Lima. S. Rose was the fourth of nine children. She and her siblings in order are:

Gaspar Flores de Oliva 1579-

Bernardina Flores de Oliva 1581-ca 1596

Hernando Flores de Oliva 1584-1627

Isabel (Rose) Flores de Oliva 1586-1617

Francisco Flores de Oliva 1590-

Juana Flores de Oliva 1592-

Antonio Flores de Oliva 1594-

Andres Flores de Oliva 1596-

Francisco Matia Flores de Oliva †

Jacinta Flores de Oliva 1603-

The population of Lima in 1600 was about 26,000. Lima has only 1300 hours of sunshine a year.

During her sojourn there was a relatively enormous presence of religious in Lima. The Dominicans, for example, had 250 friars in their convent, and the Franciscans, Augustinians and Jesuits were also there in large numbers.

St. Turibius of Mogrovejo was her archbishop until she was twenty years old, for he reigned from 1581 to 1606. St. Martin de Porres was also a contemporary and fellow citizen of Lima, for he was born December 9, 1579, in Lima, and he died there November 3, 1639. Although he receives no mention in Feuillet's account, he surely would have been known to her for he was a fellow Dominican and well-known in the city for his charitable works, as was she.

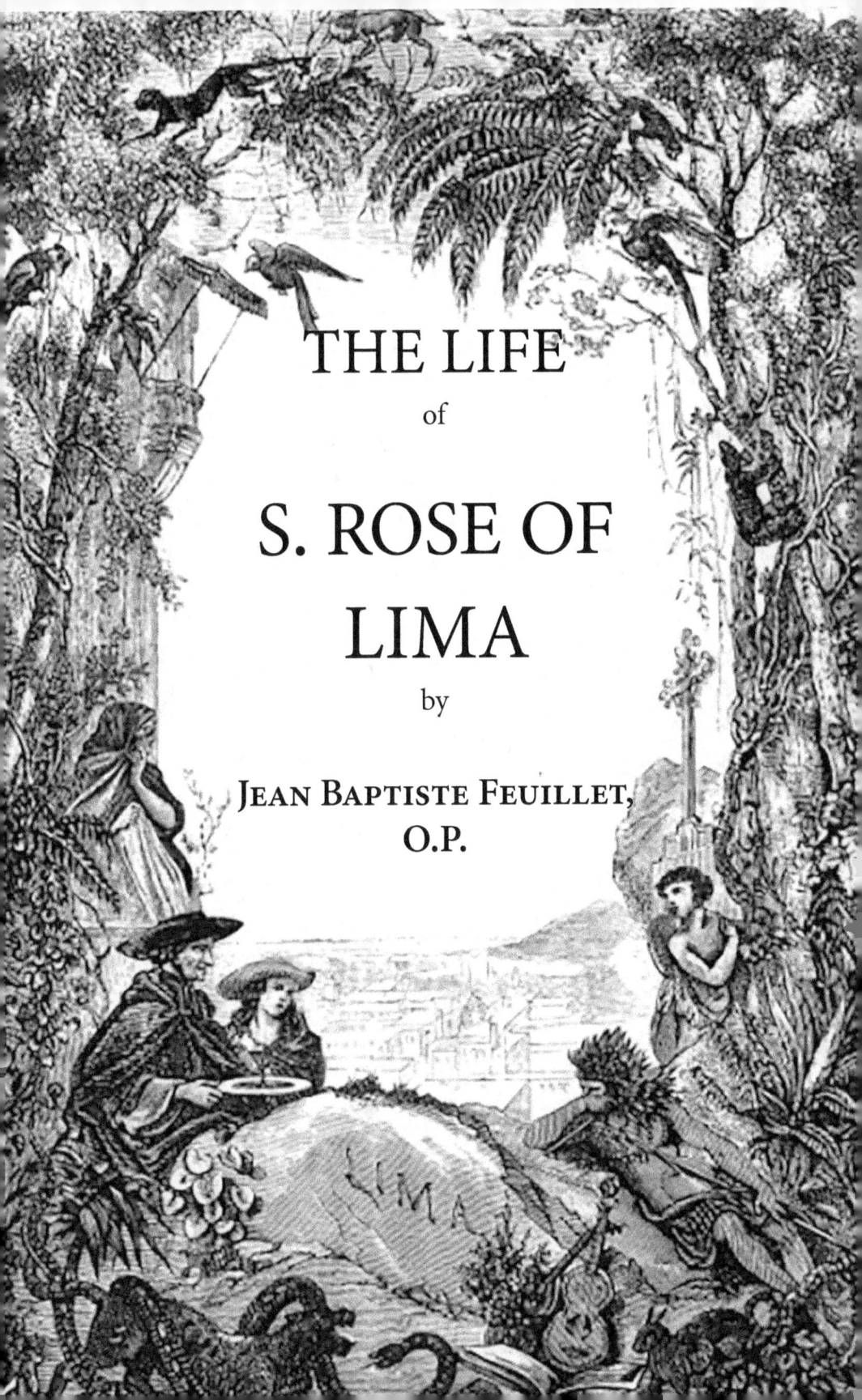

THE LIFE
of
S. ROSE OF LIMA
by
Jean Baptiste Feuillet, O.P.

THE LIFE
OF
SAINT ROSE OF LIMA.

CHAPTER I

HER COUNTRY, HER BIRTH, HER DISPOSITIONS, AND THE VOW OF VIRGINITY WHICH SHE MADE AT THE AGE OF FIVE YEARS

Our blessed Rose, the first spiritual flower which Divine Providence planted and cultivated in the richest part of the New World, was born on the 20th day of April, in the year 1586, at Lima, the capital of Peru in South America. Her father was Gasper Florez, and her mother Mary Oliva, both more considerable by their birth than by their fortune. This virtuous woman, who had been several times in danger of losing her life, by the excessive pains she had endured during her other confinements, was happily preserved from them at the birth of our Saint, who came into the world differently from other children, wrapped up in a double cuticle, like a rose, whose bud is surrounded by leaves as soon as it begins to appear.

The lady Isabel of Herrera, her mother's sister, being chosen as her godmother, gave her the name of Isabel in baptism; but three months after, as she slept in her cradle, her mother and several other persons, who did not all belong to the family, having perceived on her countenance a beautiful rose, she was called from that time by no other name than Rose, on account of this prodigy.

Her godmother, thinking herself slighted by this change of name, was offended at it, and lived at variance with her sister, till Divine Providence, who watched over the interests of our Saint, put an end to this unhappy dispute, by inspiring his Lordship, the Archbishop of Lima, to give her the name of Rose in confirmation.

Rose, when older, had some scruple about it, on learning that it was not the name she had received in baptism; she thought it was an effect of the complaisance or of the vanity of her parents, who wished to make her beauty more attractive by this agreeable name. Disturbed by this conduct, which she thought unworthy of the spirit of a Christian, she went to the Church of the Friars Preachers; and having entered the Chapel of the Rosary, she cast herself at the feet of the Blessed Virgin, to make known to her her uneasiness. Our Blessed Lady immediately consoled her, assuring her that the name of Rose was pleasing to her Son Jesus Christ and that, as a mark of her affection, she would also honour her with her own name, and that henceforward she should be called Rose of S. Mary. So that we may say, that of all the saints whose names Almighty God has changed by an extraordinary favour, our blessed Rose is the first, and perhaps the only one, whose surname has been also changed by heaven.

Her infancy had a lively resemblance to that of the seraphic saint, Catherine. Never was she troublesome by annoying cries; and never was she seen to shed tears, excepting once, when her nurse had carried her to a neighbouring house, where this sweet child wept, as if to show her sorrow in being taken from her solitude, the sweetness of which she began to taste, in the house of her father. The holy Fathers teach

us, that the just man cannot do or suffer anything virtuously without the help of grace, but that Almighty God works by His grace many wonders in His saints without their co-operation.

This was shown in the blessed Rose, who when only three months old gave proof of a heroic patience: for, some one having thoughtlessly pinched her thumb, by shutting a chest hastily, she concealed the pain it gave her. Her mother having hastened to her at the first news of the accident, she hid the finger, and did not let it appear that she had been hurt. The injury grew worse afterwards from her silence, and violent remedies were necessary, which caused her to lose a part of the nail. The surgeon employed pincers to extract by the roots that part which still remained in the flesh, and was greatly surprised to remark, that, during this painful operation, she did not shed a tear, utter a scream, or even change countenance.

It was not on this occasion alone that she gave proof of her patience; she practised it equally whenever she had anything to suffer. She endured, with an inconceivable constancy, the pain inflicted by cutting off with scissors part of her ear which had become corrupted. At the age of four years she was troubled with a sort of disorder in the head, and her mother, who loved her tenderly, wishing to dress it herself, used a certain powder, so corrosive and burning, that it caused her to shudder from head to foot; still she never complained, though this remedy caused a number of ulcers in her head, which gave her excessive pain.

As coral hardens in the waves, which are the emblem of affliction, so we might say, that the patience of our Saint increased with the greatness of her sufferings; for, during six weeks, the surgeon who attended her cut off every day a portion of flesh, that a new skin might grow in its place, and she suffered this torture with invincible patience.

Almighty God, who designed her to be a living image of His crucified life, did not leave her long without suffering, and He permitted that two years after she should be afflicted with a polyp in her nose, which grew so large that they had recourse to the surgeon to remove it, which he did in three different operations, during which she evinced a super-human patience, suffering this pain with a joy that seemed miraculous, and much resembled that which many martyrs have shown in the dreadful torments inflicted upon them by their executioners.

This early apprenticeship in the school of Calvary, where she learned from Jesus Christ Crucified, to suffer all sorts of pains and afflictions, disposed our young Rose to offer to God, from her infancy, the agreeable odour of the ardent charity with which her heart was inflamed.

She received most happily the first rays of Divine grace, and her little brother contributed to this; for playing near her one day, he threw accidentally a quantity of mud on her hair. Being naturally neat, she was vexed at his carelessness, and was on the point of going away; when he said to her with a gravity beyond his years, "My dear sister, do not be angry at this accident, for the curled ringlets of girls are hellish cords, which bind the hearts of men, and miserably draw them into eternal flames."

Rose received these words, which he uttered with the zeal of a preacher, as an oracle from Heaven: she entered into herself, and renouncing for ever the vanities of the world, she gave herself entirely to God, and conceived an extreme horror for sin. From that time she felt herself powerfully drawn to prayer; and she applied herself to it so assiduously, that she was not content with giving to it part of the day, and the greatest part of the night; we may even say, that sleep was no interruption to her prayer, for her imagination represented to her during her repose the absorbing idea she had formed to herself of her Divine Spouse in the fervour of her prayers, and of her converse with Him during the day.

In this sacred intercourse she received a lively inspiration from Almighty God to follow in the footsteps of S. Catherine

of Siena, by a perfect imitation of the virtues of this seraphic lover of God. And because virginity, joined to baptismal innocence and to the flower of youth, is a double lily, which sheds its splendour on the spouses of Jesus Christ; so Rose, moved by the spirit of God, consecrated to Him irrevocably and by vow, at the age of five years, her virginal purity, by the promise she gave Him never to have any other Spouse but Him alone. Thus we may say of S .Rose, what S. Ambrose said of S. Agnes, that her piety and virtue were above her years, and beyond the strength of nature.

As soon as she had made this vow, she cut off her hair, unknown to her mother, in order to manifest to the Spouse she had chosen, that by thus disfiguring herself she intended rather to disgust than to please men; and that she absolutely renounced the world, with which she never wished to have any intercourse. We learn from the testimony of her confessors, that she began to have the use of reason when this heavenly ardour filled her soul; and this generous action was so pleasing to Almighty God, that He showered down upon her His choicest benedictions, and enriched her with so many graces, that she preserved her baptismal innocence till her death.

The cathedral of Lima and its Sagrario where Gaspar Flores and María de Oliva y Herrera were married

CHAPTER II

HER OBEDIENCE, THE RESPECT SHE HAD FOR HER PARENTS, AND THE ASSISTANCE SHE RENDERED THEM.

To obey the parents from whom we have received our life, is only the effect of an ordinary degree of virtue; and there would have been nothing remarkable in the obedience of the blessed Rose, if she had contented herself with simply fulfilling this duty; but she infinitely increased its merit by perfectly complying with that which she owed to her parents, without failing to accomplish what Almighty God required of her. She managed so well, that she executed whatever her father and mother commanded her, without omitting the least part of her duty towards God. Her mother, like many others who love their children more for the world than for heaven, often begged her to take care of her beauty, and even desired her to use cosmetics and paint to preserve its freshness; but Rose, who knew this to be contrary to modesty and simplicity, which are the only ornaments of Christian beauty, entreated her so earnestly not to oblige her to do this, and not to imitate these mothers who sacrifice the salvation of their children to their own ambition, that she, by degrees, induced her to think differently; thus making the law of the spirit victorious over that of the flesh, and causing the secret aversion with which her Divine Spouse inspired her for this worldly custom, to triumph over the unjust command she had received to conform to it.

Another time her mother made her wear a garland of flowers on her head. Not thinking herself strong enough to effect a change in this command, she obeyed; but she sanctified her submission by the painful mortification with which she accompanied it: for God having brought to her mind the remembrance of the cruel thorns which had composed His crown in His Passion, she took the garland, and fixed it on her head with a large needle, which she plunged so deeply into her head, that it could not be drawn out without the help of a surgeon, who had much difficulty in doing it. Thus she contrived to elude without resisting the orders of her mother, when they were openly opposed to the law of God, and she punished herself severely when she obeyed her in anything that partook of the vanity of the world. This fidelity was most pleasing to her Divine Spouse, and she perceived by a remarkable circumstance, that she could not in the least depart from it without offending Him.

One day, having put on a pair of scented gloves in order to oblige her mother, she had no sooner begun to wear them than her hands became cold and benumbed, and soon after she felt in them so violent a heat, that notwithstanding the love of our Saint for suffering, she was obliged to take off the gloves, which caused this torture; and God, to show the blessed Rose that the little breath of vanity which had induced her, under the specious pretext of obedience, to wear these gloves, had inflamed the zeal of her Divine Spouse, showed her the same gloves in the night surrounded by flames. From that time she never obeyed her mother in anything that was agreeable to the world or to nature, without joining some act of mortification to her obedience. Her mother having absolutely commanded her to remove the pieces of wood which she had secretly put into her pillow, she did so; but she put in their place so great a quantity of wool, and stuffed it in such a manner, that her pillow, from its hardness, might have been taken for a log of wood covered with linen.

The stratagem which she practised in order to avoid appearing at assemblies, or accompanying her mother in the visits she paid to her friends and relations, was not less surprising; for she rubbed her eyelids with pimento, which is a very sharp burning sort of Indian pepper: by this means she escaped going into company, for it made her eyes red as fire, full of tears, and so painful, that she could not bear the light. Her mother having found out this artifice, reprimanded her for it, and mentioned the example of Ferdinand Perez, who had lost his sight by a similar act of indiscretion; Rose answered modestly, "It would be much better for me, my dear mother, to be blind all the rest of my life, than to be obliged to see the vanities and follies of the world."

After this answer, her mother seeing clearly that it was a repugnance for these visits, and for the dress she was compelled to wear on these occasions, which caused her to inflict this pain on herself, no longer urged her to accompany her, and allowed her to dress as she liked, in a poor stuff dress, which she wore with great satisfaction, for she sought nothing but contempt and abjection. In all indifferent things S. Rose obeyed willingly, and never received a command from her mother which she did not cheerfully fulfil. Her mother wishing one day to try her obedience, ordered her to embroider some flowers in the wrong way: Rose obeyed blindly, and spoiled her work, and her mother, feigning to be angry, reproved her for it. This truly obedient daughter answered, that she had perceived that her work was good for nothing, but had not dared to disobey the order given her; that it was of no consequence to her in what manner she traced a flower, but that she could not fail in obedience to her mother's orders. For this reason she never began her work without asking her mother's leave, and she told one of her friends, who seemed astonished at it, that she did it expressly to join to her work the merit of obedience.

Her obedience did not concern her mother only, to whom she was so submissive that she never drank without her permission, and dared not begin her work without her express order: it extended even to the servant of the house, whom she respected as her mistress, and whom she obeyed always joyfully, particularly when she was cross and ill-tempered.

Her mother, who was of a bilious temperament and often angry, sometimes forbade her to drink; and as she did not know that her virtuous daughter never would drink without her permission, Rose was often known to pass six days without drinking. Her parents having taken her to Canta, a very unhealthy part of the country, she was seized with a contraction of the nerves in her hands and feet, and as this arose from cold her mother made her wear skins, the hair of which was very irritating, and desired her not to take them off. Rose bore with them for several days, without mentioning the insupportable heat they caused, that she might not be wanting in obedience; but her hands and feet became so inflamed in consequence, that numbers of little blisters were formed in them, which afterwards became very painful ulcers.

Obedience generally terminates with life, but the blessed Rose manifested it even when in her tomb. The mother prioress of the Convent of Nuns of S. Dominic at Lima, commanded the picture of Rose, in virtue of the obedience which every one in the house owed to her, to enable them to find a silver spoon which a servant belonging to the monastery had lost, that they might avoid any rash judgment of innocent persons; and as if our Saint had animated the colours of her picture with that spirit of obedience, which had made her so submissive to God, and to His creatures for His love, the prioress perceived immediately on the table the lost spoon, and we might say, that the picture placed it there, to represent the perfect obedience of its original.

Who could express her exact obedience to her parents

during her whole life, her respect and the tender love she bore them? At the times when she was suffering most from weakness, she generally spent more than half the night in working to help them in their necessities, and though she devoted twelve hours every day to mental prayer, she did more work than another, who had less to do, would have done in four days, and her work had so much beauty and delicacy that it seemed to surpass art and nature.

She was a perfect mistress of needlework, either in designing flowers or executing them in embroidery or in tapestry; and what is surprising is, that though her mind was often elevated to God and absorbed in the contemplation of His perfections while she was working, yet her hand guided her work as perfectly as if her mind were solely intent upon it.

Besides her needlework she cultivated a little garden, in which she grew violets and other flowers, which she sold to help her parents in their necessities; and as all her industry was insufficient to save them from poverty, she confessed ingenuously to a great servant of God, that Jesus Christ her Divine Spouse supplied the deficiency by secret and wonderful means. She tended them in sickness with incredible assiduity; she was always at their bedside, she passed days and nights there, and only left them to perform for them elsewhere some other service. She made their bed, prepared their medicine, and was ready by day and by night to perform for them the vilest and most difficult services.

I must not conclude this chapter without speaking of the ineffable joy she procured for her mother-who would otherwise have been overwhelmed with grief, in seeing her depart out of this life. This blessed Saint, when on her death-bed, foreseeing the anguish her mother would feel at her death, earnestly begged her Divine Spouse to console her in this affliction; and He did so by bestowing upon her so great a plenitude of joy, that she juridically deposed that she felt an extraordinary joy when this death took place, which would otherwise have drawn from her abundance of tears and sighs. She further testified, that this favour not only rendered her insensible to this great loss, but took possession of her mind so powerfully, that for several days she could scarcely bear its violence, and that Almighty God had shown her, by this experience, the happiness which her holy daughter enjoyed in heaven, and the torrent of delights .which He poured out upon her soul in that happy abode.

San Sebastian, where S. Rose was baptized

CHAPTER III

S. ROSE TAKES THE HABIT OF THE THIRD ORDER OF S. DOMINIC, IN IMITATION OF S. CATHERINE OF SIENA, WHOM SHE HAD TAKEN FOR HER MODEL.

If anyone should attempt to compare the lives of S. Catherine of Siena and of S. Rose, he would find so great a resemblance between these two lovers of the Son of God, that he would have some difficulty in discovering whether this sweet flower sprang forth in the Indies, or whether it was transplanted from Italy into Peru; for in S. Rose all the characteristics of S. Catherine of Siena were to be seen, the same manner of living, the same inclinations, the same favours from God, and so great a similarity in figure and countenance, that one might easily have been taken for the other.

S. Rose having cut off her hair after making her vow of virginity, seemed thereby to have deprived anyone who might seek her in marriage of the hope of succeeding in this design. But the advantages she had received from nature, offered an innocent opposition to the resolution she had made to preserve until death the precious lily of her virginity; for her extreme beauty, the refinement of her mind, her delightful conversation, and her virtue itself, captivated many hearts by their charms, and drew towards her admirers from all parts.

In order to extinguish these rising flames in the hearts of others, she invented all sorts of means to disfigure herself;

S. Rose rejects a suitor

she made her face pale and livid with fasting, she sought to destroy her delicate white complexion, she washed her hands in hot lime to take the skin off them; and to prevent others from feeling any pleasure to which the sight of her might give rise, she shut herself up closely in the house, and went out but very seldom, and when it was quite necessary; and having been taken to Canta, a little village near one of the most celebrated mines in Peru, she remained there four entire years without leaving the house; she would not even go to see a beautiful garden, close to the door of the house where she lived, from which she might have easily viewed these famous machines called moles, for which Peru is renowned.

Notwithstanding all these precautions, she was not able to prevent several persons from seeking her in marriage. Amongst others, one of the most distinguished ladies in the city, as much delighted with her virtue as with her beauty, wished her only son to marry her; she openly made the request to S. Rose's parents, who having eleven children to provide for, received the proposal most favourably, thinking the alliance would be very advantageous to their family.

Rose was the only person to whom this offer was disagreeable; she blamed herself for it, and that frail beauty which brought upon her this great misfortune; and seeing that there was no means of escaping, but by openly declaring that she would never consent to marry, having a horror of the very thought of it, she made known her resolution with a firmness which surprised her parents, though it did not make them give up the hope of inducing her to comply with their wishes. They employed threats and caresses, and seeing her inflexible in her resolutions, they tried the effects of ill-treatment, they gave her blows, and loaded her with injuries; in a word, S. Rose had the same sufferings to endure, as were inflicted on S. Catherine of Siena by her mother, for a similar reason.

After this storm, she sought in the third order of S. Dominic, a port where she might be secure all the rest of her life from the furious tempests which the devil would be sure to raise against her purity as long as she remained in the world. When her resolution was known, the nuns of the most celebrated monasteries in

St. Turibius of Mogrovejo

Lima wished her to take their habit. Monsignor Turibius, the Archbishop of Lima, requested her to enter a convent of S. Clare, which his niece, Mary de Quignonez, had just finished building, that thus she might be the foundation-stone of the holy edifice; but Rose, who, from the age of five years, had proposed to herself S. Catherine of Siena as the model for her imitation, thought it was not sufficient to copy her innocence and her other virtues, but that she must embrace the same state of life, which would not prevent her from continuing to assist her parents.

Almighty God confirmed her in this resolution by two miracles. The first took place when she had the intention of going to the Monastery of the Incarnation, where the nuns were anxiously expecting her. Before setting out she went to bid farewell to our Blessed Lady in the Chapel of the Rosary, belonging to the convent of S. Dominic, and there remained immovable on her knees at the foot of the altar; when her prayer was finished, although she made several efforts to rise, she could not succeed; she called her brother, who was in the church, to her assistance; he took her hand, and pulled her violently without being able to move her from the spot; this appearing to her to be a sign from heaven, she resolved not to prosecute her design, but to return home. She had no sooner come to this determination than she was able to rise and leave the chapel without difficulty.

Almighty God showed her by another miracle that He would have her choose the order of Friars Preachers in preference to any other, in imitation of S. Catherine of Siena, who was one of its brightest ornaments. Amongst the almost innumerable quantity of differently coloured butterflies which are to be seen in Lima, one, prettily marked with white and black, the colours of the habit of S. Dominic's order, came and fluttered round her; she considered this as a heavenly indication that she was to accomplish the design she had formerly conceived of becoming a religious in the third order of this great patriarch. She received the habit solemnly at the age of twenty years from the hands of the Rev. Father Alphonso Velasquez, on the 10th day of August, 1606, with much satisfaction; but she would have quitted it before her profession for three reasons, if she had not been specially guided by Almighty God, whose will it was that she should remain in the order of S. Dominic.

In the first place, Don Gonzalez, a very great benefactor of hers, and who possessed great influence over her mind, pressed her earnestly to become a discalced Carmelite, offering to procure her the necessary portion, and assigning as his reason that a cloistered life was more suitable to her than remaining with her parents amid the bustle of the world.

Secondly, she thought that as she wore a white habit this dress required greater innocence than hers; and that as her life did not come up to the perfection of this new state, she was deceiving the world by a false appearance of virtue under this holy habit.

Thirdly, as she had only quitted her secular dress that she might live unknown and forgotten by men, she was surprised to find that her new state of a religious person, instead of

SHE BECOMES A DOMINICAN

keeping her concealed, showed her forth as a light in the House of God, and that her reputation was so universally diffused through the town, that she was the only subject of conversation, was pointed out in the streets, distinguished from others, and praised by every one. Her modesty suffered inconceivable pain from these praises, especially when she knew that some pious persons, from the high esteem they had of her virtue, did not hesitate to compare her to S. Catherine of Siena. Though these applauses gave her so much pain, she still persevered in wearing the habit she had obtained from heaven by so many signs; for having conceived the design of quitting it in order to live more concealed, she went to kneel before the altar of the Holy Rosary to visit the Blessed Virgin, her usual refuge in the hour of distress, and as soon as she began her prayer she became sweetly insensible. These who were in the chapel concluded immediately that she was in a rapture, and,

She takes the Dominican habit

observing her closely, they remarked that her countenance changed, being first pale, and then becoming fiery, and so luminous that it sent forth rays of brightness on every side. When she came to herself after this ecstasy, she made known by the words which she poured forth from the abundance of her heart, that Almighty God had confirmed her entrance into that holy order, and that she was resolved to live and die in it.

S. Dominic de Guzman as Pentitent

CHAPTER IV

HER HUMILITY, HER INCOMPARABLE PURITY OF HEART, AND OTHER VIRTUES.

Humility, which the holy fathers have always considered as the foundation of the other Christian virtues, was so deeply rooted in the soul of S. Rose, that her labours seem to have been directed all her life to the contempt of herself, and to the practice of every sort of humiliation and abjection.

To satisfy this predominant inclination of her heart, she did not find it sufficient to choose as her employment the vilest occupations of the house, she considered herself infinitely below the servant; and this sentiment of her miseries and unworthiness induced her often to cast herself at the feet of a poor country girl named Marianne, who worked in the house, and entreat her earnestly to strike her, to spit upon her, to trample her under foot, and to treat her as the most abject and contemptible creature in the world. When she received blows or harsh words on account of the retired life she led, she thought she well deserved them, and that by her own fault she had brought on herself this injurious treatment, and she suffered it with humility and patience. When any misfortune happened to the country or to her family, she attributed it to her sins, which had drawn down this chastisement from heaven; and her humility made her usually say that she was a burden, useless to the world and odious to nature; that she was unworthy to see the light; that she was a sink of corruption infecting the air; and that she was surprised that Almighty God did not cause the earth to open and swallow up so unhappy a creature, who for her enormous offences deserved to be annihilated.

As she was deeply penetrated with a sense of her own nothingness and misery, it was to her an insupportable cross to see herself honoured; her humility could not bear to hear a word of praise; and on this account hearing one day Michael Garrez, canon of the cathedral of Lima, who had come to visit Don Gonzalez, her intimate friend, praising her in the course of the conversation, and extolling the favours she had received from Almighty God, she retired into her chamber, where she began to strike her breast, to weep and to groan in the presence of God; and to punish herself for giving, as she thought, a false opinion of herself to men, she gave herself several violent blows on the head, to force in more deeply the iron points of the crown which she always wore concealed under her veil.

Having once performed an heroic act of virtue in something very difficult and repugnant to nature, the wife of Don Gonzalez, fearing that she would injure her health very much by these laborious works, spoke to her confessor, the Rev. Father Alphonso Velasquez, and begged him to reprimand her severely for it, and to forbid her to attempt works of piety beyond her strength. He followed this advice, reproving her for her action, and desiring her to perform nothing extraordinary, capable of injuring her health. S. Rose received this reproof respectfully, rejoicing before God to see herself despised, and to find humiliation in these acts of virtue from which she had so much reason to fear vain-glory and the esteem of men.

During the three last years of her life, which she spent with Don Gonzalez, she obeyed his children, and all his servants; she did nothing without his express permission; and her humility often made her ask on her knees for a little water for the love of God, like a beggar, whose only means of subsistence is from the alms given him. In the time of sickness she usually concealed the greater part of her sufferings; but when her symptoms and weakness made them evident, she spoke of them as the just reward of her sins; and when she made known the insupportable pains she endured in every part of her body, she did so to make others consider her as an abominable sinner, whom Almighty God chastised thus rigorously in punishment of the crimes she had committed.

She was not only thoroughly persuaded herself, that she was infinitely guilty in the sight of Almighty God; but scarcely anyone else, who saw her at confession, and witnessed the abundance of tears she shed at the feet of the priest, and heard the half-stifled sobs to which her contrite heart gave vent, would have failed to take her for some public sinner, doing penance for her crimes. Yet she never committed one single sin capable of destroying the grace of God in her soul. She led so pure and innocent a life that her confessors had often great difficulty in finding matter for absolution in these things of which she accused herself with so many tears.

She kept so strict a watch over herself, that she was never heard to speak one word louder than another, or to find the least fault with the conduct or actions of others. There was nothing in her behaviour that could give annoyance to these with whom charity or duty obliged her to converse; on the contrary, her sweet and obliging manners made her so agreeable to every one, that it was commonly said, that the name of "Rose" did not suit her, because she had not its thorns.

Her charity towards mankind was so universal that this queen of the virtues seemed to be the soul which animated her words, her actions, and her whole conduct. This love which she had for God and her neighbour filled her whole heart, and had so entirely disengaged it from earthly things, that she was insensible to the pleasures which most men love so passionately. Being asked one day if, in the midst of the

The Church of S. Agustin, one of several S. Rose visited frequently.

delights and consolations which Almighty God infused abundantly into her soul, she did not feel her heart attached to worldly things, she confessed that it was impossible for her to think of them, or to take the least pleasure in them.

By this detachment from creatures, she attained to a purity of heart, in some degree similar to that which the angels possess by the privilege of their nature; for during the course of her life, which lasted thirty-one years, she never was guilty of any venial sin of impurity; and, what is quite miraculous, she was never assailed with impure thoughts, from which even the most cherished and favoured saints of God have not been exempt. Eleven learned religious, six of the order of Friars Preachers, and five Jesuits, who have several times heard her general confessions, have deposed this on their oath.

After her face had become emaciated, and had lost its beauty from the effects of fasting, penances, and cold water, which she poured so abundantly over her body that she nearly extinguished its natural heat, every one seeing the condition to which her austerities had reduced her, held her in greater veneration than ever; and she was considered in Lima as a living image of the penitential life led by the anchorites who have sanctified the deserts by their great mortifications. As her humility feared nothing so much as this universal esteem, and her modesty suffered greatly from these applauses, she had recourse to prayer, to put an end to the cause of them; and she obtained by her prayers the restoration of the brightness of her eyes, and of that brilliant complexion which her austerities had destroyed, so that she became as fresh and beautiful as before; and it happened, one Good Friday, as she was returning home from the church at noon, with a colour on her cheeks that heightened the beauty which Almighty God had given back to her, some young libertines who saw her pass, surprised to see her looking so well, railed at her for it, as if she were returning from some feast, where she had been enjoying herself, and insolently asked her, if that were the manner in which devout people fasted; yet she had fasted all Lent, on orange pippins and water, and had just spent thirty hours in tears, prayers, and groans in the church of S. Dominic, without eating or drinking.

She was still more careful to hide from the eyes of men the spiritual graces and favours she received from God, and fearing they might be perceived in spite of all the precautions she took to keep them secret, she earnestly begged Him from her infancy, not to allow the graces He bestowed upon her to be known by men; and this having been granted by her Divine Spouse, we may easily believe that she kept to herself the greatest part of the extraordinary things that passed in her interior, and that her directors were only made acquainted with the least part of the graces she received from heaven.

We cannot be surprised at this, since the blessed Spirits, taking the part of her modesty, assisted her to hide her virtues, as is shown in the following example. One day, when she was at church, she remembered having left her discipline on her table, and as her door did not shut, she was seized with great apprehension, that some one belonging to the house would perceive this dear instrument of penance. In this uneasiness, she formed a wish within herself, that the Blessed Virgin would put it in a certain place in her room, which she interiorly pointed out to her. Returning home, she did not find her discipline where she had left it, but saw to her astonishment, that this sweet and compassionate Queen of Heaven, to satisfy her desire, and take away her fear, had shut it up in the place which she had thought of.

CHAPTER V

HER FASTS, HER DISCIPLINES, AND THE OTHER AUSTERITIES WITH WHICH SHE MACERATED HER BODY.

All the graces which Christians receive, being derived from the torn and wounded Heart of the Son of God, inspire them with a love of sufferings, and make them practise austerities so frightful, that their innocent excess in the use of them can only be excused by the necessity which baptism imposes, of dying with Him on the cross in order to reign with Him in heaven; for they know that their predestination to eternal happiness includes these mortifications, which are to assimilate them to Jesus Christ, their Head; for this reason S. Paul considers this spirit of penance in Christians, as the special characteristic of their sanctity, when he says that they that are Christ's crucify the flesh, with its vices and concupiscences.

This love of the cross was so ardent in the soul of S. Rose, that the reader would scarcely give credit to that part of her life which treats of her fasts and other mortifications, if we could not assure him, that all which is related has been taken from the juridical informations of the examination, made by the Pope's express order, that he might proceed to her beatification.

She arrived at an astonishing degree of abstinence, by the same means which S. Catherine of Siena employed. From her

S. Rose as penitent

infancy she abstained from all sorts of fruits, which are delicious in Peru. At six years of age she began to fast, three days a week, on bread and water. At fifteen she made a vow never to eat meat, unless she were obliged by these who had authority over her, and whom she thought she could not disobey without sin. When her mother took her with her to dine with some ladies of rank, who invited them out of devotion, and obliged her to eat meat at their table, her obedience caused her a pain in the chest, which brought on fever and other dangerous symptoms.

The same thing happened when meat was ordered for her by physicians: and so far was it from doing her any good, that it always made her relapse into a more dangerous state. The most expeditious method of relieving and curing her on these occasions, was to give her a piece of brown bread soaked in water; and experience proved, in several instances, that this diet restored her to her original health. Her mother, who only looked upon her with the eyes of flesh and blood, seeing her face pale and disfigured, blamed her conduct, and even wished to persuade her that she committed a mortal sin, by thus denying herself the necessary nourishment for the preservation of life. To prevent her from continuing this manner of living, she obliged her to sit at table with the rest of the family, but this enlightened daughter contrived to elude her vigilance, by begging the servant to offer her only a sort of dish made without salt, composed of a crust of coarse bread, and a handful of very bitter herbs. This food was so bad and disagreeable, that she found a voluntary mortification at the same table where others sought to gratify their appetites. She was accustomed herself to gather wild herbs in the forest, and to cultivate them carefully in her garden, that she might have the materials for her self-denial always ready at hand.

She hid under the largest tufts of these plants a vessel full of sheep's gall, with which she sprinkled her food, and washed her mouth every morning. One of her favourite repasts, which seemed to her the most delicious, as it was the bitterest, was to eat the leaves of that creeping plant, the granadille, whose flowers represent so perfectly the crown of thorns, the nails, the pillar, and the other instruments of the Passion of the Son of God, that it is commonly called the " Passion Flower" in Europe: so that we can scarcely tell whether eating or abstinence was the greatest mortification to her. Her fast was so severe and rigorous, that in twenty-four hours she took nothing but a piece of bread and a little water. These who have visited America, and felt its burning heats, will acknowledge that our Saint suffered by these austere fasts a martyrdom of which we can have no idea; for the extreme heat that prevails in that burning climate exhausts the strength so much, that it is necessary to eat frequently, as a preservative against weakness.

She had accustomed herself to fast in this manner, especially the few last years of her life; she observed very exactly the seven months' fast of her order, from the festival of the Exaltation of the Holy Cross till Easter. From the beginning of Lent, she left off bread, contenting herself with a few orange pippins every day of the forty that are consecrated to penance; on Fridays she took only five; during the rest of the year, she eat so little, that what she took in eight days was scarcely sufficient nourishment for twenty-four hours.

She was known to make a moderate sized loaf and a pitcher of water last fifty days. One time she remained seven weeks without drinking a drop of water or any other liquor; and towards the end of her life she very often passed several successive days without eating or drinking. She frequently shut herself up on Thursday in her oratory, and remained there till Saturday without food or sleep, and so completely absorbed in God in a sort of ecstasy, that she continued there immovable, and as if incapable of rising from the place where she was praying on her knees. She once passed eight entire days without any food but the bread of angels which she received in the holy communion; and her supernatural abstinence was so well known to all the inhabitants of Lima, that they were aware that she passed weeks without eating or drinking, and that when necessity compelled her to drink a little water to assuage the burning heat which consumed her, she took it warm, to mortify sensuality in the pleasure she might have felt from drinking cold water.

That which seems miraculous in her austerities is, that our Saint derived more strength from her fasts than from the nourishment she took; for while she deprived herself of natural food, she imbibed from the sacred Wound of the adorable Heart of Jesus Christ, like S. Catherine of Siena, a delicious nectar which strengthened her more efficaciously than the most solid nourishment could have done.

It was no less astonishing that she could find room on her emaciated body to engrave in it by her disciplines the wounds of the Son of God; and that she should have been able to draw from it these streams of blood which she every day caused to flow; with iron chains and her other instruments of penance, she practised such terrible austerities that her confessors were obliged to restrict her in the use of them. After she became a nun she was not content with a common sort of discipline; she made one for herself of two iron chains, with which she gave herself such blows every night, that her blood sprinkled the walls and made a stream in the middle of the room, so prodigious a quantity did she draw from her veins. She disciplined herself in this manner seven times; first, for her own sins; secondly, for souls engaged in sin; thirdly, for the pressing necessities of the Church; fourthly, when Peru or Lima were threatened with some great misfortune; fifthly, for the souls in purgatory; sixthly, for these in their agony; seventhly, in reparation of the outrages offered to God.

The people of Lima, having one day misunderstood the meaning of the words addressed to them by Father Solano, a celebrated Franciscan preacher, thought he said that the earth was going to open and swallow up the town in a few days; in consequence of this mistake the whole place was thrown into consternation. Rose, taking pity on the terrified people, retired to her oratory, and to appease the anger of God she took the discipline so severely that she was nearly dying in consequence.

As she practised this penance every night, she reopened her bleeding wounds by making new ones; and being careful to prolong her suffering, she contrived not to strike always in the same place; but she reiterated her blows so frequently that she did not allow her wounds time to close; scarcely did they begin to heal than she opened them again by fresh blows; thus her whole body was almost one entire wound.

These in the house who heard the sound of the blows she inflicted on herself had a horror of this cruel treatment, and were, at the same time, touched with pity for this innocent penitent, who felt none for herself. Father John of Laurenzana, her confessor, being informed of the manner in which she treated her body, commanded her to use moderation; she obeyed, but she begged so earnestly, that he could not refuse her the permission she asked to take five thousand more stripes in the course of three or four days. She had shown from her infancy the first sparks of that fire which inflamed her soul with the love of penance; for when she was only five years old she carried through mortification heavy tiles and stumps of trees from one place to another with great difficulty. She entreated Marianne the servant, and the dear confidant of her austerities, to load her with heavy stones in the corner where she usually prayed; and she heaped upon her so great a quantity sometimes, that Rose, overcome with the weight of this burden, fell fainting and half dead to the ground. When she was fourteen, she used to leave her room at night when every one in the house had retired to rest, and walk about barefooted in the garden, carrying a long and heavy cross on her wounded shoulders; the joy which she felt under this beloved burden rendering her insensible to the effects of the air and the season.

Her confessor having ordered her to use an ordinary discipline and leave off her iron chain, she made it into three rows, and wore it round her body, and after passing the ends through the ring of a padlock, she threw the key into a corner, where it would have been very difficult to find it. This chain very soon took the skin off, and entered so deeply into her flesh that it was no longer visible; and one night she felt so terrible a pain from it, that she fainted and was near dying. The servant having awoke at a cry she uttered, quickly ran to her assistance. Rose, seeing herself obliged to confess the truth, begged her to help her to take off the chain, before her mother, awakened by the noise, should come up to her room. Marianne found no other means than by breaking the padlock; but they could not do this, and she was obliged to

go down to the garden for a stone to break it. While she was gone, Rose, fearing her mother would surprise them, had recourse to prayer, which served as a key to open the lock, for Marianne, entering with her stone, saw the padlock open of itself and separate from the links of the chains; thus they succeeded in taking it off, though not without causing great pain and an abundant effusion of blood. Her wounds were no sooner healed than she put the chain on again; but as soon as it had entered into her flesh, her confessor ordered her to send it to him, and in obeying him she suffered the same pain and loss of blood as before. After her death, Mary of Usategni, kept some links of this bloody chain, which exhaled so sweet an odour that every one who smelt it was obliged to confess it to be supernatural.

She bound her arms from the shoulder to the elbow with thick cords, which caused her great pain by compressing tightly the muscles of this fleshy part. In order to suffer more she rubbed herself with nettles, making her body one entire blister, and with thorns, which, entering deeply into the flesh, drew forth quantities of blood. She used two hair-shirts; the first, being only two feet long, did not satisfy her desire of suffering; nevertheless, she used it till she obtained another, woven of horsehair, with two sleeves, and which hung from her shoulders to her knees. She appeared yet more glorious in the eyes of God when wearing this strange coat of arms, from her having armed it underneath with a great quantity of points of needles, to increase her excessive sufferings by this ingenious cruelty. She wore this frightful hair-shirt several years with incredible joy, and she only quitted it by the express order of her confessor, when a vomiting of blood came on.

As she was insatiable of pain, seeing her hair-shirt taken from her, she chose a sack of the coarsest stuff she could find, and made it neatly in the form of a shift. It would be impossible to express the suffering this rough dress caused her; sometimes it made the perspiration stream from her in great drops; sometimes she fell fainting under it, and was unable to take a step without great torture. These austerities were insufficient to satisfy her thirst for suffering: she watched also for the hour in which cooking was going on in the house, and, when no one could see her, she exposed the soles of her feet to the heat at the mouth of the oven, where it is the greatest, that no part of her body might be without a wound, and she kept them there till the pain of her half-roasted feet quite overcame her.

This was the treatment our Saint inflicted on her innocent body, though her frequent attacks of illness gave her plenty of occasions of suffering. She would have practised yet greater and more cruel mortifications if her confessors had not prevented her. What astonishes us in her conduct is, that she suspended the interior joy with which Almighty God favoured her in her greatest sufferings, for fear that this spiritual sweetness might extend to her body, and that by making it participate in the delight of her soul her insupportable sufferings would be softened. We may, therefore say that her pains were unmixed with any consolation; they resembled, in a manner till then unknown, these suffered by the Son of God in His Passion, during which He never permitted the superior part of His soul, which was sovereignly happy, to communicate any part of its happiness to its afflicted body. We consider this divorce of the flesh and the spirit in our Saint, as one of the great wonders that have made her the admiration of the Peruvian people. When charity induced some pious persons to exhort her to moderate her austerities, she answered, "As I cannot do any good, is it not just that I should suffer whatever I am capable of enduring?"

The Rimac, which divides Lima

CHAPTER VI

OF THE SHARP-POINTED CROWN WHICH SHE WORE AND OF THE HARDNESS OF HER BED.

THE saints being predestinated to resemble the Son of God in His state of sacrifice and immolation on the cross, according to S. Paul, who makes their greatness consist in this conformity, "whom He predestinated to be made conformable to the image of His Son," every one will allow that a crown of thorns on the head of the blessed Rose was necessary to render her a perfect image of Jesus crucified, and that the portrait would not have been faithful had it not represented the bloody thorns which crowned the head of her Divine Spouse, and which were the dearest object of her thoughts.

To copy it in reality, when very young she made herself a crown of pewter, studded with little sharp- pointed nails; she put it generously on her head without fearing the pain it would inevitably cause her. She wore it several years, but only as a preparation for a more cruel one, in which she fixed ninety-nine iron points; she wore, this during the ten last years of her life; and it furnished her with a still greater occasion of exercising her love, and her patience, for considering the crown of thorns of Jesus Christ on the head of S. Catherine of Siena, she thought she might obtain the same favour. In this ardent desire of suffering she made herself a circlet of a plate of silver three fingers broad, in which she fixed three rows of sharp points, thirty- three in each, in honour of the thirty-three years that the Son of God lived upon earth. Fearing that her hair, which was beginning to grow, would prevent these points from entering in, she cut it all off, excepting a handful which she left on her forehead, to hide this penitential crown from the eyes of men. She wore it underneath her veil, which made it the more painful, as these points, being unequally long, did not all pierce her head at the same time, but one after another, according to her different movements; so that with the least motion these iron thorns tore her flesh, and pierced her head in ninety-nine places with excessive pain; and as the muscles of this part are all connected with one another, our Saint could scarcely speak; and when she coughed or sneezed this violent effort caused the three rows of points to penetrate even to the skull with almost inconceivable pain.

As she had only invented this sort of torment to imitate the sufferings of the Son of God, she would have willingly changed this circlet for a crown of thorns, to imitate Him more closely; but her confessor thought it better for her not to change it, for fear that the holes which the thorns would make might suppurate. She followed his advice, seeing that it would be very difficult to conceal a crown of thorns, as the points would come through her veil, and reveal what she so much wished to hide; for this reason she made this silver crown, in which she fixed the points so firmly that after her death the goldsmith could not draw even one out with his instruments.

To increase the pain, she changed every day the place of this crown, causing new wounds, or reopening these which were beginning to heal. She had put strings at each end of this painful diadem, that by tying them closely she might force the points in more deeply; and in changing it, which she did every day, this crown caused her new pain. Every Friday, which she particularly consecrated to penance, she tied this circlet more tightly, and made it come down upon her forehead till it pierced the cartilage of her ears in many places. Her mother and the rest of the family did not perceive this crown for a long time, nor her endeavours to hide it from their view; but one day, when she was trying to save one of her brothers from the anger of her father, who was correcting him with too much violence, in pushing her away he placed his hand by chance on the sharp crown that encircled her head, and, as he was carried away by passion, his touch was so rough, that it caused three streams of blood to flow from her wounds; and this made known to her mother and all of them the great austerities which she secretly practised.

Rose, more afflicted at the discovery than at the pain of the blow, went quickly to her room, took off her crown, cleaned it, and after having washed her wounds and stopped the blood, she put on her veil as before. Her mother, having followed her, commanded her to take it off; she then saw her head pierced all round by the iron points; and though she felt as much horror as pity, she pretended not to see them, fearing that if she took from her this instrument of penance, she would only invent a more cruel one.

She did not fail to complain of it to her confessor who desired Rose to send to him, without delay, the pointed circlet which she wore round her head. She took it to him, but when he saw this crown stained with blood, and bristling with points, he was greatly surprised; and considering her delicate constitution, her age, and her frequent illnesses, he tried to persuade her to leave it off. Rose, seeing that he used remonstrance more than authority, represented to him so forcibly the necessity she felt of suffering this continual martyrdom, in order to be conformable to her Divine Spouse, that he gave it back to her, after having blunted

S. Rose Sewing, with her hermitage in the background

some of the sharpest points. This compassion did not, however, prevent her suffering the same pain as before, for the rest of the nails pierced her head when she struck the crown, or tied it with the strings. Every time that the devil tempted her, she pressed this crown three times on her head with her finger, in honour of the most holy Trinity, and this mortification made her always victorious over his attacks. After her death a great servant of God, kissing respectfully this instrument of penance, felt himself interiorly inflamed with the love of God, and was at the same time perfumed with a heavenly odour, which was a sign to him, that Almighty God had accepted this new sort of torture, which the blessed Rose had invented to mortify herself.

This faithful spouse of the Son of God had so perfectly imitated during her life-time her seraphic mistress in the pain of this thorny diadem, that after she was dead, as there were no flowers to be found to make her a crown, which is customary in Peru at the burial of young girls, as a sign of the glory they, reap from their virginity in the next world, they took, by divine inspiration, the crown of thorns from the head of a statue of S. Catherine of Siena, to place it on that of the blessed Rose: as if that seraphic lover wished to lend her crown to Rose to honour her triumph, and to conduct her in a more glorious manner to the throne of the Divinity. Several persons of known sanctity saw her enter heaven, with a palm in her hand, and a crown resplendent with light on her head, which our Blessed Lady had placed there, to acknowledge by this favour the services she had rendered her.

But let us return to the austerities and sufferings of our Saint, which merited for her the glory of this triumph. From her infancy she invented many means of making her bed hard, and her mother having perceived it, made her sleep with her; but Rose, contrived to mortify herself in her obedience, for as soon as her mother was asleep, she drew on one side the feather bed on which she had been lying, and slipped quietly on to the bedstead, placing a large stone under her head for a pillow. She practised this mortification till her mother, after telling her that this rigour was displeasing to her, and that she was obstinate, at last said she might seek a bed somewhere else, and sleep as she liked. Rose, quite delighted with this permission, made herself a bed in the form of a chest of rough wood and put in it a quantity of small stones of different sizes, that her body might suffer more, and might not enjoy the repose smooth planks would have, afforded it. This bed still seeming too soft, she put in three pieces of twisted and knotted wood, and she added seven more, filling up the spaces with three hundred pieces of broken tiles placed so as to wound her body.

This was the luxurious couch on which this insatiable lover of the cross took the rest necessary to recruit her exhausted strength. She always kept behind her pillow a bottle full of gall, with which she rubbed her eyes before going to bed, and washed her mouth in the morning, in memory of that which was given to Jesus Christ her Spouse on the cross. When Almighty God called her to this sort of crucified life, she had only a piece of coarse cloth doubled for a pillow; soon after, not finding this hard enough, she used bricks; but all this not being sufficient to satisfy her ardour for suffering, she took a rough stone for a pillow. Her mother becoming aware of it, from the bruises which this stone inflicted on her face, forbade her ever to use it again, and insisted on her having a bolster, like the rest of the family: she certainly obeyed, but in filling it with wool, as was mentioned at the commencement of this history, she put also vine branches, and bits of broken canes, in the place where she laid her head, and by this invention she rendered her pillow as hard and more painful than it was before.

She slept for fifteen years on this rough bed, if it would not be more correct to call it a cross; and it caused her such dreadful pain, that though she was very generous, and met with intrepid courage every sort of pain, still she never placed herself upon it without trembling and shuddering, and the blood seemed to freeze in her veins, so violent was the emotion which the inferior part manifested at the sight of the pain it was obliged to endure. On these occasions, when she was half dead, Jesus Christ several times appeared to her with a sweet and gracious countenance, saying to her, to rouse her courage, "Remember, my child, that the bed of the cross on which I died for the love of thee, was harder, narrower, and more painful than that on which thou art lying; think of the gall which I drank for thy sake, and call to mind the nails which pierced My Hands and Feet; thou wilt then feel consolation in the terrible pains thou sufferest on thy bed."

She was not wanting in resolution in these frightful austerities; but as this vigour did not extend to her body, she became so weak that her confessors ordered her to use more moderation, and take away at least these broken tiles, which gave her the most pain; but she begged so earnestly, that she was allowed to replace them, and to sleep upon them during the last two Lents she passed in this life. For some time before her death she passed the night in a corner of the room, where she was almost frozen with cold. The implacable hatred which she felt towards her body taught her to refuse it every comfort; for this reason she always worked standing, and when she could not continue so any longer, she made use of a very narrow piece of wood for a seat.

When near death she lost nothing of her desire to lie on a hard bed; she sought no other tortures than the excessive pain she endured thereon; and as they would not place her on the ground, as she desired, she obtained at last, by prayers and tears, that two crossed sticks should be placed under her head and shoulders, that she might expire on this cross, as Jesus Christ her Divine Spouse

had died upon His. Some persons of piety who saw her die, perceived on her countenance that of the Son of God, with the same appearance as He had when dying on Calvary. Blessed Raymond of Capua had formerly observed the same in visiting S. Catherine of Siena when she was ill.

The insupportable hardness of her bed shows that she watched most part of the night, as it prevented her from sleeping. She confined herself to two hours sleep, and often did not spend the whole of them in sleep; she so disposed of the remaining time, that she passed twelve hours in a perpetual application of her mind to God by prayer, and the others she spent in needlework or other employments, to relieve the poverty of her parents.

Though her fasts, her hair shirt, the hardness of her bed, her almost continual meditations, and other austerities, had given her a great facility in watching, the devil did not fail to use many artifices to induce her to sleep; but she knew how to detect them, and to overcome his efforts she struck her head roughly against the wall, gave herself hard blows, and sometimes she fixed her hands to the arms of a large cross which was in her room, and thus her body hung suspended in the air; and if in spite of all these efforts she still felt overcome with sleep, she fastened the small quantity of hair, she had left on her head to hide her crown of thorns, to a large nail fixed in the wall, and thus she triumphed over the temptation.

INSTRUMENTS OF PENANCE

"And thus she overcame the temptation."

CHAPTER VII

OF HER SOLITUDE, AND THE HERMITAGE WHICH SHE HAD BUILT IN HER FATHER'S GARDEN, THAT SHE MIGHT LIVE QUITE SEPARATED FROM MEN.

Solitude is a sort of Paradise to souls that aspire to virtue, either because being there solely occupied with the perfections of God, they are raised above the condition of mortals and become quite divine, or on account of the graces which Almighty God then pours out upon them more abundantly, and the familiarity with Himself to which He raises them. As His Spirit is incompatible with that of the world, He is pleased with solitude, and He seems to reserve His caresses for these who separate themselves from the world to enjoy the sweetness of His conversation. Thus, speaking of a soul who wishes to keep a close union, with Him, He says that He will draw her into solitude, where being disengaged, from creatures He will speak to her heart, that is, He will converse familiarly with her, to show her the path she must follow to attain heaven.

The blessed Rose, while yet a child, felt herself so forcibly drawn to solitude, that she sought the most secret corners of the house, and deprived herself of all these little amusements with which children of her age usually divert themselves, that she might attend solely to God, and not to interrupt the incredible pleasure she began to feel in her sweet

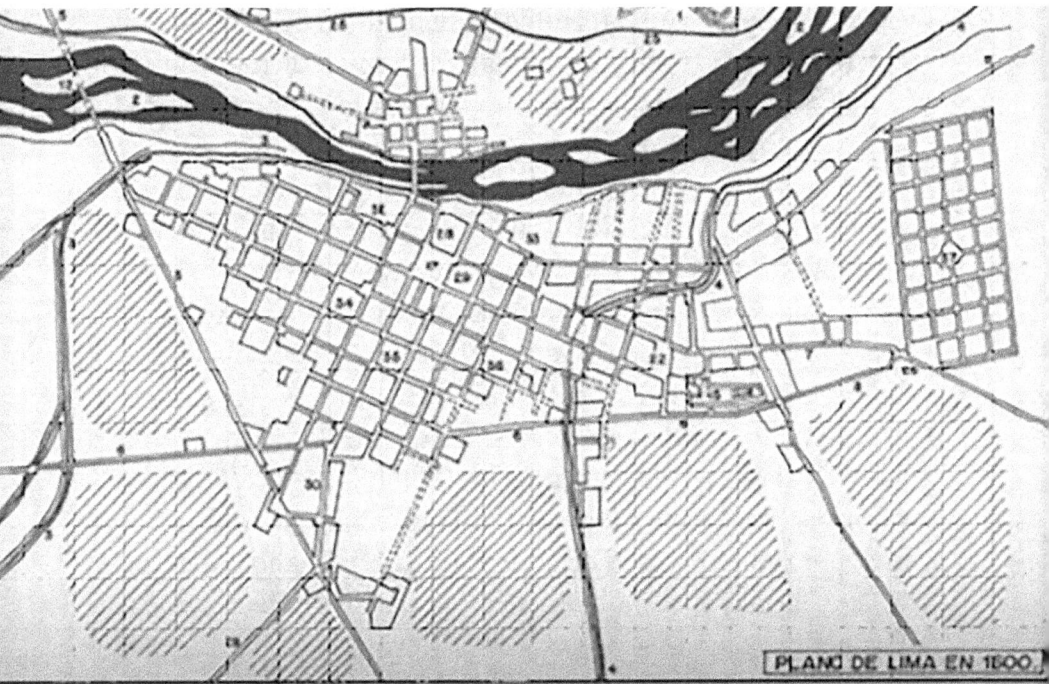

PLANO DE LIMA EN 1600

communications with Him. This desire of being hidden from the eyes of men, in order to converse more familiarly with her beloved Spouse, increasing with her age, she made a little hut in her father's garden, with palm leaves, and other branches of trees, and she wove them so carefully, that the sun had great difficulty in penetrating. She remained there nearly all day; so that it was generally said in the house, "If you wish to find Rose, you must look for her in the garden; that is her bedroom, her table, and her oratory; she never leaves it." When she was older, she could not suffer a greater torment than to be drawn from her retreat to converse with creatures. She did all she could, by prayers and tears, to prevail upon her mother to allow her some part of the house, where she would not be seen, and no longer to oblige her to go with her to the town. Though her mother did indulge her in some degree, she still required her, in spite of her repugnance, to go with her sometimes to pay her visits. One day, when she had been ordered to dress smartly on this account, she pulled out of the oven as she passed a large stone, which fell so heavily on her foot, that she was obliged to remain at home, for the wound, of which she had been herself the cause, made her walk lame, and gave her great pain.

One reason which contributed greatly to give her an aversion for company was, that the fame of her sanctity being spread over the whole town, she was spoken of in her presence as a person of great sanctity and close union with God: and these praises gave her the more pain, as she was fully persuaded of her misery and unworthiness. This made her resolve to choose another state of life, to be delivered from this slavery, and to be no longer obliged to follow the fashions and maxims of the world. Foreseeing the difficulties which her mother would oppose to this design, and believing that she should never obtain her consent without a special interposition of Providence, she had recourse to the Blessed Virgin, her ordinary refuge in her necessities; and earnestly entreated her to dispose the mind of her mother to consent to her desire of embracing a more retired life, and to allow her to make profession of a life of devotion, that she might be dispensed from the customs of the world, which she could not endure. In order to obtain this favour, which she so passionately desired, she begged the father sacristan to put on the neck of the statue of our Lady of the Rosary, a chaplet of coral which she kept in her box, assuring him that he would do her a great kindness, as it was of great consequence to her to gain the favour of the Blessed Virgin, that the Divine Infant whom she held in her arms might become her security for a grace which she fervently solicited from Him. Though these words were an enigma to the good father, he promised to present her rosary; but as the ladder was not there, he thought no more about it, till Rose, noticing his omission, repeated her petition; he then immediately sent for a ladder, and in presence of these who were in the chapel, he put the rosary on the image of the Blessed Virgin.

Some days after, the chaplet was seen in the divine hands of the Infant Jesus, as if it had been taken from the Mother, expressly to give it to the Son. This prodigy very much surprised those who frequented the church, particularly the father sacristan, who declared that no one had made the exchange, and that it must have been an effect of the power of Almighty God. Rose herself interpreted it in her favour, and saw it with great delight, knowing by this sign that our Blessed Lady had obtained the favour she had asked, and that Jesus Christ her Divine Son held this rosary, in order to answer for His blessed Mother, and to show her that He had taken upon Himself the execution of her pious design.

With this confidence she requested her mother, through the Rev. Father John of Laurenzana, Don Gonzalez and his wife, Mary of Usategni, to allow her a little room apart, into which no one of the family, or from out of doors, might enter to speak to her or visit her, except her confessor, to whom she was obliged to give an account of her proceedings from time to time. Her mother, who till then had been inflexible to her tears and entreaties, gave her leave to do as she pleased, in consideration of those who made the request. This consent being obtained, she had a little hermitage built in the garden, five feet long and four wide. One of her confessors found it too narrow, but she answered pleasantly, that it was large enough for her, and for Jesus Christ, her adorable Spouse.

Some days after she had shut herself up there, a holy woman, who had frequent ecstasies, saw in a rapture the blessed Rose like a brilliant star, the rays of which not being confined to the limits of this small cell, pierced through the walls on every side, to spread themselves over the town of Lima. She remained buried in this hermitage as a person dead to the world, always occupied either in prayer or penance, or in some work, and so absorbed in God, that living more to Him than to herself, she did not know whether her soul were separated from her body, or still animated it in its operations.

The fame of her virtue induced the first ladies of the town to visit her, to enjoy the sweetness of her conversation, and to profit by her example. As she could not forbid them the house, and as they were careful to request her mother's assistance, who enabled them to see her, and who took them to her retreat, Rose received them, though against her will, deploring the time she thought she lost in these civilities; and though they only spoke of Almighty God, our Saint said that it was much more agreeable and profitable to her to speak with God, than to speak of God.

This retired life made her much talked about, especially when she was not seen to come so often to church as before; for this is customary with devout persons, whose good example inspires piety, and often attracts to God persons who are much engaged with the world by their business or rank in life. One person being scandalized at this excessive solitude, asked her why she no longer went to mass every day; Rose answered, that not being able to leave the house without her mother, who was detained at home by the cares of her household, Jesus Christ supplied for it in a miraculous manner, favouring her so far, that while she still remained in her hermitage, she heard every mass that was said in the hospital of the Holy Ghost, and even those celebrated in the church of S. Augustine, which was four or five streets distant from her house. In fact, it was remarked several times, that our Saint had this gift from God, of assisting in spirit at all the sermons that were preached in the churches of Lima, and of giving as exact an account of them as if she had been actually present.

Her body being so obedient to the laws of her mind, and her mind so perfectly submissive to the will of God, we need not be surprised that irrational animals should have respected her virtue, and given her proofs of their obedience. The dampness of the earth, and the foliage of the trees which surrounded the hermitage of this happy solitary, drew thither an almost innumerable quantity of mosquitoes, which abound in America; and although these little insects love the shade, and always seek it, particularly at noon, when the heat of the sun is almost insupportable, and at night to be sheltered from the cold; still, not one of this legion of flies, which covered the walls, the windows, and the doors of her cell, presumed to settle upon her; they showed so much respect for her person that they seemed to honour in her the sovereign power of God, who had created them. They did not show the same deference to her mother, nor to the persons who came to see her in her retreat by the permission of her spiritual guides, for they were severely stung.

Three years before her death, she retired to the house of Don Gonzalez de la Massa, in obedience to her parents, who were anxious to allow him this favour, which he had earnestly solicited; and here she caused to be built for her a room as small as that which she had occupied at home, in which she passed her whole time, both day and night, in prayer, except when she returned, as she did from time to time, to her first hermitage, to avoid the intercourse of creatures, and to enjoy the company of Almighty God in that solitude

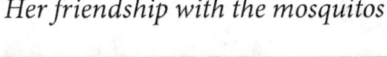

Her friendship with the mosquitos

The Espousal

CHAPTER VIII

JESUS CHRIST ESPOUSES THE BLESSED ROSE, IN THE PRESENCE OF THE EVER BLESSED VIRGIN.

Love always tends to union, and the greater the love the closer is the alliance to which it aspires; and as there is not a closer union than that which joins a man and woman in marriage, Almighty God makes use of this expression to assist us to comprehend the union which He contracts with just souls by grace and charity. Thus He assures the faithful soul that He will espouse her; that is, that He will raise her to the honour of an alliance with Him, and will give her a share in His Heart, and in His caresses. It is true that sanctifying grace procures this advantage for all the just in an invisible and hidden manner; but as there are souls singularly favoured and caressed by God, and with whom He is more closely connected, He sometimes also espouses them in a visible manner, with a ceremonial of pomp and magnificence. The blessed Rose had read in the life of S. Catherine of Siena, her dear mistress, that Jesus Christ had raised this seraphic lover to so great a degree of glory and favour, that He espoused her solemnly in the presence of the Blessed Virgin, S. Dominic, and several other Saints. Though the love she bore to the same Divine Saviour made her sigh after the enjoyment of a similar grace, the consciousness of her own misery and nothingness kept her in such profound humility, that she would have thought it a crime to harbour the thought, or to form a single desire of it; and this very humility, which made her judge herself unworthy of it, was the precious portion which captivated the Heart of the Son of God, and induced Him to honour her in a similar manner.

He disposed her for this divine alliance by miracles; for the mysterious black

"*He showed her an almost innumerable company of virgins....*"

and white butterfly, of which we have already spoken, after having long fluttered on the left side of her, at last settled exactly over her heart, and did not move till it had traced the resemblance of a heart on the dress of our Saint. At this moment she seemed to hear an interior voice saying to her with great sweetness, "Rose, My beloved, give Me thy heart," as if Jesus Christ wished her to understand by this enigmatic representation, that He would give her His Heart in exchange for hers, and renew in her person the miracle He had formerly performed in favour of S. Catherine of Siena, when He took away her heart, in order to put His own in its place.

One night when the blessed Rose was absorbed in contemplation, Jesus Christ appeared to her as a most beautiful man, and told her with a smiling countenance, that she was an object of His love; and after this delightful assurance, He showed her an almost innumerable troop of virgins resplendent with brightness, who were occupied in sawing and cutting marble, and He invited her to join the number of these chaste spouses, whom she saw employed in this hard labour. She began to consider in her mind this scene, which ravished her with admiration, and at the same instant she saw herself covered with a mantle woven of gold and precious stones, and she was placed in the company of these happy virgins.

It is painful to make known to carnal men, who comprehend not the wonders of God, and who are scandalized at the ineffable condescension which He shows to souls inflamed with His love, the present with which He honoured the blessed Rose, to invite her to the dignity of being His spouse. On Palm Sunday, a day on which the Church celebrates the solemn and triumphant entrance of the Son of God into the city of Jerusalem, amidst the acclamations of the people, the sacristan, who distributed palms to the other sisters of her order, who were in the church, passed her without giving her one, either through inadvertence, or by the special permission of God. Rose thought this must have happened through her fault, and that she must have been distracted during the distribution. Afflicted and confounded, she retired into the chapel of our Lady of the Rosary, where, placing herself on her knees, she began to sigh and weep, to expiate her fault.

While she was soliciting by her tears the pardon of the negligence she thought she had committed, she saw that the Blessed Virgin had a smiling countenance; and that after having looked upon her graciously, she turned to speak to her Son, and, as if she had received from Him a favourable answer to her request, she turned her eyes again towards the blessed Rose, as if to congratulate her on the happiness to which she was going to be raised. Our Saint, transported with a secret joy, which she did not usually feel, raised her eyes to look at the Son of God, who, looking at her again, caused a torrent of delight to flow into the soul of this chaste lover, and said to

S. Vincent Ferrer, S. Rose and S. Louis Beltran

her these tender and loving words : "Rose of My Heart, I take thee for My spouse."

Quite enraptured with the honour of this illustrious alliance, she prostrated herself humbly at the feet of Jesus Christ, and entering into the abyss of her miseries, she said to Him with profound respect, " Lord, behold Thy handmaid; I am too much honoured by the quality of Thy slave, and I bear in my soul the indelible marks of a necessary slavery, which render me unworthy of the glorious rank of Thy spouse."

The consideration of her own nothingness would have made her take this heavenly favour for an illusion, had not the Blessed Virgin assured her of the truth of this mystery by these gracious words, "Rose, the beloved of my Son, see to what an excess of glory He has raised thee; by His mercy thou art now truly His spouse." As her humility, however, made her still apprehend some delusion in this grace, of which she judged herself very unworthy, Jesus Christ, to give her confidence, graciously confirmed to her the truth of the alliance He had contracted with her in the presence of His holy Mother. Who could express the supernatural gifts of grace which she received from her Divine Spouse in consequence of this august union? We can only know what she herself made known to a learned man who directed her. When he urged her one day to declare to him what gift her Heavenly Spouse had bestowed on her as the pledge of His love and their alliance, she confessed that she was not possessed of eloquence sufficient to express the magnificent liberality which God had exercised in her regard without considering her unworthiness.

That she might always have a sensible mark of this illustrious alliance before her eyes, she begged her brother to have a ring made for her; he took the measure for it, and though he knew nothing of this mystery, he told his sister that he would have engraved upon it, "Rose of My Heart, I take thee for My spouse." This consoled her very much for she saw that Almighty God had inspired him to choose these words.

On Maundy Thursday she begged the sacristan to put this precious pledge of the love of Jesus Christ into that part of the tabernacle in which the most Adorable Sacrament is enclosed; but on Easter Sunday she was much surprised to see this ring on her finger, though she had not asked for it back, and the religious whom she had asked to enclose it had not returned it to her. She knew at once by this miracle that her Divine Spouse had communicated to this metal the property of returning to her finger, only to show her His ardent desire of being intimately united to her heart; and that as He had become everything to her by this alliance, she should make Him the sole object of her thoughts and affections. This miracle was very evident; for her mother, who was beside her in the church, and who closely watched her, saw this ring on her finger without having seen anyone approach to place it there.

A year after our Saint's death, a great servant of God, holding this ring in his hand, was sweetly ravished into an ecstasy; and among other ineffable consolations which Almighty God poured abundantly into his soul, he perceived this faithful spouse of Jesus Christ very high in glory, and honourably placed among the greatest saints in heaven. Quite enraptured with joy at this delightful spectacle, he wished to extend his hand to retain it, but he was not able: the ring seemed to have benumbed his arm. If this nuptial ring worked so great a wonder on this servant of God, who can conceive the power with which it acted on the soul of this chaste spouse?

CHAPTER IX

OF THE CLOSE UNION WITH GOD TO WHICH SHE ATTAINED BY MEANS OF MENTAL PRAYER.

The Holy Spirit having chosen the blessed Rose as His temple, became Himself her Master, and taught her from her earliest infancy how to pray. The supernatural lights with which He enriched her understanding inflamed her heart with so ardent a love for this holy exercise, that even sleep itself, which by the necessity of nature she was compelled to take, could not distract her from it; for her imagination was so completely absorbed in it, that she was often heard to repeat while asleep the same number of vocal prayers as she had said during the day. Her piety increasing with her years, she applied herself wholly to God from her twelfth year by the prayer of union, by means of which "the soul becomes one spirit with Him," according to the words of S. Paul. She had two different methods of conversing with God, one in solitude, when, having disengaged her mind from the care of earthly things, she retired to her hermitage, or to some other place apart from creatures, to attend solely and uninterruptedly to God; the other, in any place or in any employment that occupied her, for she kept her mind so united to God, and recollected in Him, that she prayed in working or in exercising charity towards the afflicted: thus, whether she walked, worked, or whatever she did, she was always in prayer.

She employed every day twelve hours in the first kind of prayer, as we have already mentioned; the second was continual, unless she was interrupted by the representations of horrible phantoms, of which we shall speak in the next chapter; so that she prayed without interruption, according to the advice of the great Apostle, for whether she slept or watched, whether she conversed, ate, read spiritual books, went abroad, or remained in her cell, God was incessantly in her thoughts, and she entertained herself with Him in loving colloquies. It is beyond the power of our imagination to conceive how, though the presence of God entirely engrossed all the interior powers of her soul, she still acted in exterior things with great presence of mind, giving the proper answers to questions, and finishing the work she commenced. Even if she were engaged in household employments, the cares which would have much embarrassed another, did not divert her from the presence of her Spouse, nor from the continual conversation she kept up with Him in her heart, in which He communicated to her His choicest favours.

In the time of prayer her senses were so recollected, that they represented nothing to her imagination which could distract her from her intercourse with God; when in the church she fixed her eyes steadfastly on the altar, and never looked at anything else; she was so absorbed in attention to the Divine mysteries, that she never knew who passed before her; and it was often remarked, that on certain occasions which inspired others with fear or surprise, she did not move a muscle, remaining motionless as a rock, while others in the church were quite terrified. After having passed hours, the whole day, and even all the night in prayer, she was often found in the position in which she had first placed herself. Towards the end of her life she remained in prayer in her hermitage from Maundy Thursday till Easter Sunday, her mind being so united to God, and so completely disengage from the senses, that her body lost all strength, and she could neither rise nor support herself.

She meditated every day three hours on the benefits of God, and the innumerable graces she had received from His mercy. She had for some time applied herself to a very sublime kind of prayer, which was, to meditate on a hundred and fifty perfections of God; after having drawn from it many holy affections which enkindled in her heart the flames of Divine love, she honoured each of these attributes separately, with an adoration of *latria*. Her mind was agitated with many different sensations during this prayer, as it formed affections conformable to the effects which we attribute to the sovereign perfections of God; fear, hope, grief, confusion, joy, desires, and compassion, had a share in her sentiments, when she contemplated His justice, His mercy, His omnipotence, His wisdom, and the other attributes which occupied her thoughts; and she felt two different sorts of agitation, similar to the two contrary pulsations which physicians recognize in our hearts, which succeed one another; now the consideration of the avenging justice of God plunged her into the depths; soon after, a reflection on His mercy elevated her to heaven.

This method of prayer was not only very agreeable to God, but our Saint testified that it was also terrible to the devils. Her love of God, which continually increased by the consideration of His Divine attributes, made her words like burning coals, which lighted up the same fire in the hearts of these with whom she conversed; for she was careful to make use of everything to lead them to love virtue and hate vice. If she walked with them in a garden, she spoke to them of the sovereign beauty of God, which spreads itself over flowers as a mirror, in which men may see the faint representation of that Source of beauty from which they derive their colour and brightness.

She made use of this means with no less advantage herself to raise her heart to God, adoring Him in all sublunary things, which she considered as animated pictures, representing to her His excellences and perfections. It usually happened that everything she saw or heard elevated her mind above her senses, even so as to throw her into a rapture. One day when she was ill, and something was being prepared for her to eat, a little bird came and perched near the window of her room, and began to sing,; where upon our Saint applied herself so earnestly to the consideration of the goodness of God, Who had given this bird so sweet a note to sing His praises, that she was ravished into an ecstasy, in which she continued transported with love, from nine in the morning till evening.

The year of her death, another bird, whose melody was most charming, placed itself opposite her room during the whole of Lent; as soon as the sun began to go down the blessed Rose ordered him to employ his notes in praising God; he obeyed, and raising his voice sang with all his strength, till this spouse of Christ, unwilling to be outdone by a bird in offering to God canticles of praise and benediction, which was more her duty than his, began to sing hymns to His glory, which she did very sweetly; when she had finished this little chorister began again, and thus together they composed a choir in which they sang alternately for an hour the praises of God. At six o'clock she dismissed him till the next day, and he was so punctual that he never failed to appear at the time fixed.

The abundant graces which she received from God in mental prayer made her exhort every one to embrace the practice of it. She spent several hours every day in reading books which taught the method of meditation, and in particular the works of Father Lewis of Granada.

She had wonderful eloquence in persuading others to it; she begged confessors to exhort their penitents, and preachers to speak of the excellence of meditation, and of its necessity

for all who wish to lead a holy life corresponding with their dignity as Christians, and with the obligation of saving their souls. Since the Rosary of the Blessed Virgin comprises both mental and vocal prayer, in the words and mysteries which compose it, she wished all who mounted the pulpit to instruct the people, and exhort them to embrace this devotion and to say at least a part of it every day. Her zeal and example induced many persons to practise it.

She collects water from a fountain

CHAPTER X

SHE IS TORMENTED WITH INTERIOR PAINS, TO SO FRIGHTFUL A DEGREE, THAT SHE IS EXAMINED BY SOME DIVINES, WHO DECLARE HER STATE TO BE FROM GOD.

The life of this Saint verifies perfectly that oracle of the Holy Ghost, that God tries those souls whom He predestines to glory, and that the greatest favours He lavishes upon them in this life, are the preludes to these interior crosses which He prepares in order to purify them.

The blessed Rose having attained to a very close and perpetual union with God, began to be attacked every day at certain intervals with such frightful darkness and obscurity, that she was often a whole hour without being able to distinguish whether she were in hell with the condemned, or in purgatory with the souls who there satisfy the justice of God. In this horrible darkness she had no thought of God, no idea of His mercies; and to fill up her chalice of bitterness, she had in her mind a confused remembrance of the love she had had for Him. As under this desolation she found herself in a very different condition from her former happy state, she imagined that she no longer knew God, and that she was reduced to the dreadful state of never being able to love Him. While these clouds of darkness obscured her mind, she thought she considered Almighty God as a stranger, an unknown person, in a word, as something as far from her thoughts and ideas, as if she had never had any union or friendship with Him.

In this species of desolation she seemed to see before her eyes an impassable wall which hindered her from escaping from this labyrinth, which made her believe that her condition differed in nothing from the pain of loss which the damned suffer in the privation of the beatific vision. As death is the termination of misfortunes to the miserable, she tried to soften the rigour of the terrible pains she suffered by the hope of dying soon; but instantly reflecting that her soul was immortal, and that death, which is so great a relief to others, would not be the end of her sorrows, this thought raised fears which would have been capable of throwing her into despair, if that same Providence of God which permitted these desolations, had not preserved her from it.

This darkness and trouble of mind tormented her for fifteen years, at least a hour and a half every day; her efforts to banish them from her mind, only made them more importunate; and this afflicted Rose found sharp thorns within herself, which lacerated her soul, from the belief she felt that she was abandoned by God.

In fine, the evil spirits filled her imagination with frightful spectres, and troubled her mind by such fearful visions, that though this courageous virgin could calmly bear the most insupportable pain, still she never could accustom herself to this sort of trial, the bare thought of which was so terrible to her, that when she felt the hour of her sufferings drawing near, she threw herself on the ground, at the feet of Jesus Christ, and, bathed in tears, she earnestly besought Him not to oblige her to drink this chalice of horror and bitterness, offering herself to the most cruel sort of death, which she would infinitely prefer, to the ceasing to love Him one moment; because God, being to her what the soul is to the body, she thought herself deprived every day of that supernatural and divine life during these storms: knowing, however, that it was by the will of God she suffered these pains, she adored it with respect, and said to Him, with a mind resigned to the orders of His Providence, "Lord, may Thy will be done, not mine; I abandon myself to Thy Divine dispensations." These anxieties, this darkness, and this species of desolation, exercised the judgment of the most famous theologians of Lima, and there were very few who gave a decided opinion; some believed that she was deluded, or that what passed in her mind was the effect of her long watchings; others, that they were illusions of the devil, which disturbed her imagination; others again attributed them to the heavy vapours which her great abstinence caused to mount from her stomach to her brain.

She listened to them humbly, and modestly said, that the little knowledge they had of her state was the effect of her stupidity, which could not explain how these things passed in her interior. She did not fail to attempt sometimes, in order to obey them, to give them some idea of her pains by comparisons; but when she had compared them to fire, which seemed most properly to express their violence, she frankly confessed that there was no relation between what she suffered in her soul, and the pain which the activity of that element causes.

When she spoke of her desolations, she said that she seemed to see herself very remote from God by a great dissimilarity, that she felt overcome by her timidity, and in these sorrowful moments she imagined herself overwhelmed by the tempest, of which the royal prophet speaks, which these sad thoughts raised in her soul; she added, that during this darkness, she wished to become anathema, that is, separated from Jesus Christ her God and her Spouse; she said, in fine, that these representations afflicted her to that degree, that they would have each day caused her death, if God had not preserved her life by a continual miracle. She was not the only soul whom Almighty God has tried in this terrible manner: we read the same thing of S. Catherine of Siena; and the history of the blessed Henry Suso, religious of the Order of Friars Preachers, relates that the Son of God often appeared to him under the form of a judge, with an inflamed countenance, and eyes sparkling with anger, pronouncing with a voice of thunder these overwhelming words: " Go, ye cursed, into everlasting fire."

Being asked if after being thus separated from God, and suffering this eclipse of the Divine Sun in her soul, she did not receive from Him some consolation; she answered, that God entered again into her mind with so brilliant a light, and enkindled so great a love in her will, that it became inflamed with ardour; after which she re-entered the Bosom of God, and was therein so perfectly transformed into her Beloved, that she seemed to be closely united with Him, and so confirmed in His grace, that not all the temptations of the flesh, the devils, or men, could ever separate her from His love.

Though God had revealed to her, and had clearly shown her that she was in the sure way of salvation and perfection; still, as she was very humble, she never refused to appear before these who wished to examine her vocation and manner of life. Besides her confessor, who studied her for a long time, many persons celebrated for their learning and piety, as well of the Order of Friars Preachers, as of the Society of Jesus, and even the famous Doctor John of Castile, a man very well versed in the mystical life, and who composed an excellent treatise upon it, carefully examined all that passed in her interior. After having conferred together several times on her life, and the extraordinary things which happened to her, they remarked, First, that from her infancy she experienced ardent desires of loving God alone, and so powerful an attraction to prayer, that she found nothing sweeter than to entertain herself with God by prayer, and to raise her mind incessantly to the contemplation of heavenly things. Secondly, that till the age of twelve years she had pursued different methods in prayer, which had all raised her to a high degree of spirituality. Thirdly, that her whole life was a continual exercise of patience under the crosses she had suffered in every way, and from the delicacy of her body, her abstinence, her want of sleep, and her sicknesses. Fourthly, that she had attained so perfect a union with God, that she could not turn her thoughts from Him, even if she had wished to apply them to something else; hence, she was never diverted from Him by her exterior occupations, nor by the violence of her illnesses, which caused her excessive pain. They remarked that Almighty God was so present to her, in all the faculties of her soul, and excited in her so sweet a hope of being favoured with His graces, that it was quite impossible for her to find any pleasure on earth, except in the continual idea she had of His mercies.

Being asked if she had ever read books treating of mystical theology; she answered humbly, that she was not aware that

S. Rose with her inquisitors

there were any bearing this title, or which taught the method of prayer, which conducts to the unitive life. When she was asked what efforts she had made to resist her evil inclinations, she answered, that, by the grace of God, she did not remember to have ever found any opposition in her soul to virtue; that on the contrary, she had felt from her infancy a strong inclination to piety, which had made her joyously embrace its practice. "1 do not mean" she said, "that I have not perceived in myself involuntary movements, but as soon as I applied my mind to the presence of God, they vanished so promptly that I had not usually time to resist them." They wished further to know if she did not find some trifling satisfaction in earthly things, when her mind became a little relaxed from its violent application to God in prayer; she said, that she could not possibly take the least pleasure in them, and that she suffered inconceivable pain when her mind was a moment unoccupied with God.

These divines, after several conferences, concluded that her life was the work of God; that she suffered in some degree the torments which the souls in purgatory endure by these representations, which oppressed her with fear, and threw her into a sort of agony; and that God permitted by a dispensation of His Providence that she should be tormented with these apprehensions of hell, and that her understanding should be obscured by this darkness, in order to keep her humble, and to purify her love more and more.

These holy men having commanded her, in virtue of obedience, to explain to them the state in which she was after this dryness and terrible desolation, she blushed at this order; she showed evidently by the colour that rose to her face the pain she felt in declaring secrets which had God alone for witness; she obeyed, but with so much confusion that her voice faltered as she declared, that after this storm Jesus Christ appeared visibly to her, now as a Child, again as of thirty years of age; that the Blessed Virgin came usually to console her with so amiable a countenance that her looks brought consolation to her soul.

She added, that these frequent visions worked in her three good effects. First, an abundance of joy, which made her insensible to all the pleasures of the world. Secondly, a love and an attachment to God, which separated her entirely from creatures. Thirdly, so admirable a tranquillity of the passions, that she knew nothing on earth capable of disturbing her peace; whence they conjectured that she was in a sure way of great perfection. Some other theologians, from the account they had heard of the profound manner in which she spoke of the inscrutable mystery of the Trinity of the Divine Persons, of the hypostatical union of the Word with the Human Nature, of the Book of Life, predestination, nature, and grace, and other mysteries of faith, had the curiosity to converse with her on these sublime subjects. After a long conference with her, they confessed that they had never known a more enlightened soul, and that our Saint had not attained the knowledge of these mysteries by the vivacity of her mind, nor by her application to study; but that God had given her the understanding of them, by an infused knowledge, and that she was only the organ of the Holy Ghost when she spoke of these elevated truths of religion.

One thing which surprised the most experienced in the mystical life was, that she had attained the unitive life with very little exercise of the laborious practices of the purgative; and they remarked with astonishment a sort of combat between God and her, without being able to determine whether God was more occupied in seeking in the secrets of His wisdom the means of exercising her by suffering, than she was disposed to suffer them for His love; for she showed an incredible avidity for crosses, and an invincible patience which rendered her victorious over her trials, and over every affliction which Almighty God sent to exercise her love and fidelity. Hence the most learned and the greatest masters of the spiritual life who had assembled to examine her, made known publicly that she was governed by the Spirit of God, and that she acted by the impulse of grace in her conduct.

Louisa of Melgarcyo, a lady of known sanctity, was so persuaded of this, that every time she met the blessed Rose she threw herself on her knees before her, notwithstanding the resistance her modesty made to prevent her; and when our Saint had passed on, this virtuous woman noticed where her feet had trod in walking, and kissed the traces with respect and veneration.

CHAPTER XI

OF THE FAMILIAR MANNER IN WHICH JESUS CHRIST, THE BLESSED VIRGIN, S. CATHERINE OF SIENA, AND HER GUARDIAN ANGEL CONVERSED WITH HER; AND OF THE VICTORIES WHICH SHE GAINED OVER THE DEVILS WHO TEMPTED HER.

If we separate love from familiarity, we deprive it of its delight and sweetness: and when Aristotle judged that there could be no friendship between God and men, it was because he considered the familiar communications which are inseparable from it derogatory to the profound respect which they owe to the Divinity, and dangerous on account of the liberty which they might allow themselves, and which would be capable of drawing down His hatred and aversion; and because this philosopher never knew the tenderness of God towards men, nor the mystery of the Incarnation, by which He has made Himself like them. The Christian religion, more enlightened in, its sentiments, recognizes a perfect friendship between God and the just man, by grace, and believes that God does not only honour by familiarity these souls who love Him tenderly, but that He bestows on them favours, which we may call a delicious foretaste of the happiness prepared for them in Heaven. The lives of the Saints are full of examples of this, and that of our Saint furnishes us with authentic proofs of it.

The Son of God not only appeared visibly to the blessed Rose at the time when her trials left her, He frequently visited her when she was reading her spiritual books, working, or embroidering, under the form of a beautiful Infant, stretching out Its little arms to caress her, and to testify the excess of Its love. Rose was so accustomed to these visions, that when her Divine Spouse was one moment later than usual in appearing, she made tender complaints to Him; and as love inspires the soul with poetry, she composed elegies, to express the pain His delay caused her.

Being once indisposed with a very bad sore throat Jesus Christ visited her more frequently than usual, and treated her with inconceivable marks of goodness; and as our Saint thought she could not have a more favourable opportunity for soliciting relief from her continual suffering, He granted what she asked, on condition that He should ask something of her. Rose having agreed, and promised to execute faithfully whatever obedience should require from her, He told her that He wished her to return to her former state of suffering: she consented, provided He would increase her pains, which was the condition of her promise. When she was one day relating these favours with great innocence and candour to her mother, to console her grief in seeing her always ill, the mother saw rays dart from the face of her daughter, which so heightened her beauty, that she seemed to her an angel from Heaven, and no longer a creature subject to so many infirmities.

One night, when she was taking her rest in the oratory, which was built in the garden, a great faintness came over her; and feeling a great want of some cordial drink to strengthen her, Jesus Christ applied the Wound of His sacred side to her mouth, and this chaste lover imbibed from it a delicious nectar, as S. Catherine of Siena had formerly done; so that after receiving this extraordinary favour, S. Rose was no longer merely the spiritual daughter of this seraphic lover; she became her foster-sister having drunk from the same source from which she derived her ardour and love.

Being at the house of a lady of quality, after a long

conversation on heavenly things, Rose left the lady to go and say her prayers: during her prayer a little girl of seven years old saw the Infant Jesus with her, in a human form, dressed in a variously coloured garment, caressing her in a thousand ways, which this child related. In the house of the Lady Isabel Mexia, the Infant Jesus was seen walking familiarly with our Saint, speaking to her, and following her everywhere. Those who witnessed these innocent familiarities, saw a dazzling light stream from the pavement on which the blessed Rose walked during their conversation. As this incomparable Spouse gave Himself wholly to her, He wished to be the sole possessor of her heart and its affections; and one day He made known to her that He was jealous of a flower which she was fond of. When she was walking one day in her garden, in which she cultivated very beautiful flowers, she saw that a quantity had been gathered; not knowing who had done her this injury, she complained of it to her Spouse, but was much surprised that instead of consoling her, He made her this loving reproof: " Why art thou attached to flowers, which the sun causes to fade? Am I not the Flower of the fields, infinitely more precious than all these which thou raisest in thy garden with so much care? Thou art a flower, and thou lovest flowers! O Rose, give Me thy love; know that it is I who pulled them, that thou mayest no longer give any creature a share in that heart which belongs to Me."

The Blessed Virgin frequently honoured her with the same caresses and familiarity. This is very evident when we mention that this Queen of Angels took upon herself the care of awaking her. The continual application of her mind to God, and her extraordinary austerities, had so heated her blood, that she had almost lost the use of sleep. Her confessors desired her for some time to use every day, lettuce, endive, and poppy seeds, in order to recover it; but as these remedies only procured a very small portion of necessary repose, she found herself so overcome with drowsiness at her usual hour of rising, that she had the greatest difficulty in waking. In this necessity she had recourse to the Blessed Virgin, whom the Church calls the "Morning Star," and earnestly entreated her to have the goodness to wake her at the appointed hour. Our Lady had the goodness to grant her this favour; she appeared to her every morning, and, after awaking her, she animated her to rise by these tender words: "Rose, my child, arise; it is time to prepare yourself for prayer." She was once so overcome with drowsiness, that she fell asleep after having been awakened. The Blessed Virgin came again, and touching her gently, said, "Arise, Rose, and do not be slothful." When the Blessed Virgin had given her this little reproof, she went away differently from her usual manner of retiring, for she always allowed Rose to see her face till she had left the room, and this time she turned her back towards her, in punishment of her idleness.

From the time that Almighty God appointed S. Catherine of Siena to be her mistress, Rose had such frequent conversations with her, that the features of this seraphic virgin seemed to have been transferred to her countenance, as it happened to Moses, who was completely transformed by God after he had spoken with Him on the mountain; for she resembled her so perfectly, that she passed in the opinion of all for a second S. Catherine of Siena.

She lived also in most familiar intercourse with her guardian angel; for when Jesus Christ, her dear Spouse, was a moment later than usual in visiting her at the ordinary time, she sent her guardian angel to seek Him.

She felt one night when in her hermitage the threatenings of a fainting fit, or some similar attack, and immediately returned to the house, for fear of being taken ill in that retired place, where no one could help her. Her mother, seeing her much changed, and with the perspiration on her forehead, thought she was going to die; she told the servant to run to the nearest confectioner's to buy some chocolate, which at

Lima is commonly composed of cocoa, lemons, and sugar, to strengthen her; but our Saint begged her mother not to buy it, assuring her that she should not have long to wait for it. Her mother grew angry, and told the servant a second time to go immediately to the place she had named. Rose, seeing her eagerness, told her to call her back, and not to trouble herself, for some would be brought to her immediately from the house of the Receiver. Scarcely had she finished speaking when a servant entered the house, and brought her a large silver cup full of chocolate from his master. Her mother, greatly surprised at so seasonable an assistance, ordered her, in virtue of her authority, to tell her how she knew that this remedy would be brought to her. Rose smiled, and confessed that as her good angel always did what she asked him, she had sent him to the Receiver's wife, to tell her of her illness, and of her want of a little chocolate to restore her strength.

Her mother opened the garden gate every night before she went to bed, that her daughter might go to her room when she returned at midnight from her hermitage. She forgot it once; and when Rose was preparing to return she saw from the window a white shadow fluttering, and apparently inviting her to follow it. She thought at once that it was her guardian angel concealed under this form: she followed, and when they arrived together at the closed door, it opened of itself the instant the shadow touched it.

She was not only familiar with the holy angel that Almighty God had appointed as her own protector, but with these of others also, as she made known to one of her friends, a religious, who having a long journey to take, came to recommend himself to her good prayers. He was fortunate at first; but when he had reached the vast plains of Truxillo, which is a fine town near the sea, he underwent great fatigue, and was twice in danger of losing his life. On his return to Lima he complained to the blessed Rose, that she had not helped him in his perils, as he had asked her before he left.

She answered, that these misfortunes happened by his own fault, as he was not then in the same state as when he came to say farewell to her. She then charitably mentioned to him some things which she could only have known through his guardian angel

If the angels loved and respected her, the devils, on the other hand, had so great an aversion for her, that there was nothing they did not attempt in order to make her feel the effects of their hatred and fury. The devil attacked her once in her cell in the form of a giant; he tried for a long time to bite her, but being prevented by the power of God from tearing her in pieces, he seized her and dragged her furiously on the ground, till this chaste virgin entreated the protection of her Divine Spouse by these words of the royal prophet, "Lord, do not abandon to the tyrannical fury of these hellish monsters these who hope in Thee." Then the enemy immediately fled. Nothing occurs more frequently in the history of her life than the insults she received from the evil spirit. He appeared to her one day, and when she showed no fear of his malice, he gave her a severe blow on the cheek; another time he threw a great stone upon her from above, which struck her fainting to the ground.

One night when she was praying at home in a corner, she saw the devil in a large basket, making a horrible noise, to divert her from her application to God; she blew out the candle, and fortifying herself with the sign of the cross, she courageously challenged him to the combat; he accepted the offer, and changing his form in a moment, he appeared in the shape of a prodigious giant; he took hold of her by the shoulders and shook her as if he would tear her in pieces. She did not lose courage, and though her bones were almost broken, and her nerves relaxed by these rough shocks, she laughed at him, and reproached him with his weakness, that appearing so strong he could not even triumph over her firmness.

It was observed that she was very often engaged in combat

with the enemies of her salvation; and that whenever she was obliged to defend herself from their temptations, she was so intrepid that she never seemed to fear them, though they assumed horrible shapes, capable of freezing the blood in the veins of the boldest and most courageous persons: on the contrary, the more frightful they appeared, the more courageously did she attack them. She was once, however, obliged to change her method of defence, and gain the victory by flight on the following occasion:—The devil appeared to her one day in her garden, under the form of a beautiful young man; at the sight of this dangerous enemy, she retired without waiting or speaking to him; and by this flight she gained a complete and glorious victory, for taking a thick iron chain which she found, she gave herself a severe discipline; and then, covered with blood, she complained to her dear Spouse, that He had abandoned her on this occasion. Jesus Christ appeared to her immediately, surrounded with brightness, and consoling her, said, "Rose, thou art deceived, if thou imaginest that I left thee alone in this extremity; know that thou hast only avoided this danger by My grace, and that if I had not been with thee in this dangerous occasion, thou wouldst not have triumphed over the devil, who wished to surprise thee."

This incident in the life of our Saint is very similar to what happened to S. Catherine of Siena on one occasion. As Rose was no less cherished and favoured by God, He communicated to her, as well as to this seraphic lover, the gift of discernment, to distinguish the true revelations of God from the deceitful illusions of the spirit of darkness. God had bestowed this grace on her from her early youth, and from that time she prescribed infallible rules for the discernment of spirits, which she drew from the effects produced in souls by them. Jesus Christ had Himself taught them to S. Catherine of Siena, and this Saint too blessed Rose, who became so experienced, that if anyone in Peru had held Plato's opinions regarding the metempsychosis of souls, he would have believed that the soul of S. Catherine of Siena had passed into the body of Rose, her spiritual daughter and fervent disciple.

S. Catherine

CHAPTER XII

OF HER INVINCIBLE PATIENCE UNDER PERSECUTION IN SICKNESS, AND IN HER OTHER SUFFERINGS.

As thorns spring forth with roses, so grief and pain seem to have been born with the blessed Rose; for her life was a tissue of sufferings, sickness, pains, and crosses, which exercised her patience from her cradle to her tomb, by a long and tedious martyrdom. When Rose was only nine months old her mother lost her milk, and as she could not afford to pay for a nurse for her, she brought her up with a little broth instead of milk. Though the sweet child suffered greatly from this privation, and from the violence used in forcing open her mouth that she might take this nourishment, she never cried; on the contrary, she seemed to derive pleasure from it. We have spoken before of the wonderful patience she exhibited at the age of three months, under the painful operation of extracting the roots of her nail with pincers, when she did not shed a tear, but appeared as unmoved as if she were insensible to pain.

Scarcely had she begun to walk, when she saw herself the subject of a dispute between her mother and godmother, each wishing to call her by the name they had given her. Her mother would have her called Rose, and her godmother could not endure the idea of giving her any other name but that of Isabel, which she had received in baptism. Whatever this blessed child did was sure to offend one or the other. If she answered to the name of Isabel, her mother punished her severely; and when she wished to correct this innocent error by acknowledging the name of Rose, her godmother, who was also her aunt, treated her with the same rigour.

As she was of a mild disposition, quite opposite to the passionate temper of her mother, it would be difficult to describe all the harsh treatment she received from her during several years. Her mother found fault with everything she did; she condemned her reserve, she blamed her fasts, she did not like her taking up so much time in prayer, nor her retired life, so opposite to the maxims of the world; for these reasons she often scolded her, and went so far as to use many abusive epithets, as if she had been an infamous person. At the least provocation she gave her blows on the cheek, but when she was carried away by anger, she put no bounds to her ill-usage; she was not content with abusing her, striking her on the face, and kicking her; she took a thick knotty stick and struck her with it, with all her strength. She began to treat her thus when she cut off her hair after having consecrated her virginity to God, and she continued the same treatment on many other occasions.

These with whom she lived were actuated towards her by so extraordinary a spirit of envy and vexation, because they saw her lead a life so different from theirs, that they did everything they could to annoy her; they even threatened to report her to the Inquisition as a deluded girl and as a hypocrite, who deceived the world by a false appearance of virtue.

Rose blessed God under these persecutions; she suffered them with joy, as she had read in the life of her seraphic mistress that she also had attained a very close union with Jesus Christ by means of sufferings. When a lady of quality asked her why she did not beg S. Catherine of Siena to free her from these persecutions, for it was commonly said in Lima, that she obtained from God, by the intercession of this

Saint, whatever she asked for herself or others, she answered, "What would this dear mistress say to me, if I were to do so? Would she not have reason to reproach me, for choosing a different path from hers? Ah! May God preserve me from this cowardice!" In fact, our Saint esteemed the sufferings of S. Catherine of Siena more highly than her consolations; and she preferred the stigmas with which the Son of God honoured her to all the sweets of His caresses, because she thought it a shameful thing for a spouse of Jesus Christ crucified to be a moment without a cross.

She desired suffering with a sort of eagerness, and when Divine Providence sent her sickness to furnish her with an occasion of it, she felt much more compassion for the trouble she gave others who waited upon her, than pity for herself, which made her often say, " Oh how advantageous and agreeable it would be to be always ill and to suffer great pains, if we did not give so much trouble to these who attend upon us !" Almighty God, who inspired her with this great desire of sufferings, furnished her with many occasions for practising patience: she was scarcely ever one moment without suffering excessive pain, and when she had nothing to afflict her exteriorly, Almighty God sent her interior pains.

When these with whom she lived relaxed their unjust persecutions a little, sickness came upon her in all sorts of shapes. She was three years in bed a paralytic, suffering great torture without shedding a tear or making the least complaint. These diseases arose from different causes, which all united to increase her suffering. Even the physicians were surprised to see her suffer so long, sometimes from tertian, sometimes from quartan fevers, which made her burn with heat and then shiver with cold; for her body was so attenuated and dried up, that

there seemed to be scarcely anything remaining to nourish fever.

She on her part adored the Hand of God in her infirmities, acknowledging that they did not proceed in her from a derangement of the system, as is the case with others, but from the particular dispensation of her Divine Spouse, who sent them to exercise her patience and to furnish her with opportunities of merit and grace. She declared to one of her most familiar friends, that she did not think there was a member of her body that had not suffered all it was capable of enduring. Her patience was invincible in these continual sufferings, and though her pains sometimes rose to the highest degree of torture, she never showed a single movement of impatience, nor uttered a word of repugnance to follow the Will of God by this path of the cross; on the contrary, she always showed an entire resignation and readiness to suffer every thing she had to bear.

It is almost impossible to enumerate her different afflictions, for we think there are very few which she did not experience in the greatest degree. First she suffered long from a quinsy; secondly, she was subject to asthma, which impeded her respiration; thirdly, she felt for several years the severe pains of sciatica, which tormented her day and night; fourthly, she was several times in danger from pleurisy; fifthly, she frequently fell into convulsions caused by the pain she suffered in the membrane which surrounds the heart; sixthly, she was scarcely ever free from fever; seventhly, we must confess that she stood in need of all her patience to bear the pain of gout in her hands and feet, and though this affliction is generally the effect and the punishment of intemperance, this chaste virgin was cruelly tormented by it, although her whole life had been spent in fasting and severe penitential exercises.

In all these violent pains, which succeeded one another, and which made the blessed Rose a daughter of affliction, she made known to those whom she saw touched with compassion for her sufferings, that she was still too well, that Almighty God treated her with too much tenderness, and that if He were to increase her pains to an infinite degree, He would do her no injustice, for she had deserved more. In the extremity of her sufferings she turned lovingly towards her crucifix, from which she derived her strength and patience, and addressed her Divine Redeemer in these tender and affectionate words, " O, my Jesus! O, my Jesus! Increase my sufferings, but increase also Thy Divine love in my soul!" We may conjecture from a vision which she had one day, that the Son of God heard the ardent prayers of this chaste spouse. He appeared to her on two very brilliant rainbows, holding a pair of golden scales, in which He weighed on one side the sufferings mankind could endure, and on the other the graces and infinite rewards which He promises; she heard Him immediately extol with magnificent praises the constancy of these who suffer generously for His love, and declare aloud that there was no other way of mounting to heaven but by the ladder of the cross.

This vision inflamed her heart with so great a desire of suffering all things for His Divine love, that she wished to go and publish to all men the inestimable advantages of affliction, and the great grace which God bestows whenever He sends sickness, losses, or any other visitation; for these apparent evils acquire for these who bear them an infinity of merits, which dispose them for the possession of sovereign happiness. The blessed Rose drew new strength from this vision, and encouragement under the paralytic seizure, which Almighty God sent to crown her patience, and which caused her to die as it were a martyr in the flower of her age.

CHAPTER XIII

OF HER LOVE FOR HER DIVINE SPOUSE JESUS CHRIST, AND OF THE MIRACLE WHICH SHE ENTREATED HIM TO WORK TO INFLAME THE HEARTS OF MEN WITH HIS DIVINE LOVE.

As charity makes saints, Almighty God, who destined S. Rose to attain a high degree of sanctity, rendered her heart, as it were, another Etna, which sent forth night and day flames of love, and which was so completely filled with this celestial fire, that the heat and sparks from it were visible on her countenance during her prayer. Fire was frequently seen issuing from her mouth and eyes, and through them she was enabled to give vent to the flames with which she was consumed while conversing with God by prayer. The ardent sighs which she continually breathed, manifested this evidently, for she was obliged to allow them to escape her, in order to moderate the violent heat of the love which burnt in her heart

This burning charity pervaded so completely all the faculties of her soul, that nothing issued from her heart, her mouth, or eyes, that did not express this celestial ardour. She had almost continually these words in her mouth, " Oh, my God ! who would not love Thee? Oh, good Jesus when shall I begin to love Thee, as I ought? How far am I from this perfect, intimate, and generous love? Alas! I know not even how to love Thee. How shameful! Of what advantage is it to have a heart, unless it be quite consumed with the love of Thee!" Inflamed with this divine charity, she composed several ejaculatory prayers, to obtain this perfect love of God, which are so moving that they might produce in the hearts of these who read them the same effects as in the heart of our Saint. The following is an example:

"Lord Jesus Christ, God and Man, my Creator and my Saviour, I am extremely sorry and sensibly grieved for having offended Thee, because Thou art what Thou art, and because I love Thee above all things. My God, Who art the Spouse of my soul and all the joy of my heart, I desire, and I desire it with all the powers of my soul, to love Thee with a very perfect love, with a very efficacious love, with a very sincere, ineffable love, the greatest that a creature can have for her God, with an incomprehensible love, with a love resolute and invincible in difficulties; in a word, I desire to love Thee as the saints and angels love Thee in heaven. Even more, O God of my heart, of my life, and all the joy of my soul, I desire to love Thee, as far as I am capable of it; as much as the Blessed Virgin, Thy Mother and my sweet Lady, loves Thee. O Salvation of my Soul! I desire to love Thee as Thou lovest Thyself. O my most sweet Jesus may I burn with the fire of Thy divine love; may it consume me, and make of my soul a holocaust to Thy glory."

She was so penetrated with this love, that it was the ordinary subject of her conversations with others; for whenever she spoke with ladies or with young girls, she always began by thesewords, " Let us love God, let us love Him With all our hearts." We may say, in a word, that the love of God was the salt with which she seasoned all her words, either in conversation, in answering questions, or when civility obliged her to speak to anyone.

All her pleasure was in speaking of this love, or in hearing others speak of it, and when anything else was made the subject of discourse in her presence, she contrived to turn the conversation, and to make it almost imperceptibly fall upon the excellence of charity, and on the happy necessity in which we are of loving God with all our soul, and with all our strength. She spoke very little, but on this occasion she was wonderfully eloquent. It was easy to perceive by the fire that sparkled in her eyes that in these delightful discourses on the love of God her tongue was the faithful interpreter of her heart, and that she drew from the abundance of the charity with which it was replenished the substance of everything she said.

It was delightful to hear her when praying in her hermitage, giving full scope to her love, and exhorting all creatures to love God, who had given them their being. She generally remained two or three hours in these transports, and these who observed her closely sometimes saw her take a harp, and joining the sweetness of her beautiful voice to the symphony of that instrument, she sang canticles of praise to God for His love towards men. As divine love is a fire, it cannot be so concealed in the soul as not sometimes to manifest its presence by actions of piety, to which the soul is impelled by the desire of pleasing God. S. Rose, reflecting one day on the charity which S. Catherine of Siena had shown towards Jesus Christ, hidden under the form of a beggar, in depriving herself of her garments to clothe Him, thought she might imitate her by making a sort of spiritual and mysterious garment for the Infant Jesus of several acts of virtue. This is the formula which was found in her own handwriting:

" Jesus.

"This year, 1616, by the grace of my Saviour, and under the protection of the Blessed Virgin Mary, I will clothe my Divine Jesus, whom the Church will soon represent to us born naked in a manger, exposed to all the severity of winter. I will make him an under garment of fifty Litanies, of nine hundred chaplets, which

I will recite, and of five days of abstinence from every sort of nourishment, in honour of the adorable mystery of the Incarnation. I will compose His swaddling clothes of nine visits to the most Blessed Sacrament, of nine Psalters of the Blessed Virgin, and of nine fasting days, to honour the nine months during which He was enclosed in her chaste womb. His covering shall consist of five days passed without eating or drinking, of five visits to the most Blessed Sacrament, and of as many Rosaries, in honour of His birth in this world. His bands shall be made of three chaplets of our Lord, of three days' abstinence from food, and of five stations which I will make before the most Blessed Sacrament. For the fringes and borders of His swaddling clothes and bands, I will make thirty-three extra communions, I will assist at thirty-three masses, I will spend thirty- three hours in mental prayer, I will recite thirty- three times the Pater Noster, thirty-three times the Ave Maria, Credo, Gloria Patri, and Salve Regina; I will also recite thirty-three Rosaries, I will fast thirty-three days, I will take three thousand stripes of the discipline, in honour of the thirty-three years He spent on earth. Lastly, I offer as a gift to my dear Jesus, my tears, my sighs, and all the acts of love which I shall make. With this I offer my heart and soul, that there may be nothing in me which is not entirely consecrated to Him."

Zeal being the fruit of love, draws its degrees of excellence from the cause which gives birth to it; so that if love be imperfect, zeal is cold and languishing : on the contrary, if love be generous, zeal is all on fire; thus, as the love of God which consumed the soul of S. Rose was most ardent, she had an incomparable zeal for His glory.

There was no one in the house bold enough to say one word in her presence contrary to modesty: they well knew that her generous zeal for the interests of God would prompt her to condemn it instantly. She could not endure a word to be spoken in the church, much less that it should be made a place for conversation; her zeal, closing her eyes to human respect and every consideration of flesh and blood, gave her a holy confidence in speaking to anyone whatever, who committed this act of irreverence. From her youth upwards, when she heard her brothers and sisters sing profane airs or immodest verses, she wept for grief, and showed them by the abundance of her tears how much the freedom of their words wounded her heart. She must indeed have felt it exceedingly, for she had so high an esteem for tears, which she said belonged to the treasury of God, and were a useful sort of money, with which we may purchase the kingdom of heaven, that she could not endure their being wasted for any earthly cause; hence, seeing her mother shedding them one day profusely for trifles, she said, " Ah mother! why do you waste this precious merchandise, which you might deposit in the treasury of God to avail towards your salvation?"

This zeal made her enter so deeply into the interests of her Divine Spouse, that she felt an incredible joy when she saw Him served and honoured by men; and a poor nun having returned to her convent after having scandalously left it, our Saint showed more pleasure on this occasion than if the crown of all America had been placed on her head; and God, to increase her joy, showed her in spirit the eminent sanctity which this repentant religious would attain through her tears and sighs. Her confessor having been requested to preach on some considerable occasion, when all the chief people in the town would be present, was attacked with a violent fever. Rose, being acquainted with his indisposition, very earnestly begged of Almighty God to send her the fever from which her confessor was suffering. In the confidence she felt that her prayer would be heard, she sent to tell him to prepare for this great action, for he would certainly be without fever when he entered the pulpit, which happened according to her desires, and be acquitted himself of this honourable employment greatly to the satisfaction of his hearers, while S. Rose was suffering the burning heats of his fever.

Almighty God testified His approbation of the eagerness of S. Rose in advancing His glory by a celebrated miracle. In 1617, the year in which she died, on the 15th of April, about five o'clock in the evening, as she was praying in the oratory of Don Gonzalez before a very beautiful statue of Jesus Christ, she felt so ardent a love of God, that, unable to moderate its violence, she rose up and began to address Him, and after some devout colloquies, she begged Him to enkindle the fire of His love in the hearts of men. At the same instant in which she made this prayer, the daughter of Don Gonzalez perceived that this image of the Son of God was quite moist with perspiration, by which He made known, in order to satisfy Rose's desire, the immensity of His charity for men, that being convinced of it by this prodigy, they might detach their affections from creatures, to consecrate them to Him and to love Him only.

Don Gonzalez hurried to the place when he heard of the miracle, and seeing the image sweat, he sent immediately for the Rev. Fathers Diego Martinez, and Diego Penalosa, that they might be eyewitnesses of this prodigy. The first being prevented, the second came, and having entered the oratory, he saw the sweat, and wiped it off himself with cotton. He perceived that this miraculous appearance augmented in proportion as he wiped it. This miracle lasted four hours, in the presence of a number of persons of consideration, whom this prodigy had drawn to the place. They saw several drops of perspiration, as large as little beads, rise successively on the face of this statue one after the other, and run down the hair and neck: the more they wiped the more abundant did the sweat

become, but it did not injure the colours of the painting; on the contrary, it seemed like a varnish which gave them additional brightness. Don Barthelemy Lobo Guerrero, then Archbishop of Lima, appointed Dr. Juan de la Roca, curate and archdeacon of the metropolitan church, judge to examine it juridically. When the examination had been made, and the depositions of the witnesses had been taken, this sweat was declared to be miraculous, not proceeding from the coldness of the place, nor from the unctuous moisture of the oil, with which the colours used in painting the statue had been mixed, but that it was an effect of the omnipotence of God, who acts when He pleases, out of the order of nature and above the rules of art.

Don Gonzalez was very uneasy about this; he feared that this prodigy might be a forerunner of the justice of God, Who intended, perhaps, to punish some secret sin, committed by some member of his family: but S. Rose removed his fear, telling him that Jesus Christ in this image had sweated to animate mankind to love Him. This miracle, which so sweetly invited men to love God, accomplished the charitable desire of our Saint, for all these who had ocular demonstration of it felt an internal fire, inflaming them with the ardour of the charity of Jesus Christ, and were happily pierced with the darts of His divine love. This miracle gave rise to another, for S. Rose having seriously injured herself by a fall, the surgeons feared she would die, or at least be a cripple the rest of her life; but she, having more confidence in the goodness of God than in the efficacy of remedies, thought that she should certainly be cured if she were to dip a little cotton in the sweat of that image, and apply it to her wounded arm; but from the delight she felt in suffering, she dared not do it without speaking first to her confessor, and obtaining his permission. He wished her to follow the first inspiration, believing that Almighty God had sent it, in order to manifest His power by some new miracle. As soon as she applied this moistened cotton to her arm, she felt the nerves return to their place, the cartilages grow stronger, the tumour sink down, and the muscles stretch out. This was a source of astonishment to the surgeons who despaired of curing this evil.

She sends her guardian angel

CHAPTER XIV

OF HER DEVOTION TOWARDS THE MOST BLESSED SACRAMENT, IN DEFENCE OF WHICH SHE ONCE PREPARED HERSELF TO SUFFER MARTYRDOM

If the union of the soul with God be the principle of its happiness and of its progress in virtue, it necessarily follows that devotion towards the most Holy Sacrament of the altar is the most efficacious means of arriving in a short time at perfection and sanctity. From this inexhaustible source of grace S. Rose drew strength, light, and heat; through this sacred channel Almighty God communicated Himself intimately to her, and, in fine, it was by the frequent use of this adorable mystery, that possessing God fully in herself, she was enabled to say with S. Paul, that she lived no longer a natural and human life, but that Jesus Christ her Divine Spouse lived in her, since the grace of this august Sacrament had quite transformed her into Him.

She communicated regularly three times a week, frequently five times, and in some circumstances of her life she communicated every day, according to the orders given her by these who regulated her conscience. As this Divine Sacrament operates according to the dispositions of the receiver, S. Rose prepared for it by confession, which she frequented not by routine, as many in the world do who profess devotion, and who confess their imperfections without any sorrow for them, but with a contrite heart, trying to blot out her sins by a river of tears, and to obtain pardon from the mercy of God by her

sighs. On the eve of her communion she fasted rigorously, on bread and water usually, and took the discipline to blood, and by these austerities she sought to imitate Jesus Christ her Spouse, who is immolated as a victim in this mystery.

She had also the holy custom of preparing her heart for Him by a number of ejaculatory prayers, to express the loving impatience she felt to possess Him; in a word, she disposed herself as carefully for each communion, as if she were going to enjoy that happiness for the last time in her life. Every time she communicated she was so transported with love, that the fire of charity which consumed her soul showed itself on her countenance, and made it appear so beautiful, and sometimes so bright, that even the priests were seized with awe and fear when they brought the Sacred Host to communicate her. She was often surrounded with light at the altar; sometimes she seemed to possess a superhuman beauty; and these who noticed this change would have taken her for an angel, had not her face resumed its ordinary expression; and many religious persons have attested, that when she was making her thanksgiving after communion, they saw issue from her eyes, her hands, and almost every part of her body, rays as brilliant as these of the sun.

Her confessors sometimes obliged her to declare the admirable effects which this adorable Sacrament operated in her soul; she obeyed, but at each word she stopped short, finding it difficult to express the sentiments of her mind, and what passed in her interior; nevertheless to give them some faint idea of these things, she told them, that her heart, her mind, and her whole self became, as it were, transported into God; that she experienced such excessive joy, that all the pleasures of the earth were not to be compared to these she tasted in this magnificent banquet, where Almighty God seems to make these whom He admits to it partakers in His happiness and in His divinity. She declared to them also, that she found in it an entire satiety; and that she derived from it such extraordinary strength, that though before communion she was quite weak from fasting, and from the loss of the blood which she drew from her veins by disciplines, so that she was sometimes obliged to rest in the middle of the church, not being able to go as far as the altar without taking breath, she went from the holy table with the same strength as the prophet Elias felt after having eaten bread baked in the ashes, which was the symbol of the blessed Eucharist, and of the strength which it communicates to these who receive it.

Those belonging to the family have borne witness, that the satiety which she found in the sacred table replenished her so completely, that she shut herself up in her room or in her hermitage without taking any nourishment, and that she remained there till night, and often till the next day, devoutly occupied and quite enraptured in the chaste embraces of her Divine Spouse. And when they called or came to seek her at the time of meals, she, who had fasted the day before, excused herself, saying, it was impossible for her to take anything; so that she was sometimes known to fast eight whole days; and, in imitation of S. Catherine of Siena, to take no other food than that which she had received at the banquet of angels in the holy communion. On her communion days she assisted at every mass that was said till noon with such great recollection, that she kept her eyes always fixed on the altar, and though a great number of persons passed and re-passed continually before her, she saw no one.

When the forty hours' prayer was taking place in any church, she went thither, and remained motionless before the most Holy Sacrament, completely absorbed in God from morning till night. She thought not of food or drink, and though the excessive heat of the country required that she should assuage her thirst with a little water, she felt in her heart a fire of love more vehement than that which heated her body, and this made her forget her necessary refreshment. The following was her method of proceeding during the Octave of the most Blessed Sacrament, and the manner in which she spent the four last years of her life. She was not satisfied with accompanying the Beloved of her heart in procession to the sepulchre on Maundy Thursday, she remained in His company for twenty-four hours, with such profound respect that she dared not sit, nor even lean ever so little against the wall, to support her extreme weakness. Anyone who saw her standing motionless, bathed in tears, now and then looking towards heaven and sighing in the bitterness of her heart, would have taken her for another Magdalen, inseparably attached to the sepulchre of her dear Master by the invisible chains of his love. When the most Blessed Sacrament was carried through the town to the sick, she felt so transported with joy at the sound of the bell, that this interior gladness pervaded her whole body. At the sight of her God, she knelt down wherever she was, and after having adored Him prostrate on the earth, she accompanied Him to the sick, and followed Him to the church with unspeakable satisfaction, thinking herself infinitely happy on these occasions of offering her homage to the Son of God, her Sovereign Lord.

She took great pleasure in washing the church linen, and in making and repairing neatly everything connected with the decoration of the altar. She made flowers of gold and silk for this purpose; and for fear that the time which she spent in these works of piety might prevent her from helping her family, who partly depended on her labours for a living, she devoted part of the night to them, taking away the hours from her sleep to consecrate them to the embellishment of the house of God. Her love for the adorable mystery of the altar was so generous, that she resolved once to defend it from the rage of heretics at the expense of her blood and life; for in her fear that they would get possession of the Blessed Sacrament, and make it the subject of profanation and sacrilege, she ran to the church to oppose their violence by force, though she could not doubt that they would despise her resistance, and tear her in pieces if she attempted to oppose their design.

It happened as follows: in the month of August, 1615, a powerful fleet of the States-General of Holland appeared on the coasts of Peru. Already the vanguard of the enemy was seen approaching the port of Lima, and the greater part of the ships belonging to this naval armament coasted so near the land, that some merchants of Lima, whom this fleet had taken by surprise, thought they saw the boats of the admiral's ship and of the other vessels put on land a quantity of soldiers. Every one was in tears; nothing was heard but the cries of women and children; and the men prepared to defend themselves in such confusion and disorder, that nothing could be expected but the total ruin of the country. Rose, who did not only look upon these heretics as the enemies of her country, but chiefly as the mortal enemies of Jesus Christ, thought of nothing in this general consternation but of defending the most Blessed Sacrament at the peril of her life, for It was exposed in all the churches of the town. She animated her companions, and exhorted them to die generously for the defence of this most august Mystery. With the resolution of suffering herself to be slain by these soldiers, she disposed herself to resist their violence courageously; she mounted on the steps of the altar with the same resolution as S. Ambrose represents Judith to have shown in approaching the camp of the enemies of God. Rose knew very well that she could not resist the violence of these who would put her to death; but she prepared to fight, to honour the belief in this great Sacrament.

From her sparkling eyes, her proud air, and the tone of her voice, which was that of a heroine exhorting the troops to combat, she might have been taken for a Christian Minerva, armed for the defence of religion, or for an angry lioness, which rushes on against the weapons of the hunters, who are carrying away its little ones. She was found in this state of preparation and resolution to die on the steps of the altar by the hand of these heretical soldiers, when news was brought that the fleet had weighed anchor, and sailed away without any manifestation of hostility. Everywhere in Lima the people were heard blessing God; each one expressed his joy and gratitude; Rose alone seemed inconsolable in this general delight, for she grieved to have lost the opportunity of martyrdom which she had thought so near. She had so earnest a desire of dying a martyr, that she every day asked of Almighty God the grace of shedding her blood, and of dying by the hand of a sacrilegious person or an executioner. She often regretted that she was not born in these times when tyrants cruelly massacred the Christians, thinking that then she should not have failed to lose her life for Jesus Christ.

This desire of martyrdom, which neither the peace of the Church, nor the little prospect she saw of being exposed to the persecution of heretics and infidels, could extinguish in her heart, often made her say, with tears in her eyes, "Would to God that I could find the opportunity and the means of going to distant pagan countries, that I might die by the hands of barbarians for Jesus Christ my dear Spouse."

CHAPTER XV

OF HER DEVOTION TO AN IMAGE OF OUR BLESSED LADY, TO THE SIGN OF THE CROSS, AND TO HER DEAR MISTRESS S. CATHERINE OF SIENA

For more than a century the people of the town of Lima had honoured a statue of the Blessed Virgin in the church of the Friars Preachers, under the name of Our Lady of the Rosary, a devotion which these monks had taught to the people at the time that they planted the faith in the most celebrated provinces of America.

But before we speak of the graces which S. Rose received by this means, we must go farther back, and show what rendered the people so devout to this image.

It was a wooden statue of our Blessed Lady, five feet high, which the first Spanish Christians who passed over into Peru with our forefathers brought from Europe with them, to be the powerful Protectress of their project. She holds the Infant Jesus with her left arm, and with the right hand offers a Rosary. When they had settled in this country, and had built this famous town now called Lima, they raised a superb church for the religious of the Order of Friars Preachers, under the name of the Holy Rosary, which was the first church and the first parish in which baptismal fonts were erected for the regeneration of spiritual children to Jesus Christ in the New World; and they placed in it this image, which was honoured

by the people with special veneration, on account of the signal favours received through the protection of the Blessed Virgin of the Holy Rosary.

The year 1535 was marked by one of these instances of her patronage. The Indians had assembled near Caxaguana, in the province of Cusco, to the number of two hundred thousand, in order to massacre the Christians; and they felt the more assured of victory as the Spanish army opposed to them consisted only of six hundred men. In this consternation the religious, having placed themselves at the head of the Christian troops, exhorted them to implore the protection of our Lady of the Holy Rosary. They did so, and, filled with confidence in her assistance, they gave battle to this great multitude of Indians. At the moment in which the engagement began, they perceived in the air the Blessed Virgin, under the same form as she is represented in the Church of the Rosary, holding a rod in her hand, and threatening the Indians with death if they did not withdraw. The infidels were so alarmed at this vision, and so dazzled with the splendour that surrounded the Blessed Virgin, that they begged for quarter, and submitted not only to Spain, but also to the yoke of Jesus Christ by becoming Christians. This memorable victory greatly increased the devotion of the people towards our Lady of the Rosary.

Philip IV, King of Spain, having placed his kingdom of Peru under the protection of the Blessed Virgin on the 27th May, 1643, and having given notice of his intention to the archbishop, the viceroy, and magistrates of Lima, exhorted them to choose some image of the Blessed Virgin, and address to it their prayers, that they might obtain succour from her in the dangers which threatened the country. When the orders of his Catholic majesty were received, the archbishop, the viceroy, and the two estates ecclesiastical and secular, chose our Lady of the Rosary to be the Protectress of the whole kingdom of

Peru, and resolved that the people should every year go in procession, on the Monday in Low Week, to the church of the Friars Preachers, to offer their prayers to her. This procession took place every year with great pomp; the image of our Lady was carried from the church through the town, the garrison being under arms; the chapter of the cathedral, the religious, the viceroy, the officers and magistrates assisted at it. The devotion towards this image was so great, that every day a crowd of people came to pray before it.

S. Rose spent some time every day in prayer on her knees before the altar on which this image was placed, with very great devotion, which increased more and more in her heart, as she perceived that this inanimate statue cast towards her looks of tenderness, and made certain signs as if it wished to caress her, and manifest to her by these miraculous movements, the love which the Blessed Virgin, of whom it was but the copy, bore to her. She noticed the same affability in the face of the Infant Jesus whom this image was represented as holding; she too saw Him sometimes smile, extending His arms to caress her, and He gave her so many visible signs that He answered the love which she bore Him, that she felt as certain of it as if she had seen His affection for her painted or engraved in large letters. It seemed to her that this Divine Infant wished to leave His Mother to throw Himself into her arms, in order to caress her with greater facility. It was looked upon in the town as certain that Rose obtained whatever she asked of Heaven when she prayed before this image, and she herself felt as sure of obtaining what she asked through the intercession of our Lady of the Rosary, as if she had received from Heaven letters patent, confirming all the graces she requested for herself or for others.

She was also very devout to another image of the Blessed Virgin, which she honoured particularly in her oratory at home, because she had remarked that this image gave signs of life, that it changed its position, approached her, smiled upon her, and offered her the same caresses as if it were truly the Blessed Virgin, and not a mere copy of the original. When a lady, who had come to see her, was relating in the presence of this image the great miracles which the Blessed Virgin worked every day at Achota, a place of devotion near Madrid in Spain, in favour of these devout persons who came to honour her, and of the sick who sought her protection to obtain from God the cure of their diseases, Rose remarked, during this conversation, that her image gave great signs of joy, looked at her with a smiling countenance, and shone more brightly than usual.

Every Saturday she took care to adorn the Chapel of the Rosary with flowers which she had cultivated expressly for this purpose. She was never known to fail in this act of devotion; and in summer, when the heat of the sun dries up all the plants, as well as in winter, when the cold renders gardens unproductive, the altar was seen as richly ornamented with flowers as in the time of spring. She had also undertaken to adorn with a robe this image, to which she had so great a devotion; but the spiritual garment which she composed of her prayers, her fasts, her disciplines, her tears, and of all the acts of virtue she practised, as an ornament for the Queen of Heaven, was much more pleasing to her than if she had clothed her with some costly material. The following is the method she practised, which she wrote down herself:—

" JESUS, MARY.

"The spiritual garment which I, Sister Rose of S. Mary, unworthy servant of the Queen of Angels, prepare, by her help, for the Blessed Virgin, Mother of God. 1st, her tunic shall consist of six hundred Ave Marias, as many Salve Reginas, and of fifteen fasting days, in honour of the spiritual joy which she felt in her holy soul when the Archangel announced to her the Incarnation of the Word in her chaste womb. 2ndly, the material for this mysterious robe shall be six hundred Ave Marias, six hundred Salve Reginas, fifteen

Rosaries, and fifteen fasting days, in honour of the joy she felt in going to visit her cousin S. Elizabeth. 3rdly, I will border it with six hundred Ave Marias, as many Salve Reginas, fifteen Rosaries, and fifteen fasting days, in honour of the joy which filled her heart when the Son of God was born into the world. 4thly, The clasps shall be made of six hundred Ave Marias, of six hundred Salve Reginas, and fifteen fasting days, in honour of her interior joy in offering her Son Jesus Christ in the Temple. 5thly, her necklace shall be composed of six hundred Ave Marias, as many Salves, of fifteen fasting days, and fifteen Rosaries, in honour of that joy she felt in finding her Son in the Temple, in the midst of the doctors, three days after having lost Him. 6thly, the sceptre that I shall place in her hand shall be made of thirty-three Paters, thirty- three Rosaries, thirty-three Gloria Patris, and thirty-three Salve Reginas, in honour of the thirty-three years which Jesus Christ, God and Man, lived on earth for our salvation." A little below she wrote: —"May God be eternally glorified, and His most pure Mother, the Virgin Mary, honoured by every creature! I have made this spiritual garment, and have acquitted myself of this devotion, by the help of the grace of my God, who has supplied for my defects."

She had a wonderful devotion to the sign of the cross; she kissed every day a large wooden cross, which she had in her cell in the garden, with such tender sentiments of love and respect, that it was easy to see that she bore its mysteries deeply engraved in her heart. Wherever she saw a cross, she knelt down to venerate it. She had the same respect for every thing which bore the figure of a cross; for when she saw any likeness of it, in pieces of wood placed across, or in the interwoven branches of trees or hedges, or in pieces of straw, or in the bolts of doors, she felt herself interiorly moved by the form of the sign of our salvation, and never passed on without showing marks of respect and veneration. Amongst the plants and flowers which she cultivated in her father's garden, she had a large rosemary, the principal branches of which formed a cross. The wife of the viceroy of Peru asked her for one of them; not being able to refuse so small a gift to a lady of her merit and quality, she sent her one, but as soon as it was planted in her garden it died. Rose's confessor having told her of it, she answered that it was not to be wondered at; for the cross cannot exist amongst the delights and vanities of the court.

The Marquess of Salinas del Río Pisuerga, 8th Viceroy of Peru

She begged that it might be sent back to her, and having replanted it, in four days it was as green and beautiful as ever.

The members of the Confraternity of S. Catherine of Siena were accustomed to carry her image round the town every year, adorned with a crown of flowers and precious stones. Rose, who honoured her as her dear mistress, and loved her as her spiritual mother, could not bear that anyone else should render her this service; she contrived so well, that she was charged with the duty of carrying it, and she acquitted herself of it, as long as she lived, with great sentiments of tenderness and devotion. Besides this commission she had obtained also the appointment of sacristan to her chapel; she adorned her image as richly as she could, but with so tender a devotion, that in doing this she gave it a thousand kisses, and expressed to her by ardent words the love she had for her. "O my dear mistress," said she one day, " how I regret not to have money to clothe you with another garment!" As she finished speaking, a slave of Madame Hierome de Gama brought her the money she had desired for this pious design.

One day in May, which is the season of winter in the torrid zone, when she wished to adorn her as usual, she went to seek flowers in her garden, but not finding any, she commanded a root of pinks to furnish her with some, and immediately there

appeared several beautiful flowers, though there had not been any ready to come out before. She gathered in the same manner a quantity of roses from a rose tree. This miracle happened so frequently that it no longer caused surprise to the people of Lima and the surrounding country. It was not without reason that she honoured with special devotion the image of this seraphic virgin; she had often seen her surrounded with heavenly light, and had been present at the miracle she worked in curing Frances de Montoya, by preserving her from the effects of a sulphurous flame which would have caused the loss of her eye, without this miraculous assistance. She had herself experienced the effects of the goodness and power of her dear mistress, when she was suffering from gout, which had swelled her hands so much that she could not move her fingers.

In the year 1616, S. Rose wishing to adorn her image to carry it in procession on the feast of S. Dominic, which was drawing near, begged her to enable her to continue the performance of her usual duties. After her prayer she put her fingers within the rings of her scissors without reflecting on her infirmity, and from the size to which her fingers were swollen she could not have done this without a miracle. This assistance, which her good mistress gave her, filled her with joy, and greatly surprised the Receiver, his wife, and several physicians, who confessed that it was an effect of the Divine Power, which bad cured her in an instant.

S. Catherine of Siena by Andrea di Vanni, one of her disciples.

CHAPTER XVI

OF HER ZEAL FOR THE SALVATION OF SOULS, AND HER CARE IN ASSISTING THE POOR IN THEIR SICKNESS AND NECESSITIES.

True love being always accompanied by zeal, it follows that we cannot perfectly love the Son of God, who takes so great an interest in the salvation of these souls whom He has redeemed with His Precious Blood, without being also zealous for the eternal welfare of sinners for whom He suffered death. As this zeal was the characteristic of S. Dominic, and as it still inflames the hearts of these among her children whom the

Church destines to gain souls, we need not be surprised that S. Rose, his beloved daughter, should have received the spirit of zeal of this great patriarch with the habit of his Order. She showed during her whole life an indefatigable zeal for the conversion of sinners, and never failed one single day to ask of God for them by her prayers, and generally also by her  blood, the grace to be restored to His friendship.

Whenever she cast her eyes on the high mountains of South America, she wept for the eternal loss of the barbarous people who dwelt amongst them. Her zeal being as boundless as her charity, she deplored also the damnation of the almost innumerable multitude of pagans in the New World, who have no knowledge of God, nor of the adorable mysteries of religion; she desired to be torn in pieces, and placed at the gate of hell, as a barrier to hinder men from precipitating themselves into it, as they do every day.

She exhorted religious persons, whenever she met them, in words of fire, to go and preach the Gospel to the idolatrous Indians, warning them especially to shun studied figures of rhetoric, which corrupt the purity of the word of God; and not to be attached to the useless subtleties of the schools, nor to the questions which are therein agitated, unless they may be useful in converting infidels. She sometimes said, in a transport of zeal, that if Almighty God had made her of a different sex, she would have applied herself to study, in order to labour with all her power for the conversion of souls, and that when her studies were finished she would have penetrated into the most distant provinces and most barbarous nations of America, to enlighten these savages with the torch of faith, or to finish her life by a  glorious martyrdom. Seeing herself incapacitated by her sex from executing this charitable design, she had resolved to adopt a child, and bring him up to study and prayer, by the help of the alms given her and the money she gained by her work, that she might send him to preach to infidels when he was capable of it.

One of her confessors being undecided about accompanying some good religious in a mission to the Indians, for which they were preparing, she made over to him half the merit she might have gained by the good works which she had performed by the grace of God, in order to animate him to this enterprise, in which the salvation of a great number of souls was in question. If she had great zeal for these poor Indians, what shall we say of that which she manifested for the salvation of Christians, who are, as S. Paul says, of the household of the faith, when she saw them in danger of losing heaven by their crimes and excesses?

She took every day severe disciplines for their conversion; and as she could not keep to herself the zeal which inflamed her, she sometimes made it known by these words: "Ah, if it were permitted to me to exercise the function of preacher, I would go by day and by night barefoot into the most public places, covered with a hair-shirt, and bearing a large cross on my shoulders, to exhort sinners to do penance, and to represent to them the fearful severity of the judgments of God." And she modestly advised these who were engaged in the apostolical ministry, to make these subjects the ordinary matter of their discourses, to renounce the ornaments of worldly rhetoric, and to abstain from these studied declamations, which are more suited to the theatre than to the pulpit, because preachers are established by Almighty God to be fishers of men, that is, to withdraw them from sin and hell by their fervent exhortations.

She was animated with the spirit of her father S. Dominic, and would have considered herself to have degenerated from the glorious quality of his daughter, if she had not imitated his ardent charity for others; therefore all her aim was to draw men to God, to bring them from vice, and to inspire them with a love for virtue. She never spoke with anyone without leading the conversation to the necessity of knowing, loving, and serving God, and to the obligation contracted by every Christian of leading a holy life, of renouncing the maxims and vanities of the world, and of clothing themselves with Jesus Christ by an imitation of these virtues which He practised for our example. She was so thoroughly persuaded of the truths she uttered, and so deeply touched by them, that she scarcely

spoke to any person without gaining him to God, and inducing him to change his life.

Almighty God often made use of her in a miraculous manner for the conversion of several persons engaged in vice. A young man of high family, but whose life did not correspond with his noble blood, despairing of marrying Rose, whom he passionately loved, sought at least some comfort in the pleasure of seeing her; he watched carefully for opportunities; he gained her mother over, and agreed with her that she should order Rose to make collars and linen for him, which he pretended to want. When her mother called her to speak to him, and to accompany him to the linen draper's shop, Almighty God made known to Rose the evil intention of this young gentleman, whose name was Don Vincent Montelis Venergas. Thus warned by heaven, she met him with civility, spoke to him strongly, and filled him with so great a fear of the judgments of God, that he left her entirely converted, and so touched with what she had said, that he, giving himself wholly to God, and applying himself diligently to the care of his salvation, he lived from that time in sentiments of exemplary piety, and generally communicated every week.

She contributed no less to the salvation of a woman, whose passionate temper caused her to fall into such excesses of impatience every minute, that it was impossible to live with her and to have a quarter of an hour's peace. She went one day to visit S. Rose in her cell, and this holy virgin made her a discourse on the meekness which the Son of God has taught us by His words and example; and she showed her so efficaciously the excellence and necessity of this virtue, which is, in some degree, the spirit of Christianity, that this woman overcame her fiery and passionate temper, telling every one that she had been delighted with the admonitions of our Saint, and that the sweetness of her eyes and words always extinguished in her the impetuous sallies of anger, to which her temper and a long indulged habit gave rise continually in her heart.

S. Rose's confessor, Father Peter of Louysa, knowing the greatness of her compassionate zeal, informed her that a certain religious was suffering dreadful pains; in his agony he was seen to sweat, shudder, and tremble with a lively apprehension of the rigour of God's judgments. She begged this good father to fortify him and to animate him to hope by the representation of the boundless mercy of Almighty God; and to offer him from her a part of all the good she had done during her life in the service of God, in order to supply what might be wanting to him before he could enter heaven; and to tell him that she should be glad to know the state of his soul after death, that she might continue her prayers and suffrages for him if he stood in need of them, he was greatly comforted by S. Rose's charity, and died in great tranquillity. Some days after Almighty God revealed to her that the soul of this person was in possession of eternal happiness.

It will perhaps appear

surprising, and not without cause, that the funeral of S. Rose should have been honoured with the cries, tears, and sighs of the poor, and that they should have been heard bitterly to lament having lost, in the person of Rose, their mother and their nurse, since she was so poor herself, and so ill provided with the goods of this life, that she was obliged to support her family partly by her own work; nevertheless, we need not be astonished at it, if we reflect that charity is powerful, and the zeal which accompanies it ingenious in devising means to help others in their necessities. She assisted them, first, by begging for them in the first houses in the town, where her virtue made her well received, and where the distribution of plentiful alms was confided to her. Secondly, by liberally dividing with them the charity which was given her for herself, as it was known that she had to support her parents and family. Thirdly, by depriving herself of the necessaries of life to help them. In this spirit of charity she abstained from food eight days, that she might give a poor man the money she would have spent in nourishment during that time. Fourthly, by bestowing upon them things of which she herself stood in need. Her mother having given her thirty-six ells of cloth to make veils and aprons, and other articles of dress, she gave them to two very poor but very virtuous young ladies. Almighty God worked several miracles to enable her to give alms, and He never failed to supply the necessities of the family by extraordinary means when S. Rose, confiding in His providence, boldly gave away what was intended for their support.

One day when she had nothing to give a poor woman, who begged her for the love of God to give her some old clothes, to cover her poor little half-naked children, she took a large cloak, belonging to her mother, and without any permission, beyond that which she interiorly received from God, who inspired her to perform this action, she bestowed it upon her. Her mother being displeased with this sort of liberality, Rose humbly entreated her not to be uneasy, and assured her that Almighty God, who had given her this thought, would make her a return beyond the cost of her cloak. She was not deceived in her expectation, for the same day a stranger came in, and gave her fifty pieces of money; three days after, Dame Mary of Sala sent her, by a servant, a piece of cloth large enough to make another cloak; and the next day the Dominicans gave her several ells of serge, as if they had all combined to return to the mother of our Saint more than her charitable daughter had given to the poor.

Her charity extended still farther; she made herself the attendant and infirmarian of the poor; She took home with her a young orphan lady, named Jane de Bobadilla, of Azevedo, who, besides her great poverty which obliged her to live at the very extremity of the suburbs of the town, had a cancer in her breast, of which no one could bear the insupportable odour. God revealed her condition to S. Rose; immediately she went to see her, offered to wait upon her, and that she might be able to do so, she persuaded her to come to her father's house, where she would render her every sort of assistance; still as she knew that her mother was a little too much attached to her own interests, she told her that she would hire a room in the house for her, and that she would give her the money to pay herself, only requiring that she should keep this a secret. Rose hired the room, brought the lady to it, whom she charitably waited upon, and worked more than usual to obtain the money necessary for the payment of the lodging, which the lady did not quit till she was perfectly recovered.

Her mother having found this out a little later, gave her leave to bring home sick persons, and after this permission Rose exercised her charity indifferently towards the poor women and girls whom she met in the streets, whatever might be their condition. She was not satisfied with giving them a lodging; she nursed them, made their beds, dressed their ulcers,

washed their clothes, and, in a word, rendered them every sort of service, making no distinction between the Spaniard and the Indian, the free and the slave, the European or the African negroes. There was no disease, however loathsome, from which these poor women were suffering, that did not call into action the indefatigable charity of S. Rose, who waited upon them night and day.

When she had no sick persons to attend at home, she went to practice charity at the hospital; and when she perceived anyone whose disease caused her aversion, she devoted herself to her service; and whatever repugnance she might feel, she made her bed, dressed her wounds, fed her, and rendered her the most abject services, although in doing so, she often soiled her habit, which she liked to keep exceedingly clean. She did not practise these virtues without a strong opposition on the part of nature; but she courageously resisted and triumphed over it by the violence she did to her feelings, of which the following is an instance. She went one day to visit a girl in the house of Isabel Mexia, who was very ill, and had been bled two days before. When our Saint saw the green and corrupted blood which had been taken from her, she felt her stomach turn at the sight. Ashamed of this weakness, she asked the servant, who was going to throw the blood away, to give it to her; and taking it with her into another room, she drank it to the last drop, imitating, by this heroic action, her good mistress S. Catherine of Siena, who, having felt the same weakness at the sight of a dreadful cancer, from which a poor woman, whom she had taken upon herself to serve, was suffering, filled a vessel with the matter that proceeded from it, and drank it courageously, to overcome the rebellion of nature.

By her charity she restored a number of sick persons to health; and we might say that the Son of God, to show forth the merit of the mercy she exercised towards them, had communicated to her hands a miraculous power to heal them;

and that, as He formerly imparted such efficacious virtue to the shadow of S. Peter that it restored health, He had renewed this wonder in our Saint, for very often the mere sight of her effected a cure. We will only cite one example, of which the whole people of Lima were witness. Don Juan de Almansa, a man of high rank, being very dangerously ill, desired very much to speak to S. Rose once more before he died: she went to see him, to afford him this satisfaction. When she entered his room, he remarked quite a heavenly beauty on her countenance, from which he conceived a firm hope that she would obtain his cure from Almighty God, Who alone could draw him from the state to which he was reduced. While she was speaking to him he fell asleep with this consoling thought, and awoke in as perfect health as if he had never been ill.

CHAPTER XVII

OF HER CONFIDENCE IN GOD, AND OF THE PROTECTION SHE RECEIVED FROM HIM IN HER NECESSITIES.

A soul which has tasted the goodness of Almighty God cannot be diffident of His mercies, for she knows that He is always disposed to protect and assist her; and the same charity which inflames her will, enlightening her understanding by its brightness, gives her so perfect a knowledge of His Divine attributes, that she finds continually fresh motives for confidence. S. Paul founds it upon three perfections of God, which are, as it were, the agents of His love and His providence, His Power, His Wisdom, and His Goodness.

As S. Rose had often experienced its effects in the loving conduct of God towards her, she had an entire confidence in Him in her spiritual and corporal necessities, and in those of others for whom she solicited graces. She took great pleasure in meditating upon, or in pronouncing these words of the prophet David, "Incline unto my aid, O God; O Lord, make haste to help me." She had them almost constantly in her mouth and in her heart. There were three things in particular, which she was as sure of obtaining as if she had had a revelation from heaven. First, she never doubted of her salvation; secondly, of the inviolable friendship of Almighty God for her: thirdly, of

His all-powerful help in the necessities and dangers in which she might have need of His protection.

She was once seized with a great fear regarding the inscrutable mystery of predestination, which is, in fact, capable of terrifying the most steadfast and virtuous souls. God did not leave her long in this anxiety; He spoke these words of consolation in the interior of her soul: " My child, know that I condemn only those, who by resisting My graces will obstinately lose their souls: continue, therefore, to make a good use of them, live in peace, and be no longer disturbed with this fear." After she received this favourable answer from her Divine Spouse, she had so firm an assurance of her salvation, that when Don Juan de Castille asked her if she had had any revelation, which had given her a certainty of salvation, she confessed to him that Jesus Christ had made known to her that she was predestinated to glory from all eternity; and even when lying on her death-bed, overwhelmed with the pains she suffered in every part of her body, she received an assurance from Heaven that her soul should not pass through the fire of purgatory, and that Almighty God was content, and His divine justice fully satisfied with what she endured from the violent pains of her illness.

In a rapture which she had once in her cell in the garden, she saw in a moment the earth around her all covered with roses. As she was much surprised to see this singular appearance in the season of winter, Jesus Christ appeared to her, and after having caressed her, He commanded her to gather these flowers. She did so, and gave them to Him, but He only asked for one, saying to her, "Thou art this Rose, of which I have a most special care." This chaste spouse understood immediately the meaning of these mysterious words; and was quite consoled to see that God kept it at His right-hand, which is the place reserved for His elect, as a rose chosen from a great number of others. She took the remainder of the

flowers, and made of them a garland, which she respectfully placed on the head of her Divine Spouse, who disappeared after having received it with a gracious countenance, and given her His benediction.

She had the same assurance of persevering in the grace and friendship of God till death, from a revelation by which He made clearly known to her that He had confirmed her in His love, and that she should never be separated from it one moment during her life. In this spirit of confidence she one day told her confessor, that he would sooner make her believe herself to be a stone or a log of wood, than persuade her that Almighty God had a horror or an aversion for her.

This great confidence fortified her mind wonderfully in all the difficulties and dangers which are inseparable from this life, and which so often disturb it. She met some furious bulls in the street without turning out of her way, though her mother and every one rushed into the nearest houses to avoid meeting them, and called to her to run away for fear of being killed; she contented herself with saying, that she was sure these bulls would not hurt her; which was verified on two occasions, to the astonishment of the spectators, who thought her death inevitable.

How great was her confidence in God for things necessary to life! One day seeing that there was no money in the house to buy provisions, nor a bit of bread to eat, she went to open the chest, in the assurance that God, Who never abandons these who trust in Him, would provide for her family. She was not deceived, for she found it full of loaves, whiter and of a different shape from these they were accustomed to eat. On another occasion the honey, which is much used in Peru, having failed, and her brothers having brought word that there was not a single drop remaining, Rose, full of confidence in God, went to the place, and found the vessel quite full of excellent honey, which lasted the family during eight months.

When her father, Gasper Florez, was sick, and oppressed with sorrow at not being able to pay the sum of fifty livres, which he owed, and which he was pressed to return, Rose, being told of it, went to the church to beg God to assist him on the occasion, and not allow him to be put to confusion. As she returned, she saw a stranger enter the house, who gave her father a little purse, containing precisely the sum he wanted to satisfy his creditor. Almighty God favoured Rose's family on many other occasions, and by miraculous means, to reward her admirable confidence in Him, in the great necessities to which her family was often reduced.

Her confidence did not merely regard temporal affairs and necessities; she manifested it particularly in things which related to the glory of God, even so far as to take upon herself, notwithstanding her extreme poverty, to furnish the funds necessary for the Monastery of S. Catherine of Siena, which was going to be erected. She told them that they had nothing to do but to begin to dig the foundations, to collect the materials and seek workmen, and that she would pay for everything; Almighty God had made known to her that her confidence pleased Him, and that He would not abandon her on this occasion. This resolution was spoken of by every one according to their caprice, but nearly all blamed it; some calling it a rash enterprise, others terming it insolence and presumption; even her mother was displeased, and called her foolish and visionary, to talk of raising a building that would cost 10,000 livres and more, when she had not a penny. Rose answered humbly, that God was the guarantee of His own word, and that in a few years she would see this monastery built. Her mother growing more angry, called her silly and extravagant. "Well, mother," answered S. Rose, with her usual mildness, "you will yourself experience the

truth of this prediction, for you will enter this monastery, you will there receive the habit of religion, make your vows, and die in the peace of our Lord." "I become a nun, I!" cried her mother, "what probability is there of that? I am old and poor, and I have never had the least thought of a religious life."

She did not fail, however, to verify her holy daughter's prediction; for in the year 1629, after her husband's death, she received the habit of the Order in this monastery, at the age of sixty. She took the name of Sister Mary of S. Mary, and when her noviceship was completed, she was professed, and died a holy death a few years later. Her poverty was no obstacle to her reception, for she filled one of the places reserved by the foundress for poor girls, who were to be received gratuitously. We shall speak of this monastery in the next chapter.

It will have been remarked from what we have said, that the care taken by S. Rose to assist the poor, and to furnish them abundantly with necessaries in their sickness, was founded only on her generous confidence in God. This was so great, that she took home indiscriminately all sorts of sick women to nurse them, without troubling herself whether or not there was any food for them, or any money to buy the necessary drugs and remedies; she confided so entirely in God, that she never doubted of His coming to her assistance in her charity towards them; and in fact she often remarked, that her family was never better off, or more comfortable, than when she had the greatest number of sick persons to provide for.

CHAPTER XVIII

GOD MAKES KNOWN TO S. ROSE THAT A MONASTERY OF NUNS WILL BE BUILT IN LIMA, UNDER THE NAME OF S. CATHERINE OF SIENA, AND REVEALS TO HER SEVERAL OTHER SECRETS

Love is always communicative; it allows of no secrets between these whose affections it unites; and it is a sort of injustice to give the heart to anyone without revealing all that it contains of any importance. The Son of God Himself gave to His apostles a most incontestable proof of His friendship for them, when He told them that He had made them partakers of all the secrets which He had learned in the bosom of His Father from all eternity. As this Blessed Saviour loved S. Rose so tenderly, and even publicly took her for His spouse, we cannot wonder that He honoured her with the gift of prophecy.

There is in Lima a celebrated monastery of two hundred nuns, of the Order of S. Dominic, built in the year 1622, by the pious liberality of Lucia Guerra de la Daga, an illustrious and very virtuous widow. God had revealed to S. Rose the foundation of this convent ten years before it was begun, and had shown it to her, sometimes by mysterious symbols, sometimes in the same form in which it at present appears, which made her speak of it with as much certainty as if she had seen it built and perfectly finished. She named the persons whom God had chosen to serve Him therein; she mentioned their number; she marked out the spot where it would be built, and sketched the design of it on a table; she told Father Louis of Bilbao, her confessor, that he would be the first to celebrate mass in it; she recognized on seeing her the person whom God had shown her as the first prioress; and transported with joy she went to embrace her, and congratulate her on her election; and by the kiss of peace she gave her, she seemed to consecrate her to that charge for which God had chosen her.

The greater number of these who heard this foundation spoken of so confidently, treated her predictions as the fancies of a heated brain, for there was then no human probability that things would fall out as she said they would. The lady of rank whom she named as the foundress was engaged in the bonds of matrimony, which deprived her of the liberty of disposing of her fortune; she had also several children; and another circumstance which seemed to destroy all hope of accomplishing this foundation was, that the person who had been sent to obtain the permission of his Catholic Majesty for it, had returned without being able to succeed. The prediction of our Saint was, however, accomplished, in all its circumstances; for the lady whom God had chosen to be the foundress soon became a widow by the death of her husband, and a few days after, her five children followed him to the grave, so that she was able to devote her property to this good work.

Almighty God removed the obstacles which the devil's malice and the envy of mankind opposed to this pious design, and so completely changed the minds of several magistrates, whose resistance and obstinacy had seemed invincible, that they not only gave their consent, but became so zealous that they themselves forwarded the execution of the project; and in a short time this famous monastery was built, which still glories in the name of the Convent of the Blessed Rose of S. Mary, though it was not built till five years after her death.

God gave S. Rose the first knowledge of it in a wonderful manner. One day having gathered a quantity of roses in her garden, she began to throw them into the air, quite inflamed with devotion, and giving vent to sighs which the thought of her heavenly Spouse forced from her. Her brother finding her thus employed, and with her eyes bathed in tears, entreated her to tell him the cause of her grief; she would not make known this mystery, but God manifested it to him by the wonders of which he was a witness, for he saw that the roses which his sister had thrown into the air remained suspended there, and having first separated, they reunited, and when all together represented a beautiful cross. He saw also that the roses which she continued to throw formed a border to this mysterious cross. S. Rose knew by divine revelation that these roses represented the great number of holy virgins who would rise above the earth by a generous contempt of its honours, riches, and pleasures, to attach themselves inseparably to the cross of Jesus Christ, by the practice of religious virtues, and the exact observance of the rules and constitutions which were to consecrate these courageous victims to penance.

On another occasion when she was praying, God showed her in spirit a spacious meadow, delightfully enamelled with roses and lilies, enclosed within a garden, which was to be separated from the profane intercourse of seculars. Father John of Villalobos, of the Company of Jesus, a religious of great merit, juridically deposed that he had several times observed in S. Rose a spirit of prophecy, and that she had discovered to him the most hidden secrets of his interior. She showed the same knowledge with regard to Father Philip de Tapia, rector of the college at Callao, and many other persons, whom she admonished of certain things, so secret that they confessed she could only have known them by revelation.

This spirit of prophecy enabled her to see what happened in other places, and she predicted some events long before they came to pass. She assured some persons who were dangerously ill and almost in their agony, that they would recover, though the physicians had given them up, and had remarked in them the prognostics of inevitable death. She foretold to several young men, and to a great number of girls, the state and condition which they would one day embrace; and by this supernatural light she told some that they would enter religion, though at that time they seemed entirely opposed to this manner of life, owing to their engagements in the world. She knew that the viceroy would change his mind, and would excuse Don Gonzalez from the difficult employment which he had destined for him, wishing more to remove him from his court than to do him honour, which change of purpose rejoiced his family, who were inconsolable at the idea of his departure.

She wrote to one of her brothers, telling him that he would have a daughter by his marriage, who would be born with the mark of a red rose on her face, warning him to take great care of her, for she would one day be a great servant of God, and that this supernatural mark was a sure sign of the wonderful progress she would make in charity and other virtues. She knew the deception of a negress, who boldly maintained that she had been baptised at Panama; S. Rose convicted her of falsehood through secret indications, and told her so many secrets regarding her interior, that this poor creature confessed her attempt to deceive, and, powerfully touched by S. Rose's exhortations, demanded baptism. Some difficulty was at first made about granting it, from the fear that she requested it more through human respect than from a true spirit of piety; but S. Rose, who knew the disposition of her soul and that death was threatening her, caused it to be given to her so opportunely, that this new Christian died the next day with every mark of perfect contrition for her sins.

Almighty God, who had enlightened her mind with so great penetration and discernment, that she knew the interior of these who came to visit her, and predicted future events to them, taught her Himself to write, as He taught S. Catherine of Siena. He also made known to her so clearly the time, the place, the day, and the hour of her death, that she spoke of her funeral, and specified particularly what would take place at that happy time.

CHAPTER XIX

OF HER LAST ILLNESS AND DEATH

The same law which obliges us all to enter the world by birth, that we may be capable of being made children of God by the grace of regeneration given to us in holy baptism, requires us to depart out of it by the door of death, in order to take possession of the inheritance of eternal glory, which the Son of God has merited for us by His sufferings, and to which the grace of our adoption gives us a title. This indispensable law of nature makes us regard the death of S. Rose, which filled the town of Lima and nearly all Peru with sighs and tears, in the same light as S. Bernard considered that of S. Malachy, which drew lamentations from all his religious, as the end of his combats, the consummation of his virtues, and his triumphant entrance into heaven.

S. Rose having learned by revelation that she should die on the day which the Church consecrates to honour S. Bartholomew, had from that time a special veneration for this feast, and she passed it in particular exercises of piety; but not considering this sufficient to honour the day, which was to be to her the first of a happy eternity, she caused several little children to fast with her on the eve, and their innocence, being very pleasing to God, greatly increased the merit of this mortification. Her mother was surprised at the extraordinary devotion she had towards this apostle; but she ceased to wonder at it, when her daughter informed her that on this day her nuptials with the Son of God would be consummated in heaven. Having attained her thirty-first year, which she knew by inspiration she should not live to complete, she made the wife of Don Gonzalez, her great benefactor, and the protector of her family, acquainted with the day and place of her death, though she was in perfect health when she gave them this sad intelligence.

The same revelation which informed her of the day of her death, made known to her also the great sufferings she was to endure at the close of her life. Almighty God showed her their number; and told her that her pains would be so violent, that each member of her body would have its own particular torment. She knew that she should have to suffer the same thirst which tormented our Blessed Saviour on the cross, and also a burning heat which would dry up the very marrow in her bones. She did not tremble at the sight of this species of martyrdom; the bitterness of the chalice which God had prepared for her did not shake her constancy; on the contrary, she lifted up her hands and eyes to heaven, to adore the sovereign goodness of her Spouse, Who wished her to partake in His cross and sufferings, that He might communicate to her His glory and His crown. With this generous disposition she entered the Chapel of our Lady of the Holy Rosary, to consecrate her soul and body to the sovereign pleasure of God. Having placed herself on her knees before the altar, she made an act of perfect resignation of herself to the holy will of God, with so great fervour and so tender a sentiment of love and piety, that the fire of charity which inflamed her soul appeared in her countenance; and Don Almansa, who saw this brilliant colour on her cheeks and so joyful an expression in her eyes, thought she must have just received some intimation of her death from her Divine Spouse.

LAST ILLNESS AND DEATH

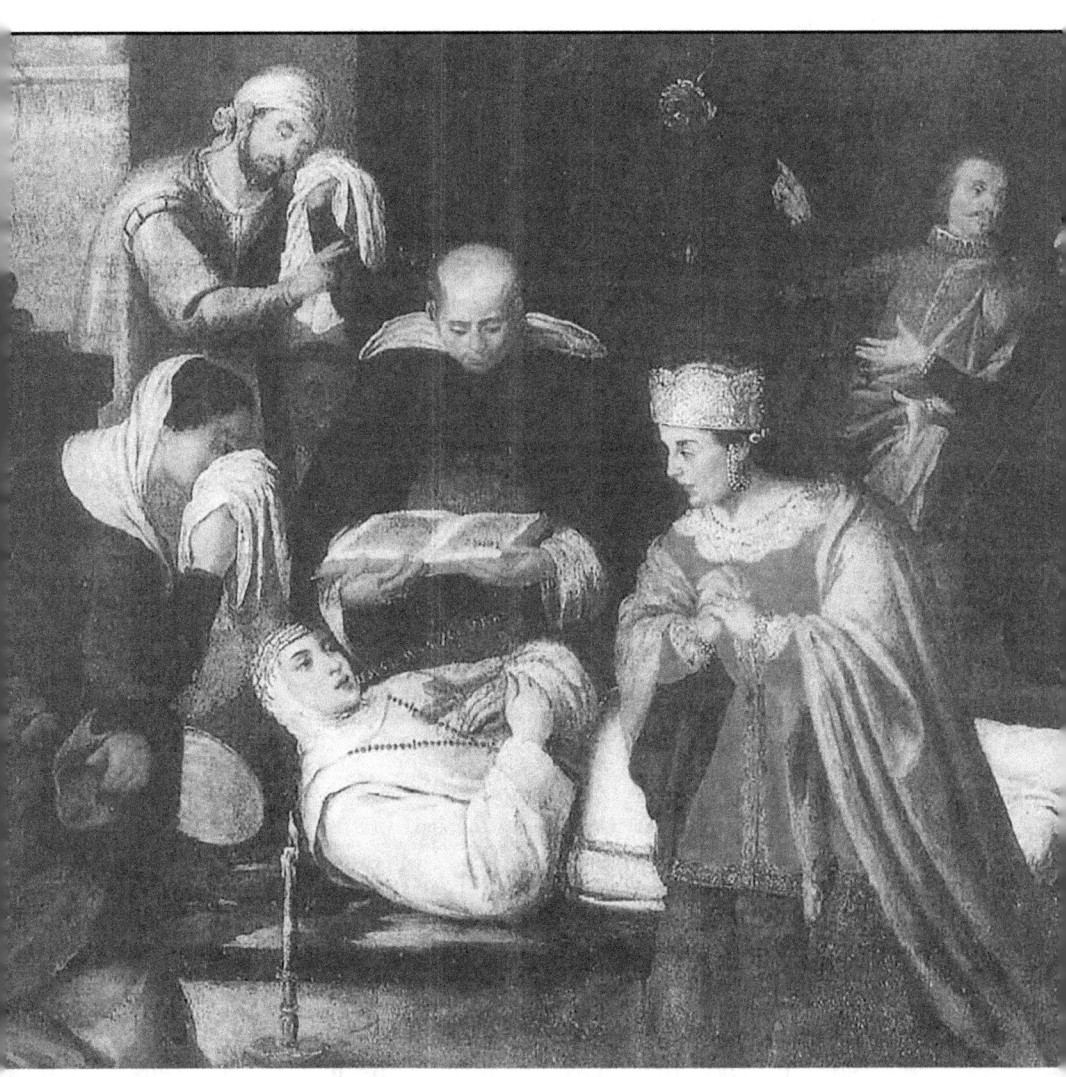

Three days before she was attacked by her last illness, she went to her father's house to bid farewell to her dear hermitage, the witness of the favours she had received from Jesus Christ, the Blessed Virgin, her guardian Angel, and from her dear mistress S. Catherine of Siena: she passed two days therein in acts of thanksgiving, prayers, and tears. In this retreat S. Rose sang, in preparation for death, canticles of praise and benediction to her adorable Spouse, Who called her to His chaste embraces. She then expressed her gratitude to S. Dominic for the care he had taken of her, and for the mercy he had shown in receiving her into his Order amongst the number of his daughters; and after this she entreated, with tears in her eyes, that he would pardon her want of correspondence to her vocation, the infidelities which she had committed in the observance of the constitutions of her Order, and the bad example which she had given to her sisters as well as to seculars. Though the stifled sobs, which her deep sorrow drew from her, choked her utterance, she could not omit to recommend her mother very particularly to him, begging him to be a father to her, and to take her under his protection.

On the first of August she went to her room at night in perfect health, but at midnight she was heard crying and groaning piteously; and the wife of Don Gonzalez, at whose house she lived, having hastened to her with several other persons, found her extended half dead on the floor, cold, without pulse, motionless, and scarcely breathing. In great alarm, they asked her what was the matter with her, and if she did not wish the physician to be sent for to give her some relief. She blushed at this word, " relief," and looking at them with half-closed eyes, she told them in a weak languishing voice, that there was nothing the matter with her, but that she felt death exercising its violence upon her; and as God alone, her sole Physician, knew her state, He alone could withdraw her from it by His power. They placed her again in her poor bed, and immediately they noticed a cold sweat on her face, and so violent a shivering seized her that she breathed with great difficulty; yet she did not cease to pronounce from time to time the sacred Name of Jesus with such tender sentiments and with so much facility, that it was evident that this Divine Name was the only comfort she found in her Sufferings.

The physicians came to visit her in this state, and having diligently examined the opposite maladies, with which she was attacked, they declared that these infirmities and sufferings were beyond human endurance, and that this union of incompatible symptoms was something miraculous: in a word, they were of opinion that her illness was not natural, and that God alone caused it to exist in her weak body, that He might make His destined spouse participate in the sufferings of His Passion.

Her confessor, who did not forsake her in this extremity, fearing that her humility would prevent her from making known the nature and the great number of her sufferings, commanded her, in virtue of obedience, to declare them to the physicians in the best manner she was able, in order to give them at least some slight idea of them. In obedience to this order, she told them that during her life she had been afflicted with every one of the different diseases from which mankind suffer, but that she did not understand that with which she was actually attacked, and that she could not explain to them the pains she endured, except by borrowing comparisons from the most painful sensations in nature. "It seems," she said, "as if a ball of fire were forced into my temples, that it descends to my feet, and that it passes across from my left side to my right, carrying an insupportable heat. I feel," continued she, "as if my heart were lacerated by a burning dagger, and the invisible hand which guides it pierces me sometimes from head to foot, and then, by crossing from side to side, engraves the figure of a cross in my body with this instrument, which burns me with the greatest violence to which fire can attain. I suffer," she added, "such sharp pains in the bowels, that it seems as if each moment they were being torn out with burning pincers; and my head burns as if heated coals, just taken from a flaming furnace, wore placed upon it. In fact, I believe that when I die my bones will be found reduced to ashes, and the marrow dried up, from the effects of the burning heat which I endure."

On this the physicians looked at each other in astonishment at hearing things so extraordinary, and being more and more confirmed in their first opinion by the recital of these dreadful pains, they concluded that her malady was supernatural. Rose, hearing the result of their consultation, ingenuously avowed to her confessor that they were not mistaken in their judgment; and therefore she needed nothing but love and patience to fulfil the designs of God, who wished her to partake in His pains and sufferings. When the physicians had retired, she begged that she might be left alone for some days, and that no one would come to speak to her, that she might be able to converse more at liberty with Jesus Christ her dear Spouse, with whom she felt herself fixed to the cross.

On the sixth day of the same month she ascended with her Beloved, not to Thabor to partake of the glory of His Transfiguration, but to Calvary to bear a part in His excessive sufferings; for on this day her whole left side was attacked by paralysis, and two days after she was seized at the same time with pleurisy, asthma, sciatica, gout, colic, and fever, as if these cruel diseases had united their different pains to make her suffer one which included them all, for she endured inconceivable torments. We may say that this happened by the special dispensation of Providence, who permitted her to be attacked by all these diseases at once, that she might suffer on her bed from the Hands of her Divine Spouse, a martyrdom as meritorious to her, as that which the saints endured on wheels and racks from their executioners.

She preserved always an admirable tranquillity of mind in the midst of her pains; she was so calm in the paroxysms of her fever, in the shooting pains of sciatica, and the sharp attacks of colic, that she appeared insensible, or as if her body were of iron, incapable of pain or change. Though she suffered so much, she never entreated her Divine Spouse to diminish her pains; on the contrary, she begged Him with all the affection of her heart to increase them, in order to punish her rigorously for the crimes of which she believed herself guilty in the sight of His Divine Majesty.

Nevertheless, as the severity of her sufferings brought on fearful paroxysms and convulsions, she began to fear they might cause delirium and loss of reason; she therefore, with tears in her eyes, implored those of her family who were nursing her, to join her in praying God to deliver her from that evil which, above all others, she dreaded. God had compassion on His servant, He was moved by her tears and sighs, and He miraculously preserved her mind sound and entire till her last breath, amidst the burning heat of the fever, which must have caused her to fall into delirium if He had not preserved her from it by His mercy; and, by a further favour, He granted her the use of her tongue, to make known her thoughts till she died. We have the greater reason to believe, that the preservation of her senses was an effect of the Omnipotence of God, as she was often seen during this last illness, as it were, out of herself, without any use of her exterior senses, or in raptures in which her soul seemed to leave her body to unite itself more closely to God.

She suffered from a thirst, which grew more violent every moment, but still she endured it till death without swallowing a drop of water to quench it: preferring to deprive herself of this relief, rather than of the consolation of dying with a burning thirst; and after the example of her Divine Spouse, she asked only for gall and vinegar to drink to increase her suffering.

During her illness she usually confessed her sins every day; and to dispose herself better for death, she made a general confession of her whole life, with such marks of deep contrition, that her sighs and groans were heard in the room adjoining. On the third day before her death she received the Holy Viaticum and Extreme Unction with interior dispositions suited to the excellence of these two sacraments, the graces of which were, in some manner, to put the seal to the merits which she had acquired by the practice of all the virtues.

It was noticed when the Blessed Sacrament was brought to her, that she changed colour, her face became shining and inflamed, and amidst the transports of joy which filled her, she fell into an ecstasy; and after receiving this Bread of angels, which was to fortify her, for the passage from earth to heaven, she remained motionless and totally absorbed in God. In receiving Extreme Unction she disposed her limbs herself, though she had been before quite incapable of moving them, and these around her knew that this holy oil prepared her rather for the glory of her triumph, than for these fearful invisible combats to which the agonizing are exposed; she was indeed assured of her salvation, and Almighty God had revealed to her that her soul, on leaving her body, would go straight to heaven, without passing through the flames of purgatory.

She often declared in an audible voice, that she was a Christian, and desired to die in the faith of the Church, and that she was a daughter of the great S. Dominic. To give proof of this, she kissed her scapular respectfully, and would have it always laid upon her in her sickness. Finally, to imitate the charity of the Son of God, she prayed with all her heart for those who had offended her in word or deed, begging Him

S. Rose of Lima, August 24, 1617

to load them with His graces, and to show them the same mercy which she hoped to experience from His goodness; and holding a little crucifix in her hand, she could not satisfy herself with kissing it, and repeating tenderly, "Father, forgive them."

After having so perfectly copied His love, she had only to imitate His humility before her death; for this purpose she begged that the servants of the house might be sent for, and though she had never disobliged one of them in any manner, she begged their pardon with tears in her eyes. She showed a sensible grief that she had been so great a burden to her mother, and that she should give her yet a great deal of trouble, during the two days she had still to live. She thanked Don Gonzalez very gratefully for his goodness to her, telling him that he would soon be freed from this miserable sinner, who had given so much uneasiness and trouble to his whole family. There was not a person who did not shed tears at these words, and who did not admire the wonderful humility of this spouse of Jesus Christ, who had so profound a contempt for herself, while every one considered her as a Saint.

Don Gonzalez feared that some dispute might arise between the curate of her parish and the religious of S. Dominic, concerning the right of possessing S. Rose's body after death, each having a claim to keep it in their church, the one as his parishioner, for she had died in a house which came under his jurisdiction; the others as their sister, from her being a religious of their Order. To avoid this dispute he thought it would be advisable that she should ask the religious to have the charity to give her burial amongst them, as to one of their sisters, by manner of supplication, rather than by will, for fear that she might become aware of the eagerness which the convent and parish would show to possess her body. She had no difficulty in following this judicious advice, for she knew it was the custom for religious of the third Order of S. Dominic to be buried in the church of his children, and fearing that this favour might be refused to her, owing to the disedification she thought she had given, she begged them with many entreaties to grant her this consolation.

A short time before her death, she was continually in raptures and ecstasies, in which she had a foretaste of the ineffable sweetness she would possess in heaven for all eternity. This violent application of the mind fatigued her weak body very much, and gradually disposed it to die; but her soul acquiring new strength at the approach of the blessed moment which was to unite her for ever to her Spouse, she felt a joy which was perceptible in her eyes and in her words. Two hours before she expired, coming to herself from a long ecstasy, she turned to Father Francis Nieto, and said to him in confidence, "O father, what great things I could tell you of the pleasures and abundant consolations which God will bestow upon His saints for all eternity! I go with inconceivable satisfaction to contemplate the adorable Face of God, whom I have all my life desired to possess."

She then thanked her parents, these who had nursed her in her illness, and particularly Don Gonzalez and his wife, for all the kindness and charity they had shown her. She exhorted their daughters with all the strength that remained to her and with words of fire, to the love of God and the practice of virtue; after this, she spoke privately with her two brothers, and conjured them to lead good lives, and to honour and assist their good mother.

Towards midnight she heard a mysterious noise, which announced to her the coming of her Divine Spouse; she welcomed it with joy; and seeing herself on the point of expiring, she requested her brother to remove the bolster from beneath her head, and to place pieces of wood in its stead. She thanked him for this act of kindness, and placed her head upon them, and as if she had only waited for these pieces of wood, to die upon a sort of cross, she said twice, "Jesus, be with me; Jesus, be with me," and immediately afterwards her pure soul quitted her mortal body, and took its flight into the Bosom of God, to take possession of that heavenly inheritance prepared for it from all eternity. Her death took place on the 24th August, the feast of S. Bartholomew, in the year 1617, her age being thirty-one years and five months.

The same night Aloysia de Serrano had a revelation of her death; and as S. Rose and she had promised one another, that the one who died first would make it known to the other, S. Rose kept her word and informed her of her death and of the happiness she enjoyed.

CHAPTER XX

OF THE HONOUR WHICH SAINT ROSE RECEIVED AFTER DEATH, AND OF THE TRANSLATION OF HER BODY, WHICH TOOK PLACE SOME TIME AFTERWARDS

THE death of the just is attended with circumstances which render it sweet and agreeable: it is not only precious in the sight of God, as their introduction to a throne of which they take possession as conquerors laden with the glorious spoils they have taken from the world, the flesh, and the devil; it is even precious in the sight of men, when they remark on the countenances of the illustrious dead the respect which death pays to their ashes, freeing them from that hideous deformity which gives us a sort of horror even for these persons who were the most beloved by us. The honours which are paid to them after death make us regard it rather as a triumph than as a shameful defeat, and we can scarcely believe that they have paid this indispensable debt of nature, since their virtue makes them live in the esteem of men, while their bodies are lifeless and without motion. In this sense S. Gregory Nazianzen calls the generous Machabees the rivals of a precious death, since they sought it covered with blood and dust in the midst of combats, as a source of life and glory which would render them immortal in the memory of men.

Death appeared so lovely on the countenance of S. Rose, that these who remarked the freshness of her complexion and the redness of her lips, which were separated so as to form a pleasing smile, doubted for a long time whether her soul had quitted her body; for they saw so much brightness in her eyes, and such apparent marks of life, that they could not be satisfied till they had placed a mirror before her mouth, and had perceived that she did not in the least tarnish its lustre by her breath; then they knew that she was dead.

In place of the tears and sighs that would naturally have been expected from the persons who were present at her death, and who had been very dear to her, either by the alliance of blood or by the bands of a close friendship, so great a joy was visible on their countenances, that the house seemed more like the scene of a wedding than a place of tears and mourning.

A person who was present at her death saw a number of angels around her bed during her agony, and she deposed upon oath, that God had revealed to her several days before the death of S. Rose, that her passage from earth to heaven would be glorious and her tomb magnificent; and He had expressly forbidden the use of black drapery, which is a sign of sadness, and desired that they should employ white hangings, as being much more suitable to our Saint's glorious triumph.

In fact, she was placed under ground with as much pomp as would be granted to a heroine, who during life had performed a multitude of great actions; for scarcely had the day-light appeared, before a prodigious crowd of people of all ranks came to the door of the house of Don Gonzalez, in which she had breathed her last; and this surprised the people of the house extremely, for they could not imagine how they had heard of her death, since no one had gone out afterwards. The crowd was so great that it did not merely comprise the heads of families: poor and rich, gentlemen and merchants, priests, religious, seculars, Spaniards, and native Indians entered in confusion and surrounded the body of our Saint. Some kissed her feet with profound sentiments of respect and devotion; others cut off some piece of her dress. They had taken care to close her eyes; but it was impossible to keep them in this position, for they reopened immediately, as if our Saint took pleasure in looking on the inhabitants of Lima, who had had such esteem and veneration for her.

The news of her death having spread itself over the town and neighbourhood, so many people came, that they filled not only the house in which her body was laid out, but the street also; the viceroy was obliged to send soldiers to make a passage through the crowd, in order to carry her to the church, and the multitude was so great in the streets through which they had to pass, that they were several hours without being able to advance.

The Archbishop of Lima, who had quitted his palace to convey the body with his clergy, not being able to reach the house of Don Gonzalez, went to wait for the convoy at the church of the Dominicans, which was about a thousand paces distant. All the religious communities, and all the

Fellow Dominicans carry her to San Domenico

confraternities of the town, came to join in honouring her; and though the chapter of the metropolitan church does not usually attend on these occasions, except for the archbishop's funeral, it was nevertheless present, to increase the splendour of this ceremony. The foreign ambassadors also showed her the same honours as they usually paid only to the viceroys of the country.

The streets through which the body of S. Rose passed on its way to the Convent of S. Dominic were very narrow, and therefore a great number of virtuous and illustrious ladies were obliged to place themselves at windows, that they might have the satisfaction of seeing once more this virginal body, which had been during life the living temple of the Holy Ghost. The poorer people mounted on the roofs to satisfy their pious curiosity; in a word, all the town was present at her funeral, every one wishing to show by this last mark of respect the esteem they had felt for our Saint during her life. The Canons of the Cathedral carried the body a considerable distance, but the eagerness of the principal people in the town to partake in this honour, made them change bearers in every street; the most illustrious amongst the senators succeeded the chapter; after, them the superiors of all the monasteries carried her one after another. Everywhere the people were heard crying out that Rose was a Saint in heaven; and not being satisfied with this vocal testimony, they tried to obtain some portion of her relics, and if the soldiers had not opposed their devotion, they would certainly have cut off all her clothes.

The body being at the church door, certain signs of joy were remarked on her face; and the statue of our Blessed Lady which was in the Chapel of the Rosary sent forth rays of light, which every one took for a miraculous indication of the pleasure she had in again seeing our Saint, who had honoured her with so much love and tenderness. Every one ran to see this prodigy; they observed with astonishment the light which issued from the countenance of this holy image, and there were some who declared that they saw drops of perspiration distilling from it. The Father Prior of the Convent of S. Dominic appointed his senior religious to surround this holy body, as much to prevent the pious thefts of the people, as to bring near the blind, the lame, the deaf and dumb, and a great number of sick people, whom the hope of obtaining a cure through the merits of S. Rose had attracted; and they were not disappointed in their expectation, as we shall shortly see.

The guard of the viceroy and the soldiers of the garrison having made the people retire, they began to prepare for the interment; but so great a tumult was raised, that they were obliged to postpone the ceremony, and unless they had given a promise to the people to delay it, not one would have gone home. This promise having caused these who were in the church to disperse, so great a number of others entered, that the archbishop, seeing that it would be impossible to bury her, made a sign to the religious to carry the corpse into the sacristy; as these fathers thought it was not very safe there they took it away, and placed it in the Chapel of the Novitiate as the most proper place, and the most retired part of the convent, to which seculars have no access. The archbishop being now at liberty to pay his respects to this virtuous servant of God, he placed himself devoutly on his knees before the corpse to kiss her hand, and he found the fingers as pliable and supple as when she was alive.

The next day, as soon as the father sacristan had opened the church doors, and the religious had placed our Saint's body in the nave, an immense crowd of people entered, not only from the town, but even from six or seven leagues' distance from Lima, to be present at her interment. In spite of all the efforts of the soldiers and the viceroy's guard, they could not keep back the people, who all rushed forward violently; some pushed others to enable them to touch this holy body with garments for the sick, with rosaries, prayer-books, or medals: never was there witnessed such a scene of confusion; cripples begged to be allowed to pass that they might be cured by touching her relics; children were lifted from hand to hand over the heads of the people, to kiss her clothes; and with all their precautions, it was not possible to prevent them from cutting her habit, her veil, and her gimp, which were obliged to be changed six times.

The church resounded with the voices of these who were present, imploring her intercession as a Saint reigning with God. The noise was so great, that they were obliged to give a signal to the choir by a bell, whenever it was necessary to answer the Bishop of Guatemala, who was celebrating mass; and it would never have been finished, if the cantors had not left their places to be nearer the altar that they might be able to hear. This illustrious prelate having descended from his throne to approach the coffin, and proceed to the ceremony of interment, was surrounded by a quantity of people, who redoubled their cries and groans; and having given by this means a signal to these who were at a greater distance, that the body of S. Rose was going to be put into the ground, a more numerous troop joined them, and added to the confusion. The religious, fearing some sedition, or that the people would try to seize by force some part of her dress, or of her body, appeased their violent devotion, by making a second promise to defer the burial till the next day.

The people willingly believed this, as there was no appearance of corruption in the body from the heat, for so much beauty was remarked in her countenance, so agreeable an odour was perceived, that everyone believed that Almighty God was renewing in the person of S. Rose the miracle He had so often worked in favour of His saints, by preserving her body from corruption; they thought the body would be exposed for several days to satisfy the people, who were never satiated with seeing her; for during thirty-six hours no

Another view of the crowd and of her Dominican pallbearers

change had appeared in her, either in her complexion or the brightness of her eyes, though the dampness of the place, and the heated breath of the crowds who had filled the church from morning till night, would have been sufficient to effect some alteration in her countenance.

Towards noon the doors of the church were closed, and without waiting for the return of the people, who were troublesome even by their piety, they placed the body of S. Rose in a coffin made of cedar wood, and buried it in the Chapter of the Religious. When the ceremony was completed, the doors were opened to a crowd of people, whose impatience made them furious, and who were ready to break them open with violence. When they saw that they had been deceived, they ran to the grave, and having watered it with their tears, they carried home some of the earth through devotion, to make use of it as a sovereign remedy in their diseases, hoping to be delivered from them by the intercession of this happy Spouse of Jesus Christ. After her death her father's house was every day surrounded by the carriages of the first persons in the city, who wished to see the hermitage which S. Rose had sanctified by her sighs and rigorous penances, and in which she had passed the greatest part of her life, separated from the intercourse of men, but singularly favoured by God.

The frequent miracles which took place in Lima and in the whole kingdom of Peru made her tomb so famous, that the people thought they had not paid sufficient honour to her memory; and it was resolved in the council of state, that a service should be performed for her with greater pomp and magnificence than at first. The archbishop and the viceroy had some little difficulty in fixing the day, that they might both be able to be present; at last they chose the 4th of September, without reflecting that it was consecrated to honour S. Rose of Viterbo in Italy. The people all came to the church on the appointed day, and while the archbishop, the clergy, and the religious communities recommended aloud the soul of S. Rose to God, the people begged her prayers by tears and groans as a great servant of God, the fame of whose sanctity had already spread over all the towns and villages of Peru. The town of Pontozzi, which is about three hundred leagues from Lima, was one of the first to show its respect for the memory of S. Rose, by the ringing of bells, the thunder of artillery, and by placing a great number of lights at the windows. The other towns of Peru vied with each other in showing their confidence in our Saint, by the vows they offered up at her tomb.

The miracles which Almighty God worked there every day to honour her, who during life had immolated herself entirely to His service, drew thither a number of persons from all parts, some to return thanks for the health which they had received from heaven by her intercession, others to implore her suffrages with God to be cured of their infirmities. This fervour never relaxed, as is usually the case with these popular devotions, which begin warmly but insensibly diminish in their progress, till in time they are quite extinguished. On the contrary, it increased so much by the quantity of miracles which were witnessed at her tomb, that all the dignitaries of the city, ecclesiastical or secular, with the principal officers of the council and police, concluded that the body of S. Rose being the precious treasure with which God had enriched the town of Lima, it ought to be made public and withdrawn from the cloister of the religious where it had been buried, to be placed in an honourable position in their church, to satisfy the devotion of the people.

The archbishop joyfully consented; and having given the necessary orders for this august ceremony, he took from the earth the body of S. Rose on the 27th of February, in the year 1619, in the presence of all the religious of the town, of the nobility and the people. As soon as the grave was opened an

agreeable odour issued from it, which appeared miraculous to the numerous assemblage, and they redoubled their joy and respect when they saw this holy body as entire, and the complexion as fresh, as when it was put into the coffin. It was transported from the cloister of the religious into their church, with all the pomp and magnificence that this great servant of God merited, and that could be imagined by the people to show their respect and affection. Father Louis Bilbao, a religious of the Order, a doctor in theology, and a very celebrated preacher, who had long been her confessor, pronounced her panegyric, and extolled with great eloquence the admirable virtues of our Saint. When her *eulogium* was finished she was carried to a little vault on the right side of the high altar; but as the crowd continually hastened thither, as to a second ark, to implore assistance, and persons of all ranks and ages were seen praying there, and offering presents, and leaving their sticks and crutches as glorious trophies of their gratitude for having been cured by her intercession, they were obliged, out of reverence to the adorable Sacrament, to remove these precious relics to the chapel of S. Catherine of Siena, where the people could satisfy their devotion more conveniently, and without fear of irreverence.

In the year 1630, on the 17th of March, an Apostolic Brief was received at Lima, by which the Sacred Congregation of Rites established a tribunal, and allowed the Father Inquisitors to examine canonically into the life, actions, and miracles of the servant of God, Sister Rose of S. Mary, religious of the third Order of S. Dominic. Two years were employed in hearing juridically a hundred and eighty persons, who presented themselves and deposed to what they had seen. Nothing more remained to terminate the proceedings but to visit the relics. They went to her tomb, and having opened it fifteen years after her death, they found her bones entire, covered with dry flesh, which exhaled a delightful odour like that of roses: from thence they went to the Chapter, where she had been at first interred, to see the grave from which the people every day took earth, to which God had communicated virtue to cure fever and other diseases. They found it quite full, with the exception of about five pounds' weight of soil, though several bushels had been carried away during these fifteen years.

In 1640, the Procurator General of the Order of Friars Preachers, hearing of the extraordinary devotion of the people, and the public veneration shown to the relics of this spouse of Jesus Christ, wrote to the fathers of the Convent at Lima, telling them to prevent this exterior honour, for fear of incurring the censures which Pope Urban VIII had fulminated in 1634 against these who should publicly show marks of veneration at the tomb of these who had died in the odour of sanctity, before the Holy See had declared them blessed. In consequence of this order they resolved to prevent the honour which was shown in their church to S. Rose. As soon as this resolution was known in the town, a number of people ran tumultuously to the church, where they loudly complained of this proceeding. And as a rumour was spread that the body of S. Rose had been secretly taken away to be transported from Lima into Spain, the religious were in danger of being murdered, and whatever they could say to the people to undeceive them had no effect, for they were too excited to be capable of hearing their excuses, or understanding their innocence. But their fury having subsided a little, they were told that they had been misinformed; that the body of S. Rose was still in the chapel of S. Catherine of Siena, and that what was done was in obedience to the commands of the Sovereign Pontiff, and that they might proceed to the Beatification of this servant of Jesus Christ in the forms prescribed by the Church, which they must obey, in order to obtain the favour which all the people desired for their fellow-citizen.

CHAPTER XXI

OF THE REVELATIONS WHICH SEVERAL PERSONS HAD OF THE GLORY OF S. ROSE.

There is no saint in heaven, of whom we may not say what S. Bernard said in pronouncing the *eulogium* of S. Victor the martyr, namely, that he instructed us by his example, and employed his credit with Almighty God for our advantage; for the saints were not raised to this eminent sanctity solely for their own perfection, but that the example of their virtues might be an inducement to others to practise the same. And as men cannot imitate their actions, nor call upon them in their necessities, unless they are informed of their happiness, God makes known their merits by extraordinary means, such as revelations and apparitions, that being persuaded of the excellence of their state, they may aspire to their sanctity, and seek to procure by their intercession, grace to attain to it, and relief in their afflictions of soul or body.

By these miraculous means God revealed to many persons the immortal glory of S. Rose, and He made use of her prayers to soften the hearts of a great number of sinners, whose unhappy obstinacy had hitherto given little hopes of their salvation. But before we relate these particular circumstances, we are glad to be able to assure the reader, that nothing is advanced which has not been taken from the authentic examinations which were made of the virtues, graces, and miracles of our Saint. As Aloysia de Serrano, who has been mentioned before, was united with our Saint by an intimate friendship, she was the first to whom God made known the glory which she possessed. One day when she was absorbed in God, she saw the Blessed Virgin before a magnificent throne, holding a rich and bright crown in her hand to place it on the head of some one for whom she seemed to be waiting; on the other side she beheld a multitude of virgins encircling S. Rose, and bringing her joyfully to the feet of the Mother of God. All these illustrious virgins were crowned, and carried palms in their hands; Rose alone was without a crown, and had only a palm; but a moment after she saw the Blessed Virgin place upon her head the brilliant crown she had held in her hand. A person of the greatest experience in mystical theology confessed to Don Gonzalez, his intimate friend, and also gave testimony by words and in writing before the apostolical commissioners, that S. Rose had appeared to him twenty-two times during the three weeks after her death, surrounded with glory.

The physician, Don Juan de Castile, so well known for his virtue,, made oath before the same commissioners, that S. Rose had appeared to him several times, fifteen years after her death, environed with an extraordinary light, and that he saw her in the midst of this light clothed in her habit of religion, but so majestic and glorious that he could not find words to explain her splendour; she held a lily in her right hand, the emblem of her virginity; and during these visions she spoke of the happiness of the saints in so sublime a manner, that he could not express their glory. In the last examination made at Lima, in 1631, he deposed on oath, that for six months, whenever he made his meditation, either by day or night, he had been allowed to see the royal magnificence with which Almighty God rewarded the merits of S. Rose, by means of an angel whom she sent from heaven to invite him to witness this delightful spectacle.

S. Dominic presents S. Rose to the Celestial Court

That which happened to Diego Hyacinth Paceco, a Spaniard, is very wonderful. He was a poor man who earned his bread at Lima by copying writings for lawyers; and Diego Morales, a notary in S. Rose's cause, having pressed him to engross in a very short time, two thousand rolls of writings belonging to the proceedings, and other authentic deeds concerning the examinations which had been made of the life and miracles of S. Rose, he despaired of being able to finish them, on account of the shortness of the time given him, and also partly because his fingers were benumbed with fatigue, and the nerves of his hand entirely relaxed. During the night S. Rose appeared to him; she approached him, and taking his arm she pressed it violently; the pain having awakened him he thought it was a dream; but finding himself perfectly cured he perceived that it was a reality, and that our Saint had truly appeared to him and cured his hand, that he might finish what he had begun in her cause.

She appeared to several other persons after her death, surrounded with odoriferous roses in the delicious garden of her Divine Spouse, particularly to a good widow, who lived at Lima in the odour of sanctity. One day when she was enraptured to see our Saint amidst a great multitude of angels and saints, Rose said to her, "Mother, this state of glory is only acquired by generous efforts; we should work hard, for the recompense with which God crowns our labours is exceedingly great; you see how His mercy rewards abundantly, and even beyond my hopes, the pains I suffered and the few good actions I performed while on earth."

As she was very charitable towards the inhabitants of Lima during her life, she testified to them by several apparitions, that she felt the same interest for them now that she was in heaven; for this widow, when recommending the town to her prayers one day, was ravished into an ecstasy, and in her rapture saw S. Rose, who consoling her said, "Mother, I will do what you ask me, and God has promised to grant me for this dear people whatever regards their salvation; I remember perfectly these things which have been recommended to my intercession, and I will not fail to ask for them."

This is conformable to what sister Catherine of S. Mary testified before the commissioners, to the effect that S. Rose had appeared twice to her after her death. On the first occasion, our Saint encouraged her in the extraordinary pains which tormented her, and in her afflictions; and the second time, she saw S. Rose in the air above her sepulcher, supplicating on her knees the Majesty of God for the town of Lima.

The cure of Father Augustin de Vega, a celebrated religious of the Order of Friars Preachers, and Provincial of the kingdom of Peru, is very remarkable. His life was despaired of, the physicians had given him up, they had ceased to give him remedies for some days, every one being of opinion that his illness was incurable, and that he would never recover. S. Rose appeared, during the night in which his death was expected, to Don Christoforo de Ortega, and desired him to go very early the next morning to the provincial at the convent of his Order in Lima, and to assure him from her that he would recover from this sickness, and that Almighty God had chosen him for a bishop, that he might labour in the service of the Church, and employ the great talents which He had given him. He went, spoke to this dying priest, and making known to him what had happened during the night, delivered the message with which S. Rose had entrusted him: from this time the father began to improve; and some time after he was elected Bishop of Paraguay, and became one of the most celebrated and learned prelates who have governed the Church of Jesus Christ in the New World.

CHAPTER XXII

OF THE MIRACLES WHICH ALMIGHTY GOD WORKED THROUGH THE MERITS OF S. ROSE.

As miracles belong to the number of these gratuitous graces, which God grants rather for the good of others, than for the particular advantage of the person by whom He works them, they are not the essential marks of sanctity; for S. John the Baptist, the greatest among the children of men, never performed any, according to the testimony of Jesus Christ Himself. Still, as they are a subject of astonishment to men, and as they oblige them to acknowledge a Sovereign Power, which has absolute dominion over nature, the Son of God has made use of them to establish religion in every part of the world, and to confirm its excellence and truth; wherefore S. Augustine says, *"semen fidei sunt virtutes."*

We need not then be surprised, if Almighty God has worked so many miracles through S. Rose, a nun of the third Order of S. Dominic, in the New World, where the faith was only just beginning to spring up; for they were necessary to confirm the newly converted, and to strengthen them in the faith. For this reason, though the life of S. Rose was a continual and very famous miracle, God also worked through her means a great number of prodigies, for the salvation of many persons. We do not undertake to relate them all, for the number is so great that a volume might be composed of them; we will content ourselves with noticing the most remarkable.

1.

OF THE CONVERSIONS WHICH THE PRAYERS OF S. ROSE OBTAINED

As the conversion of sinners from crime to innocence, and from sin to grace, is a more noble effect of the charity of the Saints, and a more glorious mark of their power with Almighty God than the restoring diseased and languishing bodies to health, we may say that God has given glorious proofs of the sanctity of His spouse: for a number of hardened sinners, who had been for years in the habit of sin, were struck with compunction and sorrow for having offended God, at the time in which they touched the body of S. Rose, or even beheld it exposed in the church. Father Nicholas de Aguero, of the Order of Friars Preachers, then Vicar General of Peru, testifies in his circular letter of the 1st of September, 1617, that many openly confessed their crimes and disorders, and gave proof by the abundance of their tears and their loud cries, that they were truly converted.

It was remarked, that some young libertines, who came to the church merely to gaze upon the ravishing beauty of this chaste spouse of Jesus Christ, whom they had not been able to look upon attentively during life, returned home penetrated with great contrition, and resolved to change their lives. Some days after S. Rose's death, several persons went to visit Mary Oliva, her mother, and bestowed plentiful alms upon her, in gratitude for the graces which they said they bad received from God through the merits of her holy daughter, who had undoubtedly obtained their conversion from a state of sin in which they had long been.

For several years there had appeared little hope of the

conversion of a man who lived more like an atheist than a Christian, and whose scandalous life was a tissue of all sorts of crimes and disorders; he had never made a good confession in his life, and these who knew his terrible obstinacy looked upon him as lost, for he would not hear anyone speak of doing penance. A pious person, who was sensibly touched by the deplorable loss of a soul for which Jesus Christ had shed His Precious Blood, addressed herself to S. Rose a few days after her death, and entreated her to obtain from God the conversion of this poor soul. Her power with Almighty God was soon manifested; for this man awoke from the lethargy of sin, and the fear of God softening the hardness of his heart, he was converted, and during the rest of his life had as great a horror of sin as he had before had pleasure in committing it. This conversion was much talked of, and greatly augmented the respect which was shown to the merits of S. Rose.

He was not the only person who experienced the favourable effects of her intercession; it is mentioned in the depositions which were taken on the 11th of January, 1617, before the apostolical commissioners, that the number of persons who were converted to God through S. Rose's intercession, and who did penance for their past crimes, was so great in Lima and the whole kingdom of Peru, that a short time after her death so many disciplines, iron chains, hair-shirts, etc. were sold, that the stock of the merchants was exhausted. Father Antonio do la Vega Louysa, the Jesuit, remarks this circumstance particularly; for according to the common opinion of doctors, these conversions are the most certain marks of the sanctity of these who obtain them.

The most infamous public sinners were seen with astonishment to quit their sinful habits and embrace the sweet yoke of chastity, to live for God alone in the practice of rigorous penance, and to apply themselves solely to the important affair of their salvation, seeing in the penitential and crucified life of S. Rose the stringent obligation we are under of attending to it. The priests declared that since S. Rose's entrance into heaven there had been a complete change of manners in Peru, and they knew, by the numerous and remarkable conversions they every day witnessed, that she was powerfully soliciting the salvation of her countrymen. Worldly women renounced their vanity, and left off wearing these rich garments which only serve to nourish pride and ambition, to clothe themselves in the garb of modesty. Religious persons, animated by the example of this innocent penitent, renewed their first fervours so courageously, that nothing was heard in cloisters but the sound of the disciplines, which they took to imitate her mortification. Confessors were besieged in their tribunals by a great number of persons, who testified by their tears and groans the sensible sorrow which they felt for having offended God.

This wonderful change caused a man of rank to give testimony before the Inquisitors, that since the Gospel was preached in Peru by the Dominicans, who were the first missionaries there, no preacher had ever inspired the people with such sentiments of penance, or inflamed them with so great a love of God, as S. Rose had done since her death.

She not only gave her assistance to these who were engaged in sin to withdraw them from it; she also animated very good men to a more perfect and holy manner of life. We may cite as an example Father John of Villalobos, Prefect of the College of the Society of Jesus in Lima, who having visited S. Rose in her last illness, and earnestly entreated her to draw him to the practice of her virtues, felt such interior unction, and received after her death such supernatural lights, as made known to him that she had obtained for him the grace he had solicited.

We may say, in fact, that there was no person, however rebellious to grace and obstinate in sin, whom S. Rose did not induce to enter into himself and rise from his unhappy

. The inhabitants of Lima were greatly scandalized by the aversion which Mary Xuara, the wife of one of the richest and most influential persons in the country, bore towards some cousins of Francis and Alexander de Columa, two brothers who were sons of her husband by his first wife. Francis de Columa took care of these ten little orphans, but his stepmother was not at all moved by their great poverty; on the contrary, she made her will without leaving them anything, and to satisfy her hatred she even did not name them in it. These two brothers being, however, obliged by their business to go into the country and leave these poor orphans at Lima, Francis, touched with compassion at their misery, addressed himself to S. Rose, and looking on her picture he begged her to soften the heart of this obstinate woman, and to inspire her with sentiments of humanity for these little children. The next day this woman, who during eighteen years would not see him, sent for him, and told him that she had passed a miserable night, and that the misery of the ten orphans had been constantly in her thoughts; she begged him to fetch a lawyer to draw up another will in their favour; and this was executed.

Louisa Barba, being almost in her agony, was exhorted by her confessor to have confidence in God, for she would not die of this illness, because S. Rose had made known by revelation that she would be a nun, and would end her life in the cloister. She did not die, but she felt no inclination whatever to embrace this holy state; she had, on the contrary, as great a horror for religion as she would have had for the frightful head of Medusa. Nevertheless, a short time after S. Rose's death, when she went to pray at her tomb, that God would make known to her the state of life for which His Divine Providence destined her, she felt herself so powerfully attracted by Almighty God, that being no longer desirous to resist grace, which had dissipated her unreasonable sentiments, she became a nun of

the third Order of S. Dominic, and was called Sister Louisa of S. Mary.

2.

TWO DEAD PERSONS RAISED TO LIFE, AND MANY MIRACULOUSLY CURED BY TOUCHING THE BODY OF S. ROSE, AND INVOKING HER ASSISTANCE IN THEIR INFIRMITIES

The authenticated miracle of the resurrection of Magdalen de Torrez; which happened in October, 1627, should be placed first on the list, as the most admirable effect of the supernatural power which God communicates to His saints. She was the daughter of a poor labourer, who dwelt in the outskirts of Lima. She was seized with a violent fever and diarrhea, of which she died. She was placed on straw, where she remained from the night she died till the next day: everything was ready for her burial, when her mother, placing her confidence in God and in S. Rose's protection, put on the mouth of her dead daughter a piece of a garment which had belonged to our Saint. Wonderful to relate, this girl, who was quite cold, and whose body had become stiff, opened her eyes, and in the presence of her father and several others who were in her room, rose from the mattress in full vigour and as perfect health as if she had not been ill.

In the year 1631, Anthony Bran, a servant of Madame Jeanne Barette, received a similar favour from heaven through the merits of the same Saint. He had been ill of a fever for three months, and his strength being gradually exhausted, at length he died. These who witnessed his death informed his mistress of it, who seeing him dead, cold, and breathless, lifted up her eyes to heaven, and said, sighing, "God has taken from me this faithful servant, who was so useful to me in my affairs and in the management of my household; may

His holy Name be for ever blessed!" While she was making this act of resignation, she perceived near the dead man's bed a paper picture of S. Rose, and immediately she entreated her protection in her affliction, and earnestly begged her to obtain from God the life of this servant. Full of confidence that she should obtain her request, she placed the picture on the corpse, and while she was on her knees praying with those who were in the room, Anthony came to life, rose up in a sitting position, and published aloud the favour he had received through the intercession of S. Rose, and went the same day to her tomb to thank her.

While the corpse of our Saint was exposed in the church before burial, Elizabeth Durand went thither to touch it, that she might recover the use of her arm, of which she had been long deprived, and which the surgeons pronounced incurable, for none of their remedies could restore its natural heat; but having touched this holy body she returned perfectly cured. A poor slave, a native of Guinea, named Helen, had been tormented for seven years by a quantity of worms, which having exhausted her strength had reduced her to a state in which her life was despaired of. She was attacked by a violent fever, with swellings of the legs and feet, which were sure prognostics of approaching death. Her master, John Merin, being sorry to lose her, hearing of the miracles which were wrought by the intercession of S. Rose, who had been dead three days, persuaded this dying negress to recommend herself to her prayers, and to promise to make a novena at her tomb. She followed his advice: she was carried to the Saint's tomb, and on the last day of the Novena she felt as well as if she had never had this illness.

Beatrice Gavez, who had been afflicted for four years with disease of the chest, from which suffocation was apprehended, having heard of S. Rose's death, slipped with the crowd into the house of Don Gonzalez, in which she had died; and after having recommended herself to her prayers she touched the bier on which her holy body was placed, in the hope of being relieved; from that moment she breathed freely, and her chest was perfectly cured.

The miracle which Almighty God worked in favour of Alphonsus Diaz, through S. Rose's intercession, is not less authentic. He was a poor cripple, well known to every one, who begged his bread from door to door in Lima; he dragged himself along with difficulty on little crutches, on account of a contraction of the nerves, which had some years back so dried up and shortened his feet that he could not support himself on them; as soon as he had offered up his prayers near the coffin of S. Rose, whose assistance he invoked from the bottom of his heart, that he might be cured through her means, he felt his feet stretch out, and having tried his weight upon them to see if he could walk, he found himself perfectly cured.

A negro child, aged twelve years, whose name is not mentioned, and who could only walk with crutches, hearing the miracles spoken of which were worked at the Church of S. Dominic by the merits of S. Rose, crept under the bier on which the body of our Saint was laid and having invoked her assistance, he received so miraculous a cure that he began to run about the church in the presence of a crowd of people, who gave testimony of the miracle. George de Aranda Valdivia, a priest, who had been in the war of Chile against the revolted Indians, and had afterwards embraced the ecclesiastical state, had received in battle several wounds in his left arm, which, not having been well dressed, had caused in the course of time a tumour and inflammation, which prevented him from saying mass, as he could not raise his left arm. Being much afflicted at this circumstance, he went to the cloister of the religious in which the body of S. Rose was to be interred, and having prayed and recommended himself to our Saint, he found himself perfectly cured, and his arm free from swelling and inflammation, and as flexible as the other. Transported with joy, he entered the church, in which were Father Christopher of Azevedo and several seculars, and prostrating himself before the altar of our Lady of the Holy Rosary, he publicly gave thanks to God for the miraculous cure which he had obtained through the merits of S. Rose.

Father Diego de Arasca, Prior of the Convent of Friars Preachers in the town of Panama, having set out for Lima during the great heats, was seized with fever, which reduced him to so deplorable a state, that the physicians seeing his body begin to swell, gave notice to the Father Provincial, Gabriel de Zarata, that the administration of the last Sacraments should not be deferred. The good father received them with exemplary piety, and while the physicians and his brother religious despaired of his life, he recommended himself to S. Rose. His prayer being finished, the swelling and fever disappeared, and the next day he went to the sepulchre of our Saint to return thanks.

Isidora de Montalvo, a very old woman, had been ill for eight months of fever with violent paroxysms, and the physicians thinking her great age rendered her incapable of bearing remedies, had left her. In her extremity she called upon S. Rose, and immediately found herself free from fever. She lived a long time after receiving this favour through her intercession.

There was at Lima a wretched woman, whose name is not given, who hated her husband to such a degree that she poisoned him; and that she might not fail in her design she chose a violent poison, that he might die before assistance could be had. As soon as he had taken the wine with which she had mixed the poison, his body began to swell, a perspiration came over him, and he appeared like a dying person; in the midst of these convulsions he cried out suddenly, "S. Rose, assist me, I promise to make a Novena at your tomb!" His cruel wife, who expected only his death, was terrified at these words, and fearing to be punished for her abominable crime, she stabbed herself with a knife. Her husband recovered at that very hour, and the next day went to begin his Novena, which he finished as an offering of thanks to our Saint.

3.

AFTER S. ROSE'S DEATH MANY SICK PERSONS WERE RESTORED TO HEALTH, AND SEVERAL WOMEN ASSISTED IN THEIR LABOUR, BY TOUCHING HER VEIL, OR SOME PART OF HER DRESS

Elenora Ruiy de Sandoza had long suffered from an almost insupportable pain in the head, which rendered her incapable of mental application. With the design of gaining the jubilee in the metropolitan church at Lima, she put a piece of S. Rose's dress on her head, and was instantly relieved from the pain she had endured for several years.

Another person, named Philippa de Vargas, who suffered from continual fever, felt in its paroxysms a violent pain in her head, as if some one had forced sharp thorns into it; having tried all sorts of remedies in vain, she had recourse to S. Rose, and full of confidence she put a piece of her dress on her head; she fell asleep immediately, and after a pleasant slumber she awoke without fever or headache.

The prioress of the monastery of S. Catherine of Siena at Lima, used the same means to be cured of a severe headache and pain in her chest, which cure she obtained by applying a piece of the dress of S. Rose.

Sister Marina of S. Joseph, a Barefooted Carmelite, had so hurt her eyes by a fall, that she could neither raise nor cast them down; besides this, she suffered continual pain in them. In this affliction she applied a piece of the veil which our Saint had used, and was cured the same day.

Isabel of Mendoza had in her house a little slave girl, three

years old, named Margaret, who had lost the sight of one eye, and the other was so weak that she could scarcely see with it, so that it was thought she would become blind. Her mistress having seen persons in the church of the Friars Preachers thanking God for the health they had miraculously obtained through the merits of S. Rose, thought that her little slave might perhaps recover her sight through her intercession. In this confidence she asked the Father Sacristan for some relic of our Saint, and he gave her a piece of S. Rose's dress. In the evening she placed the relic upon the child's eyes, and having bandaged them she was put to bed. The next morning the skin which had covered her eye was found attached to the bandage on removing it, and both eyes were perfectly cured.

Louisa de Faxado, a widow, who lived at Lima, had lost two of her children, a son aged seventeen, and a daughter ten months old, by epileptic fits; she had only one little boy left, named Francis de Contreras, who was so tormented by the same malady, that he sometimes lay on the ground for fifteen hours in convulsions, foaming at the mouth and struggling, and his mother despaired of his recovery. In this extremity she had recourse to God; and knowing the miracles which He worked through the intercession of S. Rose, she thought she might obtain her son's cure through her merits. When he was one day attacked by a fit of his malady, she placed a piece of our Saint's scapular on his breast: his convulsions ceased at once, he came to himself, and had no return of fits from that time.

The year of our Saint's death, John Rodrignez Samanez, a painter, was troubled with asthma, accompanied by a great oppression of the stomach: this disease had three years before attacked his lungs, and he could only breathe by coughing, or not without a whistling sound that proceeded from his chest. When nothing but his death was expected, Mary de Mesta applied some relics of S. Rose to his stomach; as soon as he had recommended himself to the Saint he fell asleep, and when he awoke found his chest relieved and entirely cured.

A lay brother of our Order, named John Garcias, finding the door of S. Rose's hermitage too narrow to allow him to draw out a footstool, took a knife to cut off part of the wood, but in his eagerness he plunged, the instrument so deeply into his hand that he cut off a large piece of flesh, which hung from his arm in a frightful manner. He had recourse to S. Rose, and taking a piece of her veil he applied it to the wound, and wrapped up the hand in his handkerchief, and an hour afterwards he found his wound as perfectly cured as if it had been dressed by the most skilful surgeons in the country. More than twenty persons witnessed this miracle.

Another still more famous miracle was operated in favour of Blanche de Zuniga, wife of Don Anthony de Contreras, governor of the province of Guilas, in the kingdom of Peru. This lady, who had been eight months with child, being at a country house with her husband, perceived one day that her child no longer moved, and concluded that it must be dead: she remained in this fear five days, and feeling already dangerously ill, she prepared to receive the last Sacraments. While all the family were in the greatest affliction at this two-fold misfortune, some pieces of S. Rose's dress were brought from Lima to her husband; as soon as he received them he ran to his wife's chamber, and giving them to her she placed them on her body, and in the space of an Ave Maria, during which time she was occupied in invoking the protection of our Saint, she was delivered of a dead child already putrified and livid, after which she was restored to health.

S. Rose's intercession was particularly available to women, in freeing them from the cruel pangs of child-birth, and preserving their offspring: and for this reason, after her death, a great number of children in Lima had the name of Rose given to them, as a mark of their mothers' gratitude for her assistance in their labour. Nature has sometimes imprinted a mark upon these children, as a glorious testimony of the power which S. Rose had received from God to assist them, of which Peter de Guixano is an example. This child was placed in a cross position in his mother's womb, which by preventing her delivery put them both in evident danger of death in this extremity the mother called upon S. Rose, and when her prayer was finished the infant moved and came easily into the world, with a red rose on the eyelid of the right eye, which nature seemed to have engraved there in memory of this miracle.

4.

SEVERAL PERSONS AFFLICTED WITH DYSENTERY, QUINSY, FEVER, FRENZY, AND OTHER MALADIES, HAVE BEEN MIRACULOUSLY CURED BY EARTH FROM THE SEPULCHRE OF OUR SAINT.

It would seem as if Almighty God had communicated a medicinal and vivifying nature to this earth, in recompense for its having preserved the body of S. Rose from corruption; for the convent of Friars Preachers at Lima being always composed of three hundred religious, they were obliged to procure from Panama a sandy and burning soil, in order to fill up the chapter cemetery, that the bodies being quickly consumed by it there might be room to inter all the religious who died. Extraordinary to relate! that part alone of the ground which received the body of S. Rose changed its quality: it became solid, the earth grew hard as stone, and not being able to scratch it up with their hands to obtain the dust, they were obliged to break it with a hammer, though the rest of the soil in the cemetery was quite light. Almighty God caused this miraculous earth to be, as it were, an inexhaustible source for the relief of the inhabitants of Peru; which was

manifested visibly in 1632, when, after a prodigious quantity had been taken from this sepulchre to be distributed amongst the villages, towns, and provinces of this great kingdom, it did not appear as if more than four pounds' weight had been carried away; for F. Bernardin Marquez, who had been obliged to plunge his arm into the hole, to draw out the great quantity which was sent all over Peru, and even into Spain, perceived with astonishment on taking some out that this earth had increased underneath, and that the space which he had left empty was so completely filled that he could not put his hand into it. This dust worked such miraculous cures that persons came from all parts to fetch it, so much the more eagerly as they witnessed its wonderful effects. We will cite some remarkable examples.

A little girl of six years old had the tonsils of her throat very much swollen by a quinsey; an ulcer had formed; but what made the surgeon fear she would die was that gangrene had commenced in the wound, and the mortified flesh was beginning to fall away in small pieces: they gave her some of this earth mixed with a cooling drink, and the next day she was perfectly cured.

For twenty years the abbess of the Monastery of the Nuns of S. Clare, in Truxillo, had had a swollen leg, which gave her great pain, for there were more than forty ulcers in it, with so much inflammation that she was never without fever: she recovered her health by swallowing some of the earth from S. Rose's tomb, though she had sought it without success for several years in the experience of surgeons and the remedies of medicine.

Sister Grimaneca de Valverde, a nun of the Monastery of S. Clare, lost her sleep so completely with a burning fever and continual loss of blood, that she was fifteen days and nights without closing her eyes, which brought on delirium. The attendants were watching for an interval of reason to give her the last Sacraments and prepare her for death, for the physicians said she had not more than eight hours to live. Isabel of Fuente, the abbess, thought they must have recourse to the mercy of God, and to the merits of S. Rose. In this confidence she went to fetch some of the dust from her sepulchre, and begged the confessor to mix it with water and give it to this dying nun to drink. He did so, she drank it, the fever diminished, the other symptoms disappeared, her senses returned, and after having slept she found herself perfectly well the next day.

Father Ferdinand of Esquivel, sub-prior at Lima in the Convent of S. Mary Magdalen, was troubled with a rupture, which prevented him from preaching or making any journey. One day when he was in affliction at this circumstance, which prevented him from discharging his missionary duties, he was inspired by God to go to the sepulchre of S. Rose. He obeyed the thought, he went to her tomb, and after having prayed that our Saint would assist him in this infirmity, and applied some of the earth, he never felt afterwards any pain, and was so perfectly cured that he resumed the office of preaching which this indisposition had interrupted, and undertook long journeys by sea and land without any inconvenience.

Anne Cortes received the same assistance in a more dangerous and pressing infirmity. After two months of fever she was attacked by pleurisy, which so increased her fever that she became quite purple; she had lost appetite and sleep, and began to prepare for death, which she thought inevitable. Her mother recommended her to S. Rose, and remembering that she had a little of the earth from her grave, she encouraged her daughter to have confidence in the merits of our Saint, and to swallow this earth in some broth; she said some prayers first, and after taking it the purple colour disappeared, the fever left her, she went to sleep and was entirely cured.

Stephen of Cabrera having broken a rib by a fall, felt so much pain from it that he could not sleep; he asked for some of this earth, and having applied it to his side the swelling went down, and he fell into a slumber which relieved his pain; on awaking he found himself perfectly recovered.

In 1618, on the 21st of March, Catherine of Artiaga was attacked in the presence of several ladies of rank by a violent bleeding at the nose, which no remedies seemed capable of stopping, and she prepared for death. A lady having with her some of the earth from S. Rose's grave, put a little into a piece of linen and hung it round Catherine's neck, and immediately the blood ceased to flow, of which several persons were witness.

Father Anthony Montoya, and Father Juan de Estrada, both novices in the Dominican Order, were going to receive holy orders in the town of Guamangan: and as they were passing through a village named Guando, a man, thinking they were two priests, came in terror to request them to go and give absolution to a poor Indian woman who was in her agony, as there was no priest in the village: these two Friars were much grieved that they had not the power of absolving this poor sick woman, and went with the man to exhort her and make the recommendation of her soul. They found her motionless, incapable of speech, and apparently near her end. As they were praying at the foot of her bed, Brother Anthony remembered that he had some of this earth with him, and when the prayers were finished he related to these who were present the miracles which God worked every day by means of it to honour our Saint, and he exhorted them to call upon her for this sick person: he put some in a spoon, and having mixed it with water he made her swallow it. Two hours later these novices being ready to quit the village came again to see her, and on their entrance they found her husband as joyful as he had been sad, and the woman sitting up and eating with a good appetite. When she was told that this earth had cured her she thanked them, and was from that time very devout to S. Rose, and said publicly that she owed her life to her.

The number of these who were cured of fever is so great that it will be sufficient to mention a few names. Joseph do Castro was cured by taking some of the dust in broth. Jane of Mendoza used the same means with success. Father Diego de Palomino, a very learned religious of the Order of Friars Preachers, finding no medicine give him relief in his fever, addressed his prayer to S. Rose, swallowed some of the earth, and was that day cured of his disease. Maria Velasquez, wife of Captain Diego Ruiz de Campos, was freed from a fever and other symptoms which put her life in danger by drinking water with which this dust had been mixed. John of Palomorez was cured of fever and asthma by the same remedy. A short time after, his wife, who had been with child seven months, was attacked by fever, which greatly reduced her; and being unable to use the remedies of medicine, she put her confidence in S. Rose's protection, and took some of the dust from her tomb, which cured her the same day.

We should never finish if we were to try to name all the others; suffice it to say, that with all the care that was taken to keep a list of them, the number of the cured was too great for the pious intention of these who undertook it. John Lobo, a priest, swore solemnly before the Apostolic Commissioners, that he had seen a great number of persons of every rank and age, at Chusco, Potozzi, Orura, and other places of Peru, cured in a moment of their infirmities, and chiefly of fever, after having taken in water a little of the earth from her grave.

5.

PICTURES OF S. ROSE APPLIED TO PERSONS AFFLICTED WITH LEPROSY, QUINSY, GOUT, HEADACHE, AND OTHER

INFIRMITIES, HAVE BEEN THE MEANS OF RESTORING HEALTH TO THEM

THE devotion of the people to S. Rose was so great after her death, that there was scarcely a family, not only in Lima, but in all the towns and villages of Peru, that did not possess one of her pictures engraved and printed at Rome, whence they were sent to America. The miracles which God worked through these pictures caused the sick to have recourse to them in their infirmities.

Mary de Vera, the widow of Louis Nunez, had a violent fever with other symptoms, which reduced her to the last extremity, and obliged her to receive the Sacraments in preparation for death, as the physicians assured her she would not survive the next day. She sent, however, to beg Marianne, an Indian woman, who when young had been brought up with S. Rose, to send her a little picture of our Saint which she possessed: as soon as she received it, she kissed it with devotion, and holding it in her hands, she fell into a slumber which lasted till the next morning. On awaking she found herself in perfect health; and full of joy she lighted a wax taper on each side of this picture, and placing herself on her knees she thanked S. Rose for having obtained her health from God for her. This miraculous cure being made known in the town, public thanksgivings were offered to God for it.

In 1631, during the month of December, Mary de los Royes, a little girl of nine years old, was miraculously cured in nearly the same manner. For a year this child had had a disorder in the head which nothing had been able to remove. Her mother took her to the church of S. Dominic, and taking off her cap, touched the picture of S. Rose devoutly with one of her bandages, and hoping to obtain from God her daughter's cure she replaced it on her head; two days afterwards this child was found as perfectly cured as if nothing had been the matter with her.

In the November of the same year a little orphan, ten months old, named Mary, lived with Jerome de Soto Alvarado, who had taken her through charity. This child was so afflicted with leprosy, that she was a horrible object. The servant of the house, seeing that the physicians despaired of curing her, went to pick up in the church of S. Dominic some roses which had been placed on a statue of S. Rose; she took them home, and without mentioning her design she applied them to all the marks of leprosy which appeared on the child's body: having wrapped her up well, she carried her to bed, and found her the next morning cured of her leprosy: in ecstasies of joy she ran to acquaint her master, who hastened to view the miracle, and who went to give testimony of it before the Apostolical Commissioners who were examining the life and miracles of our Saint. This miracle was so well authenticated and so public, that to keep it in mind they ordered that the little girl should be called Mary Rose, which name she bore all her life.

Sebastiana de Vega, the wife of Cyprian de Medina, a doctor of laws and royal advocate, being in the act of mounting a mule to go into the country with her husband, fell when she had her foot in the stirrup, and dislocated a bone, which gave her very great pain, and rendered her incapable of changing her position in bed. One night when she was in great suffering, she desired the servant to bring her a paper picture of S. Rose; she placed it on the dislocated bone with so much confidence, that on awaking from a slumber into which she had fallen while holding this picture, she found herself cured and free from pain.

A poor slave, named Elizabeth Biafora, being very near her confinement, was seized with pleurisy, violent fever, and vomiting; the physicians seeing these symptoms in a person who was not in a state to use their remedies, caused her to receive the last Sacraments, thinking she could not recover. This poor woman seeing there was no human hope, put all her confidence in God; she earnestly asked for a picture of S. Rose, which she applied to the side in which she felt pain, and left it there all night. The next morning the physicians

being come to try to save at least the child's life, were much surprised to find her in perfect health and asking for something to eat. The day after this miracle her confinement took place happily, and she was able to nurse the child herself.

In 1632 Angelica de Albido, wife of Francis de las Cuentas, who was with child of twins, was delivered of one, but the other still remained, and the matrons who attended her thought she would die. Her husband was inconsolable; and in this consternation the sick person had recourse to S. Rose, and asking for one of her pictures, she had it fixed to the foot of her bed, that it might be always before her eyes. While she was heartily praying to her to help her in this extremity, she felt pains come on, and in the same moment a second daughter came into the world. In memory of this miracle they were named in baptism Mary and Frances de Rose. The history of her life from which these miracles have been taken relates twelve more which are well authenticated, and which were wrought by the application of her pictures.

CHAPTER XXIII

OF THE EFFORTS MADE AT ROME TO OBTAIN FROM THE POPE HER CANONIZATION.

As honour is the reward of virtue, it has always in every country been rendered to illustrious men who have signalized themselves by glorious actions, or who have well served the people or the state; and as in the idea of pagans apotheosis constituted the height of glory, supreme honours have been offered to these emperors and heroes who had made themselves renowned by the mildness of their government, or by the splendour of their triumph. The Christian religion, more enlightened in the discernment of the honour she pays, and more just in the recompense which she awards to virtue, consecrates the more solid and the more noble rewards to these who have perfectly imitated the Son of God by the exact practice of the heroic virtues which He preached on earth by word and example; she praises their merit, she pronounces panegyrics in their honour, and to render them immortal in the memory of man she grants them the honour of a sacred apotheosis, declaring to the people that they are reigning with God, and that they may offer to them public testimonies of honour and respect. The eminent virtue of S. Rose, sustained by such great and continual miracles, rendered her so faithful a copy of the virtues of Jesus Christ, that we may say in her praise what Hildebert said of a lady who was very pious and closely united to God, "*In ea praeter virtutem, nihil virtus invenit.*"

We need not be astonished that after her death the kingdom of Peru most earnestly solicited the honours of canonization for her from the Holy See. The metropolitan church of Lima, all the religious Orders of S. Francis, S. Augustine, the Carmelites, the Order of Mercy, of S. John of God, and Father Nicholas Mastrillo, Provincial of the Society of Jesus, in the name of the whole Society, wrote letters to the Pope, in which they very humbly entreated His Holiness to proceed to the canonization of the admirable servant of God, Sister Rose of S. Mary, whom the people honoured for her virtues, and whose miracles rendered her illustrious throughout the New World. The viceroy, the council of state, the governors of the province, and the magistrates of the towns, united for the same end, and joining their solicitations to these of the prelates, the clergy, and all the religious communities, entreated not only for her canonization, but that S. Rose might also be given as Patroness to Lima, the capital of the kingdom of Peru. A brief was dispatched from Rome, by which His Holiness appointed Apostolic Commissioners to examine on the spot her life, her conduct, and the miracles wrought at her tomb. It was thought that the depositions of a hundred and eighty-three witnesses would soon enable them to see the desires of all Christian America satisfied; for on the 22nd of March, in 1625, Cardinal Peretti, Prefect of the Congregation of Rites, having examined the depositions which had been juridically taken at Lima of the life and miracles of S. Rose, issued a decree in which he declared that His Holiness might cause information to be taken by apostolic authority.

On the appearance of this decree Pope Urban VIII sent a Brief to the Archbishop of Lima, and in his absence to the Bishop of Guatemala, giving him for coadjutors the dean and the archdeacon of the church of Lima. They were so diligent, that the proceedings were finished and presented to the Congregation of Rites on the 22nd of July, 1634. Cardinal Torrez, who had succeeded Cardinal Peretti, acknowledged their authenticity; but a Brief which His Holiness published the year following, prohibiting new devotions, stopped the whole affair. After the death of Urban VIII, the solicitations were continued under Innocent X, but delays were caused by unavoidable circumstances.

Urban VIII

Under Alexander VII the petition was renewed, and Father Anthony Gonzalez, Definitor of Peru, and Procurator in this affair, was so active in the business, that on the 13th of September, 1663, Cardinal Azzolini having made a discourse in the Congregation of Rites before His Holiness on the heroic virtues of S. Rose, and also on the miracles which God daily worked through her merits, it was resolved to proceed to her canonization. Father Gonzalez repeated the solicitations which had been made to three preceding Popes, in the name of the clergy, the nobility, and the people of Peru. He presented to the Pope the requests of nine religious Orders, three letters from the King of Spain, and three from the Cardinal of Arragon, on the same subject.

The Very Reverend Father John Baptist de Marinis, of the Order of Friars Preachers, presented to him two requests in the name of his whole Order, by which he made known to His Holiness the persevering devotion of all Peru, in honouring the Venerable Sister Rose of S. Mary as a Saint, whose merits it had pleased God to exalt by a hundred and nineteen new miracles;

Alexeander VII

but the war with the Turks in Hungary, and other affairs, caused the decree to be delayed a little longer: Divine Providence had reserved the glory of the accomplishment of the proceedings to our Holy Father Pope Clement IX. The Queen-Regent of Spain pressed the matter so earnestly that His Holiness commanded the Congregation of Rites to assemble for this purpose. After several meetings their decree was published on the 10th of December, 1667, by which they declared that His Holiness might proceed to the canonization of this servant of God, and might permit her in the meantime to be honoured under the name of Blessed.

Clement IX

The Brief of Clement IX for the beatification of S. Rose is dated the 12th of February, 1668; and she was canonized three years later, 1671, by Clement X., who appointed the 30th of August for her feast. Thus solemnly has the Church of God set the seal of her unerring approval upon that series of wonders, that endless chain of miracles, which, reaching from her cradle to her grave, make up the life of this American virgin.

There was never a time and never a land when and where it was more needful for the daughters of the Church to learn how to make for themselves a cloister in the world than England in the present age; and it is precisely this lesson which the Life of S. Rose conveys. Amidst so much that is false and hollow, heartless and unreal, how beautiful before Almighty God, would be the childlike simplicity of this virgin of the South, copied even faintly in the lives of our Catholic countrywomen!

Clement X

For it is this simplicity which was her fairest ornament; indeed, so completely child-like was she herself, and so child-like the wonders with which her Divine Spouse encircled her, that in reading her Life it seems hardly ever to strike us that she was anything but a little girl. It is as though she grew no older, but remained still the baby, cradled in the arms of Jesus, as when the vermilion rose bloomed miraculously on her little face when three months old. Let us also thank Almighty God in the fervent simplicity of our faith for the seal His Church has set upon these authentic wonders; wonders not lost in dubious antiquity, but adequately proved in the face of modern criticism so short a time ago; and remembering that this bold exhibition of the marvellous is by no less an authority than the Catholic Church presented to our veneration and our love, let us take it like awestruck children, as a page from the lost chronicles of Eden, and strive to unlearn that bold timidity with which we have too often been inclined to court favour where we shall never get it, and to avoid sneers which are to us as an heritage and vouchers of our truths, by smiling with the profane and doubting with the sceptical. For one of the faithful to try to look as like an unbeliever as he can is a sight which never won a soul to Christ, or gained for the Church the

1586 - 1617

esteem of an opponent. Rose of Lima is now raised upon the altars of the Church by the decree of her canonization; she is a Catholic Saint: no sneer of man can wither the marvellous blooming of her leaves; but he will find a thorn who shall dare to handle roughly this sweet mysterious Rose which S. Dominic planted in the garden of his Master.

F.W. Faber.

B. Columba de Reate. V.

The Life

of

BLESSED COLOMBA OF RIETI

by

Sebastiano degli Angeli, O.P.

THE LIFE

of

BLESSED COLOMBA OF RIETI

--

PART I

WHICH CONTAINS THE LIFE COLOMBA LED IN RIETI HER NATIVE COUNTRY, AND DURING THE TIME WHICH PRECEDED HER ARRIVAL IN PERUGIA

CHAPTER I

ORIGIN, BIRTH, AND INFANCY OF COLOMBA.—EXTRAORDINARY EVENTS WHICH PREDICT HER FUTURE SANCTITY.

Colomba was born of honest and virtuous parent at Rieti, an ancient and celebrated city of Sabina, at break of day, on the 2nd of February, 1467. Contemporary writers do not mention her family, for it soon became extinct in Rieti; authors who wrote at a later period assure us, however, with good foundation, that Colomba's father belonged to the family of Guadagnioli, which originally came from Collisepoli, a town situated on the hill not far from Narni. In fact, this family of Guadagnioli was existing in Collisepoli in the year 1650, and by authentic monuments belonging to them this descent is clearly proved; and it appears that Colomba's father, leaving his country in 1450, took up his abode in Rieti, to carry on business as a merchant, as we are assured by Ludovico Jacobilli, a writer of Foligno, who cites witnesses worthy of credit. This family of Guadagnioli kept also in their house with great veneration an ancient picture of our Saint, with an inscription signifying that she belonged to their family: and in fine, Cardinal Rapaccioli, a native of Collisepoli, thought himself honoured in belonging to the country whence Colomba's father drew his origin.

Angiolo Antonio Guadagnioli was the name of her father, and that of her mother Giovanna: they were both rich in solid piety and religion. Giovanna was only fifteen, when during the last three months which preceded the birth of this child, she suffered so much from nausea and disgust for every sort of food, that a few fruits and wild grapes were the only food she took, which circumstance was considered as an indication of the future extraordinary abstinence of Colomba.

Scarcely had this happy infant appeared in the world, than Heaven, which had destined her for great things, deigned to honour her with an apparition of angels. The truth of our narration requires that it should be related here as contemporary writers make it known to us. Several venerable matrons having assembled, as is the custom, to assist at the confinement of Giovanna, one of them, a virtuous woman named Barbara, when holding the new-born infant in her arms, heard herself repeatedly called by her name from the street. Hastily depositing the tender babe on the bare ground, she ran to the window to see who called her, and was followed by all the women present, who were attracted by curiosity. All were amazed to see passing in the street under the windows a magnificent chariot, filled with youths of an angelical appearance, who signified their joy by songs and the sound of instruments. In the midst of this angelic company arose, as if in triumph, a statue of wax. It was placed in the centre of a golden circle, crowned with seven lighted torches, and supported by three seraphim. After an hour had elapsed this mysterious vision disappeared, and filled with astonishment at the novelty of the wonderful sight they had witnessed, they lifted up the child from the ground, where it had remained without giving the least sign of uneasiness. From this circumstance they began joyfully to conclude, that this heavenly apparition was meant to announce the future sanctity of the new-born infant; it was therefore decided by unanimous consent, that the child should receive in holy baptism the name of Angiola.

The wonders did not terminate here; for when the child was taken to be baptized, and the accustomed exorcisms had been completed, scarcely had she been presented at the sacred font, when a white dove was seen to fly into the church, which, after several flights round the font, placed itself at last on the head of the infant Angiola. The assistants were surprised at so novel an event, and they judged that this was no less a presage than that which happened to S. Ambrose, in whose mouth a swarm of bees settled, and might be taken as an indication of the innocence of the future life of the child.

When the sacred function was finished, and the news of what had occurred in the church had spread through the streets, a great number of people, excited by a holy curiosity, came in crowds, some to see the happy babe, others to know the real circumstances of the fact from the matrons, who returned home filled with admiration, surprise, and joy. So lively an impression did this singular event make on the mind of every one, that the name of Angiola given to the child in baptism seemed to be forgotten, and she was called usually by no other name than that of Colomba. Thus Almighty God deigned to manifest to the faithful by sensible signs, His predilection for this soul, which He had chosen to be the worthy temple of the Holy Ghost.

The parents of Colomba being made aware by these extraordinary occurrences of the precious pledge they had received from Heaven, spared no pains in observing attentively everything she did in her infancy; and they applied themselves to it with greater earnestness when they began to discover in Colomba extraordinary and wonderful signs of a love for mortification and penance, superior to her age. It was at that time the custom to wash infants in a sort of bath, made for the purpose, of bronze or some other metal; and the child when placed in one of them refused with unusual cries and tears to remain there; but the mother trying the experiment of placing her in a common wooden vessel, Colomba then showed by her tranquillity and her smiles her innate love for mortification and humility.

Her mother observed that the infant only took milk once in the day on Fridays, and at first she was rather disquieted, fearing her child would be ill; but when she reflected that this only occurred on Fridays, and not on other days, and saw her healthy and robust, she admired with reason in this abstinence a supernatural and hidden virtue, which already began to show itself in her daughter.

She was often found by her father and mother out of the cradle, lying on the bare ground, and when they were alarmed and ran to take her up, they perceived by her smiles and tranquillity that this could not be ascribed to accident, but to a supernatural power, which inflamed this tender heart more and more with the love of the Cross, to make it a living image of Jesus Christ.

In fact, when scarcely three years old, (who would believe it?) Colomba secretly scattered branches of thorns under the sheets of her little bed, to disturb the repose of her limbs which were still so delicate; and at four years of age she obtained leave from her pious parents to fast every Friday on bread and water.

All her diversions at this age bore signs of piety, devotion, and mortification; she never appeared more cheerful or happy than when she found herself before some holy picture, or saw a cross which she eagerly endeavoured to embrace and kiss, diligently making similar ones with her own hands. But what besides the love of the cross, which had already inflamed her noble heart, could have taught Colomba at this tender age to make industriously with her own hands painful hair-shirts, to afflict her tender limbs? She was only five years old when she was found by her mother in a distant corner of the house, in the act of making a shirt of horse-hair, which she had herself collected from an old sieve. When asked by her mother what she was making, she answered that her work might be made useful in the house. This shirt is still preserved with great veneration by the nuns of S. Agnes at Rieti.

That her parents might not prevent her from walking barefoot, she ingeniously removed the soles of her shoes, covering her foot with the upper leather. Ribbons, lace, pins, and other feminine ornaments which children are generally so eager to possess, and which her father often gave her, she converted into disciplines or other instruments of penance. She passed many hours of the day on her knees before a crucifix or a picture of the Blessed Virgin and when she heard mass in the church, at seven years of age, she seemed immoveable on her knees like a statue, so great was her attention. These were the delightful pastimes which occupied the time of Colomba's wonderful infancy.

CHAPTER II

COLOMBA'S CHILDHOOD AND YOUTH, HER PROGRESS IN VIRTUE.—SHE MAKES A VOW OF VIRGINITY DURING A HEAVENLY VISION.

When a tender shrub, planted in the best soil, and watered by a neighbouring stream, begins to shoot forth its branches, we have no doubt of its becoming a large tree. Thus, as Colomba had given such noble signs of Christian fervour in her infancy, at which period of life vices are generally lightly thought of, and almost considered innocent, she was seen to acquire the practice of all virtues as soon as ever she came to the use of reason.

Prevented by grace in restraining her senses before she experienced their tumult, and in hating the vanities of the world before she tasted them, this courageous child found no difficulty in attaining even in her childhood to the possession of these virtues which are said to belong to "purified souls" and thus her heart being at peace, she was enabled to exercise their acts in perfect calmness, with ease, promptitude, and delight.

She laid a solid foundation for her elevated fabric by assiduity in prayer, and not content with these she daily said, hearing one day, when she was seven years of age, the nuns of the third Order of S. Dominic reciting their office, filled with a holy desire, she immediately begged of these sisters to admit her into the choir for the recital of the canonical hours, and being received there, her quickness in learning and devotion in praying were so great, as quite to delight the hearts of these religious.

This holy institution of the third Order of S. Dominic, called "of penance," has been greatly praised by Sovereign Pontiffs, and enriched with many privileges, from its having at all times added splendour to the Church of Jesus Christ. It was greatly extended by means of the glorious and seraphic S. Catherine of Siena, and brought to live in community, and it flourished very vigorously at this time, especially in the provinces of Italy, producing a copious fruit of noble and illustrious virgins, who signalized their names by the sanctity of their lives and miracles. There were in Rieti nuns of this third Order who enjoyed a high reputation for sanctity, from the number of learned and pious religious who directed them. From them Almighty God was pleased that Colomba should receive the milk of her spiritual life.

When Colomba had become intimate with these nuns, a vast field was opened to her, from which she might derive more abundant pasture to satisfy her spiritual hunger. She made frequent visits to the nuns, and as she enjoyed their holy conversation she looked forward with grief to the hour when she must depart. Having obtained her parents' permission to spend more time, especially on festival days, in these conversations, she passed the whole of these days in reading spiritual books with the nuns, and in prayer in the church of S. Dominic.

In this church the virtuous child fixed her eyes particularly on a holy image of Jesus crucified, before which, kneeling often in contemplation, she melted into tears, which moved those who were present, and entreated her Divine Saviour to make her a partaker in His sufferings, and to direct her in His holy service.

Leaving the church one day, after making her accustomed

petition before the crucifix, she returned to the nuns, and though she was always eager to read spiritual books, she seemed to be seized with an unusual avidity for this holy exercise, and she began earnestly to beg the nuns to read some devout book. It happened that one of them, to satisfy her, took up and read the Life of S. Catherine of Siena, whom at that time particularly all the sisters were ardently desirous of imitating.

Colomba's attention was so riveted that she remained all the time motionless and in an ecstasy; and contemplating the Calvary of sufferings which Catherine the spouse of Jesus Christ formed for herself, to please her heavenly Bridegroom, the child was inflamed with holy fervour, and her countenance becoming, as it were, on fire, she formed to herself her own Calvary on the model of that of Catherine, without placing any bounds to it, resolving to suffer for Christ alone as much as she possibly could, and to find the happiness of her whole life in suffering.

This was the first conspicuous and fundamental fruit which Colomba at the age of seven years gathered from her continual prayer—enlightenment of the mind to discern well, and strength of heart to resolve firmly.

The innocent child, delighted to see the vast field which she had purchased, delayed not to set her hand to the plough, and without ever looking back to plant therein the chosen Vine of our Lord. She laid down to herself first an inviolable law, never to allow any delicacy or repose to her body, under any pretext whatever; for she could not arrest that fire of divine love with which she was inflamed. Seeing a new course of penance, formed by her love of God, open before her, she began to observe rigorously the fasts of Lent, Advent, and the Vigils of precept. Her disciplines and hair-shirts were no longer composed of little cords, but of iron, which drew blood. She requested from her confessor, a Dominican religious, the habit of the third Order of S. Dominic, which was allowed to be worn underneath at that time, and she began to wear woollen clothes instead of linen.

This rigorous manner of life was intended by her as a declaration of her love for virtue, and also of perpetual warfare against sin, for which she had so great a hatred, that she turned pale and trembled from head to foot at the mere name of "sin." It was a wonderful and edifying sight for the whole city, to behold this tender child, who, excepting her age, had nothing childish about her, so sedate and sensible, so modest in her looks, so humble and simple in her manners, devout in her conversation, obedient to the smallest sign without hesitation, patient on every occasion without complaining, an enemy to idleness, and desirous always to assist others.

These were the virtues which adorned the childhood of Colomba, when she had scarcely come to the use of reason; and they were not merely the effects of a happy disposition, but also the fruits of her ardent charity, which, like a flame impatient, as it were, of confinement, tried to diffuse itself, and to make others participate in the gifts she had received from God.

In fact, who would not have been astonished to see a child of eight or nine years old, seated as a mistress in the midst of a circle of chosen playfellows whom she had contrived to assemble, and whilst she attended to her work, encouraging them in pious and devout conversation, instructing them in the holy fear of God, and animating them with the hope of the rewards promised to virtue? This was, however, the daily practice of Colomba, who was chosen by Heaven not merely for her own sanctification, but to propagate divine love in the hearts of others. "Know, my dear companions," said Colomba to them, "that the happiness of heaven, the company of the angels, and glory of the saints, is a gift that is only known by him who enjoys it, and no one can enjoy it who does not keep his heart united to Jesus Christ. He is the heavenly Bridegroom who introduces into heaven these virgins who are faithful to Him, and calls them His spouses; but to be really His spouses, we must despise the pleasures and vanities of the world, abhor its pomps, fly from vice, and love virtue. Be then humble, devout, patient, and meek, because our dear Jesus is so."

Sentiments like these clearly indicated that Jesus alone was the centre of her thoughts, the object and the repose of her desires. Jesus Christ Himself deigned to show how true this was, and how pleasing to Heaven was the heart of this child, by visiting her, honouring her with His visible presence, and confirming her in His holy service.

Colomba had attained the age of ten years, when, enamoured of the priceless worth of the virginity of the most holy Mary, which was so pleasing to the most Blessed Trinity, she meditated day and night, moved by an interior impulse, on making a solemn offering of her own virginity to her Lord, and consecrating herself to be His spouse.

One night when she was at prayer in her room, begging our Lord that He would vouchsafe to receive her offering, suddenly an unusual light filled the apartment, as if the sun itself had entered into it. Terrified and trembling at this singular occurrence, she saw presented before her eyes a royal throne of gold, studded with precious stones, on which was seated our Divine Redeemer Jesus Christ, around Whom in attendance upon Him were the glorious apostles S. Peter and S. Paul, S. Leo the Pope, S. Jerome, and the Patriarch S. Dominic. The happy child falling prostrate, with profound humility entreated her Divine Saviour's benediction, and Jesus raising His merciful Hand, blessed her, looking on her with a sweet and gracious countenance. Colomba then took courage, and feeling within herself a supernatural strength, she presented to our Lord her meditated vow of virginity, which she promised to observe till death in spite of every obstacle. Jesus having given her a promise of His Divine aid on every occasion, then disappeared from her sight; the Pontiff S. Leo alone remained with Colomba, and spent the night in sweet discourses on eternal happiness: the holy Pope also disappeared at break of day, leaving the room filled with a most fragrant odour. The young virgin remained for some hours in ecstatic contemplation, and, like Moses after his conversation with God, she appeared in public with so joyful a countenance, and so much fervour in her heart, that she showed forth wonderfully the beauty of that Divine love which inflamed her.

A few days after her heavenly Spouse deigned again to delight her heart, by showing to her the reward promised to the vow she had made. Colomba was in the church of S. Scholastica, praying before an image of the Blessed Virgin, when she was presented with a large piece of gold by two angels, who invested her with a white girdle, saying to her, "Receive this, daughter, it will be the reward of thy vow and of thy labours." And at the same time Colomba saw her youngest brother also girded by angels: he became a Dominican Friar, and was named Father Giovanni. The young virgin was much strengthened by these two heavenly visions, and being greatly encouraged in her holy resolution, she soon manifested her invincible firmness in sustaining combats and gaining the victory.

CHAPTER III

COLOMBA SUFFERS MUCH IN KEEPING HER VOW—SHE REFUSES THE MARRIAGE ARRANGED BY HER PARENTS. SHE CUTS OFF HER HAIR.—SHE IS BEATEN BY THE DEVIL.

When a soul that is in the enjoyment of spiritual consolations does not derive from them greater strength and vigour in loving and suffering, but stops at the mere enjoyment of these delights, it gives good reason for suspecting that its visions are mere delusions, and rather a deception of self-love than the true gifts of God. The vision of Jesus glorified on Mount Thabor, granted to the apostles, was intended to excite in their hearts a love of sufferings and labours; and the sight of Jesus Christ glorified in heaven, which S. Stephen enjoyed, made him strong in enduring, and even made the stones appear sweet to him. Thus Colomba manifested by her actions that the heavenly visions she enjoyed were not idle entertainments, but true gifts of a fervent love, and that she had chosen to follow Christ not only to Mount Thabor, but even to the bloody heights of Calvary. At twelve years of age she began her voyage through the stormy sea of the world, but by the aid of Divine grace she avoided its rocks, and, like a skilful sailor, arrived safely at the port.

The first obstacle she encountered and courageously overcame was the opposition made by her parents to her holy vow. The saintly life which the child had always led till the age of twelve years, which had been, moreover, illustrated by signal graces and favours from Heaven, ought to have inspired her parents with a prompt condescension to their daughter's wishes, for there was no room to doubt that they were the designs of Heaven; and these same parents had frequently experienced the effect of Colomba's desires, in obtaining through her prayers a ready and abundant assistance for the necessities of their family, deliverance from some misfortune, or an instantaneous restoration to health. Almighty God nevertheless permitted that the contrary should happen for the purification of His chosen servant's love.

Colomba had been gifted by nature with beautiful features, and with a quantity of fair and flowing hair, which ornament was at that time in great esteem among women; so that her charms appeared, even amidst the shadows and obscurity of her humble and mortified behaviour. Her modest and chaste beauty, joined to her piety, which was known to the whole city, drew the eyes of many towards her to seek her in marriage.

In the meantime her parents arranged a match for her without her consent, in favour of a rich, and, as some say, a noble youth, and they began to procure for her a set of rich bridal dresses; but observing that this step, instead of being agreeable to Colomba, only gave her great pain and annoyance, they made known to her the contract which they had already agreed to for her future nuptials.

The young virgin turned pale, and using the most efficacious means which her mind and heart suggested to her, she made known to them her repugnance, concealing at first the spiritual espousals in which she was already engaged. Her parents, who had gone rather too far, did not yield at all to the respectful entreaties of their child, and hoping to vanquish her easily with caresses and diversions, they tried every means of this sort, and even engaged her confessor to dissuade her from her holy purpose, and to command her to relax her rigorous system. All these attempts being incapable of altering the child's determination, they resolved at length to oblige her by a command.

For this purpose, several of her relations being met together with her parents one day, all with one accord began the attack, some with entreaties, others with commands. Colomba defended herself respectfully for some time, but finding the assault grow stronger, and seeing herself attacked on every side, filled with holy fervour and courage she thus began to speak: "Be no longer in doubt and suspense, my dear parents and beloved relations, for my refusal is not an empty ceremony, but an eternal truth. I am no longer able to agree to your wishes, nor to consent to have any earthly spouse, for I am already espoused to the Monarch of Heaven, and to Him I have consecrated my virginity by vow; I will belong to Him alone, and to no other, and no vain honour, no grandeur, no fear, or torment, will be able to make me change my resolution. Do not, O my dear friends, dispute with me these honours and favours which God has given me, nor oppose yourselves to what He works in me. Reflect, my dear parents, that the Spouse whom I have chosen is more noble, more worthy, and more beautiful, than any who are of this world."

This holy discourse was not completed, when her indiscreet assailants, who, instead of being moved, were inflamed with anger, began to ill-treat the servant of Christ, some with abuse, others with threats and blows, and at last they left her. The brave young girl did not lose courage in the least, but when she found herself alone she fell on her knees before Jesus Crucified, and repeatedly thanked Him that He had made her worthy to begin to suffer for His love.

The battle against the holy young virgin was not yet terminated, but on the contrary, growing stronger, her relations, without regarding reason, when a little time had elapsed prepared to carry this fortress by treachery and violence. They fixed the day for her marriage without her knowledge, being resolved to extort her consent in the midst of the banquet. But as the arrangements of men are in the sight of God as spiders' webs, without substance, Heaven permitted that this lover of the cross should endure labours and sufferings, whence she might gather delights in the erection of her Calvary, but Divine grace willed that at the same time she should gain a memorable trophy of her second glorious victory.

During the night which preceded the day fixed for her nuptials, as Colomba was praying according to her custom, she heard a voice and saw appear before her two religious clothed in the habit of S. Dominic, who said to her, "Colomba, confide in God, and go to-morrow to S. Mauro, (a church situated on a hill outside the walls of the city) there thou wilt find a nun who will instruct thee what to do. Be of good courage, and do not fear." The child, not comprehending this mystery, thought the rest of the night a thousand years while she was waiting for morning to go to S. Mauro. She easily obtained the permission of her mother, who was anxious not to do any thing to displease her daughter at that time, and in the company of her mother and several other devout women she set out for Monte Mauro. Colomba, however, who walking more quickly than her companions, had left them a little behind, knelt down to pray before a cross by the road side, and she soon saw appear before her the nun pointed out to her in her vision, who, approaching her, spoke to this effect: "Know, daughter, that to-day at the hour of vespers thy relations will bring to thee the spouse they have destined for thee, and they will do all in their power to extort thy consent, and to celebrate the marriage to-day; but be firm and constant in thy resolution, and keep the faith which thou hast sworn to Christ. Fear not threats, and imitate S. Catherine of Siena."

Having said this the nun disappeared from Colomba's sight, and rising up and joining the others, who had not perceived this interview, she prosecuted her walk to the church, concealing for the time the bitter grief which oppressed her. But scarcely had she entered the church, where she could unbosom herself alone before the crucifix, than bursting into a flood of tears, she thus addressed our Lord: "Judge my cause, O my Divine Love, for it is Thy cause; in Thy mercy come to defend me against the insults which are preparing for me. If Thou dost not assist me, what will become of me? In Thee alone, O my Jesus, I confide, and be Thine alone all the care of preserving for me that which is Thine. Grant that I may suffer any torment, and a thousand cruel deaths, rather than give my consent to another spouse."

When she came back she went before returning home to consult her confessor on what had happened, to take his advice, and receive an explanation of the words, " to imitate S. Catherine of Siena." Her confessor explained to her the example of this Saint, who on a similar occasion cut off her hair; and the child hearing this was satisfied, and returned home joyful and consoled, preparing herself for her defence by continual invocations of the Divine assistance.

When the hour destined for the conflict had arrived, and her relations, among whom, according to some writers, was also the intended bridegroom, were come to the house, the afflicted Colomba was called, to whom they intimated with resolute words that she was to give her consent to the husband they had chosen; but the prudent child submissively asked for a little time to return to her room, from which she would quickly return to them with her answer. Her relations flattered themselves in the meantime that they had already vanquished her firmness, and expected to receive her consent on her return; when suddenly they saw her present herself before them holding in her hand her hair, which she had cut off, and throwing it contemptuously on the ground she said to them, " This is the gift which I make to you, and for which my Spouse cares not at all; do now with me what you please, for I fear nothing, having Jesus for my defence: take care, however, unfortunate people, not to incur His indignation. I am sorry that the ill-advised young man will have to pay dearly for his error, and to do penance for it."

The bystanders, astonished and stunned at the sight of this unexpected courage, and confused with the boldness of Colomba's words, from whose countenance there beamed something supernatural and divine, did not know what to say in reply; and because no strength can resist the Holy Ghost, they all departed in confusion and anger. The nuns of S. Agnes in Rieti still preserve this hair, which, like the sling in the hand of the youthful David, overcame the monstrous giant. The young and innocent virgin being left alone, but absolute mistress of the field, after having thanked her Divine crucified Saviour, thought it expedient to withdraw from the first fury of her relations' indignation. The urgent motive which induced her to take this resolution, was the threat of her eldest half-brother, who having struck her declared he would kill her, and he would perhaps have put his horrible design into execution, had he not been terrified by a vision which arrested the blow and recalled him to repentance.

Colomba resolved in the meantime to fly from her father's house, in order to retire to the church of S. Scholastica, a monastery near their house, where she had first enjoyed the sweet vision of the angels, who invested her with a girdle; but deprived of all human help, and obliged by force to leave the church, she took refuge with a widow of her acquaintance, till the extraordinary event became divulged over the town, when many persons who admired this great constancy manifested by a child, and judging with reason great and extraordinary things of her, interposed to appease the anger of her friends that she might return home. Being again received there, she was comforted by Heaven; for being at prayer during the night, S. Dominic with S. Catherine of Siena appeared to her, and blessing her, assured the servant of God that she should be their daughter. Much time had not elapsed before the eagerness of her parents for their daughter's marriage diminished, as the intended spouse, assailed by interior remorse and alarm which consumed him, resolved of his own accord to break off the contract, and a few months later he died.

Hell was enraged at the sight of so much constancy and bravery in Colomba, and was still more furious on account of the number of souls whom her beautiful virtues and her fame as a true servant of God drew along with her. Therefore, after having wonderfully triumphed over the world, she was obliged to enter another field of battle, the more dangerous on account of the strength and power of her adversary. The devil began to attempt to frighten her during her prayers at night with obscene phantoms, with noises, and finally with blows. At the sight of so powerful and unknown an enemy the innocent child was alarmed, for she was yet inexperienced in such assaults; and she began with sighs and sobs to examine deeply into her conscience, to ascertain if by her fault the divine and just Judge had abandoned her in this abyss of torments, when remembering that at the age of six years she had happened by chance to name the devil, when she was treated with impatience, though she had soon confessed this fault, yet judging these diabolical assaults to be the punishment of this error, she went trembling to the feet of her confessor, to renew her accusation and perform rigorous penance for it.

Being desired by her spiritual father to throw herself into the arms of God with strong confidence, and not to let herself be cast down by these diabolical insults, she derived so much courage and such help and light from God, that she put the enemy to flight by the sign of the cross alone. She rejoiced if she were dragged along the ground, or received many blows from the infuriated enemy of her salvation; she provoked him to ill-treat her, desiring to carry the cross with Jesus; and she endured all this with perfect tranquillity and interior peace of mind, keeping these tribulations secret from the rest of the family.

CHAPTER IV.

PROGRESS OF COLOMBA IN PERFECTION.—HER LANGUISHING LOVE FOR GOD AND HUNGER AFTER HOLY COMMUNION ARE REFRESHED FROM HEAVEN. VISIONS AND ECSTASIES WHICH SHE ENJOYS IN HER FATHER'S HOUSE.

If among the encomiums which the Holy Ghost pronounces on the just soul, one is, that "in a short space she fulfilled a long time," we may with reason call the lovely soul of Colomba "just;" for at the age of only eighteen years, having wonderfully triumphed over herself, the world, and the devil, she was already loaded with these victorious spoils which usually adorn mature age. It cannot therefore appear surprising that her parents, convinced by her many holy actions that divine grace worked in their daughter without obstacle, determined to leave her in peace in her holy manner of life. This concession enabled her to advance with rapid steps to the higher degrees of perfection.

Her exterior actions being all happily guided by an interior light, which always beamed in her soul, were not only irreproachable, but even admirable. A lover of silence and an enemy to idleness, she was always occupied in some sort of work. She never cared about any recompense, but if any thing were spontaneously offered to her, she generally employed it in relieving the poor, whom she often attended when sick, instructed in piety and devotion, but above all exhorted with great fervour to hate sin.

Still more wonderful, however, was the task which our Saint proposed to herself in secret in her interior life before the eyes of Almighty God. Filled with an ardent desire of being clothed with the habit of S. Dominic, she began to dispose herself for it by copying in herself the life of the holy patriarch. Very short was the sleep she allowed to her body, while she spent a long time in prayer. She disciplined herself to blood three times each night, once for herself, once for sinners, and the third time for the souls in Purgatory.

She began to keep five Lents, or rather to observe five periods of fasting. The first was from All Saints to Christmas day. The second from Septuagesima till Easter. The third from the Rogation Days to Pentecost. The fourth from Trinity Sunday to the Octave of Corpus Christi. The fifth from the feast of S. Dominic to the Assumption.

This fast, at the mere name of which others would turn pale, was not chosen by Colomba only for the maceration of her innocent body, but also on account of the absolute nausea which she had for earthly food; not proceeding from her constitution, nor from indisposition, but from the great desire which made her hunger only after the Bread of Heaven. Scarcely had this angel tasted the Bread of Angels, than inebriated with spiritual sweetness she conceived a disgust for all earthly relish. In fact, she began by little and little to deprive herself of the use of bread, nourishing herself with fruit only, and her hunger after the Eucharistic Bread alone constantly increasing, grew so insatiable that she obtained at last permission to communicate every feast day. Her confessor was induced to grant her this favour, when he ascertained that Colomba had been one day miraculously communicated.

She was praying in the Cathedral Church, with her eyes fixed on the Sacred Tabernacle, to which she ardently aspired, when she saw issue from it a little cloud, which passing over her head sprinkled her as with a light rain, and a beautiful Babe proceeding from the cloud, placed Himself in her arms, and then taking the form of a Host communicated the Saint. This prodigy could not remain concealed; for her mother and others having observed her clothes bathed in this celestial dew, asked her with surprise if she had been in the river, and she was obliged to make known the heavenly favour she had received.

The more frequent use of the Eucharistic Food was so profitable and appropriate a nourishment for the spouse of Christ, that she increased wonderfully not only in spiritual strength but also in bodily vigour. The mental illuminations she received, her ecstasies and raptures, soon demonstrated the heavenly conversation and the high degree of union with God in which she lived.

Every thing she asked of God she obtained with facility. She had a desire to see the stable at Bethlehem, that she might more easily contemplate this great mystery, and falling into an ecstasy she received consolation from heaven. During the night of the Epiphany she was meditating on that bright star which served as a guide to the three holy Kings, when there appeared a large and shining globe over the dwelling of our Saint, which not only filled her chamber with brightness, but was a cause of admiration and wonder to many spectators, her confessor among the number. She was contemplating one day at mass the crucifixion of our Lord, and at the elevation of the chalice she behold above it Jesus crucified, all covered with livid wounds and blood, at which sight, pierced with sorrow, she fell half lifeless to the ground: recovering after a little time, she turned to her confessor, who had come to her assistance, and said, " Ah ! father, pray to Jesus, that He may not again permit me to see Him in this wounded and exhausted condition, for I cannot bear so sorrowful a spectacle."

She was left alone in the house one day to take care of her youngest brother, and being absorbed in contemplation, while standing near the fire, she let him fall on the burning coals. The child began to cry violently, and a neighbour coming in and witnessing this doleful sight, joined her cries to these of the infant, believing him to be terribly burnt, but on lifting him up he was found by his mother and others who had come to assist him not to have received the least injury from the fire, not even the loss of a single hair.

She was frequently found in an ecstasy, her body immoveable as a corpse; sometimes again she was elevated from the earth, and when her senses returned she discoursed so well and with so much fervour on heavenly things, and especially on the most august Sacrament of the altar, that she ravished with wonder the minds of her hearers. Her mother reproved her one day, because in her ecstasies she did not finish the work she had in hand, and Colomba humbly answered, "Have pity on me, but I cannot refuse the gifts with which Heaven favours me; and if we are not too solicitous about earthly things, Almighty God will not allow us to want for anything."

The fame of her angelical manner of life was not confined within the limits of Rieti, it spread over the whole of Italy, and especially in Rome; and coming to the ears of a Spanish bishop who was there, who was a great lover of perfection and holiness, and experienced in the discernment of spirits, he became desirous to know and examine the spirit of Colomba, and he resolved to go to Rieti to see and converse with her. Being arrived in the city he entered the cathedral church to pray, and after a long space of time looking round the church he saw a bright star over the head of a young girl who was kneeling in prayer. The bishop concluded at once that this must be Colomba, as in fact it was, and rising up he went towards her without delay; and Colomba's aunt turning towards the prelate and reverently accosting him, asked him what he desired, the prelate answered that he wished to speak with Colomba, to which her aunt willingly acquiesced, retiring to a separate chapel out of the church.

The bishop began to examine her spirit attentively, questioning her minutely regarding her manner of life, what was her desire of serving God, what was the nature of her prayer, what mortifications and penances she practised, what nourishment she took, what pleasure and facility she found in the exercise of virtues, what favours and graces she received from God, and what use she made of them. Colomba was then nineteen, and she answered all his questions so humbly and with so great elevation of mind, that the prelate was greatly consoled, admiring in her the spirit of God which guided her; and discovering in the Saint true purity of heart, and a spirit disengaged from earthly things, with a will inflamed with pure love, which is accustomed to be rewarded by familiarity with God, he judged that our Saint had attained this happy state of union. He finally interrogated her respecting Holy Communion; and as Colomba had an excessive hunger after it, changing countenance immediately, and her face becoming quite inflamed, she manifested the great spiritual avidity which she felt for this Food; but immediately entering into herself she answered with profound humility, that her baseness was too great to receive it.

The bishop recognized herein the effect of the first impression which a languishing love makes upon the soul; and encouraging her, he told her to obey him and communicate every day; and after exhorting her to holy perseverance in her fervent life, he assured her that she would obtain from Heaven what she desired. He desired her to recite every day in remembrance of him the Psalm "Qui habitat" and he gave her a little silver cross filled with holy relics, which she immediately placed round her neck, while she received his blessing. The holy bishop told several religious that Colomba was full of the true spirit of God, and that she had made great progress in contemplation.

Sᵃ COLUMBA DE REATI, VIRGEN del Orden de Predicadᵒʳ á 20. de Mayo.
Palomᵒ sculp.

CHAPTER V.

COLOMBA'S SPIRITUAL HUNGER INCREASES AND IS AGAIN MIRACULOUSLY ASSUAGED.—HER EXTRAORDINARY RAPTURE.—SHE TAKES THE HABIT OF THE THIRD ORDER.

As spiritual pleasures and delights, instead of satiating him who enjoys them, increase the appetite, in opposition to the effect of earthly satisfactions, so the daily Communion of Colomba made her hunger still more after this heavenly Food. The spirit of this longing contemplative became so inebriated with holy transports in God, that she could never take her eyes off the sacred Tabernacle. She had good reason to act thus, for her Divine Lover, Jesus, continually responded to her love by tokens of His favour. She was several times communicated by Angels when assisting at the holy Sacrifice of the Mass, and one night when contemplating the most august Sacrament of the altar, she suddenly heard a voice saying, "Come to receive the holy Communion, Colomba, it is now time."

She was at this time in the church before the altar, and she thought she received communion from the hands of her spiritual father as usual, but when morning was come, and the priest did not see Colomba come to Communion in the church as usual, fearing something had happened he went to see her to find out the reason. The Saint was astonished at this unexpected question, and assured the priest that she had received the holy Communion from him, proving it to him by mentioning the place in which he had put the key of the Tabernacle. The religious returned to the church to ascertain the fact, and observing that the sacred Particle was really missing from the Pyx, he justly concluded that she had been miraculously communicated by the ministry of angels.

So many celestial favours bestowed on this angelic young girl, opened her parents' eyes, and they determined no longer to resist the operations of the Holy Ghost, and granted leave to their daughter to take the habit she desired. Her maternal uncle, who had been her strongest assailant, was the first not only to give his consent, but to concur willingly in defraying the necessary expenses, as if he wished thereby to make reparation and show sorrow for his fault in using too much violence. It was in the year of our Lord, 1486, and the nineteenth of Colomba's age, that she received this great consolation, and saw fully verified the promises which S. Dominic had repeatedly made to her in her visions, and for this she immediately offered her thanks to the Almighty. Her very innocent life and wonderful actions had rendered her a desirable subject to all the monasteries in her country; and as each of the religious orders considered that it would be a great honour to possess her in their community, many applications were made by the different monasteries to her relations, for the acquisition of this treasure. But Colomba, who had been several times spiritually favoured and visited by S. Dominic, S. Catherine of Siena, and other Saints of the same Order, adhered constantly to her resolution of receiving the habit of the third Order named "of penance," that she might thus follow the footsteps of the seraphic Catherine of Siena.

The languishing love of Colomba suggested to her to take the holy habit immediately, but active love prevailed over her, and by placing before her her own vileness made her resolve to take a little time to make preparation for the holy function. It is the property of this sort of love to do great things and esteem them little, to work much and to think it has scarcely

SHE BECOMES A DOMINICAN

done anything; and, hence, as if hitherto her fasts and austere manner of living had been nothing, she resolved, with the approbation of her confessor, to make an addition to her fasts and prayers during the forty days which preceded her clothing.

She therefore deprived herself entirely during that space of time, not only of the use of bread, but also of vegetables, and on many days of fruit also. Her body certainly suffered by this austerity, becoming greatly extenuated, but Heaven abundantly manifested by new prodigies how acceptable to Almighty God was this rigorous preparation of His servant. Celestial visions, holy colloquies, long raptures, and many other favours received by Colomba from Heaven, were almost of daily occurrence. She was taken in spirit to see and venerate that wonderful crucifix which spoke to S. Thomas Aquinas, and which is kept in Naples, and she described its form very minutely. She went in spirit another time to visit the Holy Places of Jerusalem, leaving her body extended on the ground, half lifeless, and so wonderful was this rapture, that it lasted five successive days, to the surprise not only of her parents but of many other spectators of this prodigy; and when her senses returned, though her strength was considerably diminished, she was able to particularize every thing she had seen in these holy places.

Her father, moved with compassion to tears of joy and fear, wished his daughter to restore her strength by swallowing a couple of eggs. The obedient daughter consented to take one, excusing herself by saying that two were too much, and begging her father to take the other. Her consent not appearing real to her father, he took his egg first to induce his daughter to take the second, and on his presenting it to her, it was found quite empty, to the astonishment of the bystanders and of her father, who heard at the same time a clear voice which pronounced in his ear these words, "The care of this child shall not be thine, but Mine."

In the midst, however, of these extraordinary celestial favours, Almighty God permitted His servant to be much annoyed by the devil, to prove her constancy. She endured great insults during all this time from her infernal enemy, who tried every art to prevail over her firmness, and draw her away from her holy resolution; but finding himself always defeated, he attacked her with blows, by which her face was much bruised, and one of her teeth knocked out. The end of the forty days devoted to her preparation drawing near, after which her solemn clothing was to take place, the devil retreated in confusion, leaving the firm and constant virgin mistress of the field, and filled with joy, because she had placed all her joy and pleasure in sufferings. Heaven manifested its approval of the holy preparation she had made, and deigned to honour her with sensible signs of contentment. A few days before her clothing there appeared at night a large globe of fire over the chamber of Colomba, which appeared to be in flames, and this was observed not only by her parents but by many others also.

At length the happy day arrived which Colomba had so long and so earnestly desired, the day fixed for her clothing. This was Palm Sunday in the year 1486, which fell on the 19th of March, the festival of the glorious patriarch S. Joseph, Colomba being then in the twentieth year of her age. She went to the church of S. Dominic, accompanied by her mother and other of her relations; and as the whole city had a veneration for this holy virgin, a great concourse of people of every rank came thither, all exulting and rejoicing at the happiness of Colomba, who manifested so plainly in her humble countenance with what an internal joy her heart was inundated, that it drew tears of admiration from the spectators. She received the habit from Father Thomas of Foligno, who was the Father Prior of the Convent of S. Dominic at Rieti. All the sisters of the third Order of S. Dominic rejoiced greatly, understanding well that by the acquisition of this new associate the honour and glory of their whole Order was not a little increased.

CHAPTER VI

COLOMBA'S PROCEEDINGS AFTER TAKING THE HABIT. HER PILGRIMAGE TO VITERBO, TO VISIT OUR LADY "OF THE OAK," AND THE MIRACLES WHICH TOOK PLACE.

Colomba had no occasion to go through her novitiate, for though she was newly clothed with the holy exterior habit, she was already an experienced religious in her interior, and mistress in the observance of everything laid down in her rules. Her first thought, notwithstanding, was to observe an entire submission and exact obedience, not only to the superioress, but to all the other sisters. She lived in her father's house after her clothing, but joined the other sisters punctually in all their duties, and executed them with so much exactness and fervour, that she was an example and a source of admiration to all. She employed herself in teaching a great number of children, whom she instructed in prayer and work, and so well did she bring them up that she seemed destined by Heaven for this care.

To console the afflicted, and visit the sick, and to help the needy, were her most agreeable entertainments. Labour and sufferings, however long, seemed to her very short, as she advanced with rapid steps in active love. She had a most contemptuous opinion of herself, and though the esteem of the people for her continually increased, it could never gain the least attention from Colomba, nor could her heart be induced to take any pleasure in it; and the heavenly favours she received, which were now more frequently than ever bestowed upon her, could never arrest her active love in its course.

The very great devotion which she always nourished for the Blessed Virgin Mary, gave birth to her pious desire of undertaking a short pilgrimage to visit the holy miraculous picture of our Lady of the Oak, which had made a wonderful appearance about that time at Viterbo, a mile distant from the town. In the year 1487, Colomba having made known her wish to her parents and superiors, and obtained their consent, prepared to depart in the company of her mother, her uncle, and other pious persons, among whom were three sisters of the third Order, twelve in number altogether, a number chosen by Colomba, who in every choice was accustomed to fix upon a number which had reference to some truth of revealed religion. Her mother ordered her not to walk barefoot, as she desired. Colomba obeyed, but after she had proceeded a few miles her feet began to swell so much, that not being able to bear her shoes on, she asked leave of her mother to take them off, which was granted. She employed the time during the journey in continual prayer and holy conversation with her companions, who forgot all their fatigue while listening to her heavenly instructions. When they had reached a hill, from which the town of Narni could be discerned, the heavens became obscured, and Colomba's uncle was unwilling to proceed for fear of rain, but our Saint having made a short prayer, encouraged her companions, assuring them that they would not get wet at all during their journey, which the event verified. As they drew near to Narni, numbers of the citizens, who knew of our Saint's coming, and had a high opinion of her sanctity, moved by devout curiosity came out to meet her, striving with one another to receive her. A noble matron desired to have this honour all to herself, and

having observed the swelling of Colomba's feet, she would not allow her to continue her journey the next morning on foot, but provided her with a horse. Colomba accepted her kind offer, and though the horse given to her was naturally frisky and troublesome, he became immediately tame and quiet. They passed the second day in continual prayer without any accident, excepting that towards evening, approaching the place where they were to rest, which, according to some writers, was Soriano, one of the sisters, a novice, who had been clothed with Colomba, perceived that she had lost her cloak; but Colomba, after a short prayer, comforted her afflicted, and weeping companion, assuring her that her cloak would be recovered, and one of their company having gone in search of it, found it untouched in the middle of the road at eight miles' distance.

As they left Soriano early in the morning, passing by a wood they were assailed by some wicked persons, who, advancing boldly, seemed inclined to offer them some insult, which terrified the devout company. Colomba then endeavoured to encourage them to put their confidence in God, and turning towards these unfortunate people, said, "If you dare to advance towards us, I assure you, my brethren, on the part of Almighty God that you will be severely punished, and will never eat anything again; so if you think it will do you any good, come forward." Colomba's words had the same effect in the ears of these highwaymen, as the orders of a military commander have when he proclaims a retreat, so speedy were they in running away.

Having happily completed their journey, and being arrived at Viterbo, Colomba went first with her companions to present herself to the superior of the Order to receive his blessing, and then went to venerate the miraculous picture of the Oak. Being come to the place, Colomba and her companions found it very difficult to gain admittance into the church, for they were hindered by a great crowd of people who had assembled there to see a female that was possessed by the devil dragged by force to this miraculous picture by her parents.

Moved with compassion at this pitiable spectacle, Colomba, as soon as she entered the church, began to pray to our Blessed Lady for the deliverance of this unfortunate creature. After a long prayer she rose up, and going towards the possessed woman she declared in a loud voice to all the bystanders that there was a charm fastened under the right arm of this unhappy person. The evil spirit finding himself thus discovered and publicly covered with shame, loaded our Saint with insults by the mouth of the possessed female, threatening to vent upon her all his infernal rage; but our Saint disregarding these threats, over which she had already several times triumphed, repeated more loudly her entreaties that they would untie the charm from her arm, and to animate the spectators to help her, she began first, and aided by the others they found and took from her this charm, which they immediately threw into the fire. The spectators then saw with admiration and joy Colomba take this unfortunate woman by the hand, and conduct her to the miraculous image of Mary, and there with boldness command the unclean spirit in the names of Jesus and Mary to depart, which happy event immediately followed.

The fame of so wonderful an occurrence spread rapidly through the town of Viterbo, and the officials of the town determined to use every means in their power to detain in Viterbo and treat with due respect a religious so agreeable to God; but the spouse of Christ foreseeing in prayer these preparations in her honour, resolved to withdraw from the peril by a sudden and secret flight. Her prayer in the church being finished, rising up she made a sign to her companions to follow her, and turning towards them in leaving the church, she said, "Let us depart quickly, otherwise we ran the risk of not being able to go."

In fact, the people in the church, who did not lose sight of Colomba, began to put themselves in motion to follow her, and when she arrived at the threshold she was obliged to stop, seeing before her the woman who had been delivered from the devil, and who loudly thanked her for the benefit conferred. Colomba quickly left her with a few short words, telling her to thank God and to be mindful to lead a holy life, and with rapid steps carefully avoiding the crowd she succeeded with her companions in concealing herself, and under favour of the night they were enabled safely to set out on their road home, going that evening to Soriano.

Continuing their journey the next morning, the air became suddenly dark when they were on the top of a hill near Narni, and the wind, lighting, and thunder threatened a furious storm, an effect of the vengeance with which the devil by the mouth of the woman had menaced Colomba. These devout travellers, alarmed at not having shelter, and still more at the continual roar of the thunder, turned to Colomba and began almost to reproach her, that her promise would not be verified, "that during their whole journey they should not be wet." The servant of God encouraged these timid souls, assuring them on the part of God that not one of them should get wet. Having said this, riding on she fell into an ecstasy in prayer, and a heavy shower of rain accompanied with hail came on, pouring down on every side, but leaving untouched Colomba and her companions, who pursued their journey with dry feet, whilst many who preceded and followed them on the same road were not only wet but killed, being drowned along with a number of cattle. Colomba's mother shed tears of tenderness and consolation, thanking Almighty God, who granted things so extraordinary to her daughter, and all of them, struck with astonishment, praised God that He had allowed them to participate in so great graces and honours through the prayers of His servant.

Colomba could not, however, hide herself and escape the applause and signal honours which were prepared for her at Narni, not only for her reception, but to detain her amongst them in their town. The news of the miracle at our Lady of the Oak had already been spread at Narni, and the people conceiving from thence a greater esteem and opinion of her, determined to go to meet her and invite her to fix her abode amongst them. This design was executed with so great a concourse of people of every rank, that it seemed like a triumphal entrance, the people crying, "Long live the Saint!" The humble virgin was not a little confused, and her companions astonished, and she resolved to retreat immediately from a city which paid her so much attention, not even remaining there one night; therefore, having restored the horse to her benefactress, she continued her journey towards Rieti on foot with her companions, constantly reciting devout prayers.

When they were arrived at the lake named Pie' di Luco, they resolved, in order to hasten their return home, to perform the rest of their journey by water. Colomba was the first to enter the boat, carrying in her hand a green olive branch, and turning to her companions who followed, she thus addressed them: "Know, my dear ones, that we shall have to suffer a furious storm, for the malignant spirit who spoke through the possessed woman seeks to persecute us; but I beseech you not to be at all alarmed, for the help of Jesus will be with us." Having said this, and placed herself in prayer, she was ravished into an ecstasy, and they had not gone far when a most violent tempest arose, and the boat being tossed about by the wind, and beaten back by the waves, the boatmen seemed to have lost command over her, and their courage sinking they expected death every moment; but at this instant, Colomba coming to herself and rising up, the winds ceased, the waves grew calm, and they happily continued their journey. Our Saint conversed on heavenly things, so as to engage the attention of all, till they arrived at their destination, carrying with her the olive branch by which Heaven had wrought such miracles.

CHAPTER VII

MIRACLES WROUGHT BY COLOMBA IN RIETI.—A MYSTERIOUS VISION WHICH SHE HAS THERE, AND HER WONDERFUL DEPARTURE.

Though the veneration and esteem in which Colomba was held in her own country, for the innocence of her life and the number of her virtues, was already great, it increased yet more when the wonders worked by Heaven during her journey were related at Rieti. It was then, that discovering in her, besides sanctity of life, a great familiarity with Almighty God, which was manifested by the efficacy of her prayers, they began to regard her as their mediatrix in their necessities. Nor did they rely upon her in vain; for God, who had destined His servant for great undertakings in another place, willed that before He took her from her own people, they should receive great benefits through her means.

Many were the miracles wrought by Almighty God in Rieti through her prayers in less than a year, that is, from her return home from Viterbo till her departure. The inhabitants often saw with surprise bread multiplied for the relief of the poor, and it was once entirely provided by a miracle. She said to a woman named Barbara, who was grieving because she had not bread enough to carry to the workmen, " Go home, you will there find a provision," and Barbara found to her surprise on her arrival at home twelve large loaves of bread, which were abundantly sufficient for her wants.

Many persons seriously ill, and whose lives were despaired of by the physicians, were cured by her, and she foretold their recovery in the spirit of prophecy. She predicted to a man condemned to death for homicide, without hope of pardon, that he would be set free, exhorting him to make a general confession; and it happened as she foretold. She predicted to a lady who had been married eight years without having any family, that she should have a son, and she mentioned the name which would be given him in holy baptism, all of which occurred as she said. She preserved unhurt from the flames a person who fell into the fire. She foretold to the magistrate a nocturnal fire which would take place in the suburbs of the city, at the Porta d'Arei, and would be caused by a troop of banditti trying to gain an entrance, which was verified. In fine, the great charity of Colomba was extended during this short time to every rank of persons for the good and benefit of all.

While this beloved of her Celestial Spouse was obtaining from Him so great and so abundant graces, she was warned by a vision that she was destined to increase elsewhere the glory of God. She saw in prayer the patriarch S. Dominic, with the seraphic S. Catherine of Siena, who pointed out to her a wide straight road leading from Rieti, which terminated at a church dedicated to S. Dominic, commanding her on the part of Almighty God to enter this road and go to this church without again returning to her own country. Colomba punctually obeyed the order; but when in the vision she had set out on the road, she saw herself assailed almost on every side by serpents, wild beasts, and other animals: she trembled, and stopping began to invoke the Divine assistance, whereupon these ferocious beasts retired without injuring her, and left her a free passage; then pursuing her road in the vision she happily arrived at the church indicated, where she was graciously received by the holy patriarch, by S. Catherine of Siena, and other saints, and presented before the throne of Jesus Christ, who gave her His holy benediction.

Colomba became very pensive after this vision, and was several times heard to speak in her raptures of her departure, especially in the chapel of S. Thomas Aquinas, where, being in a rapture in prayer in the presence of several persons, she was heard not only to speak of her departure, but a voice of an invisible person was heard addressing itself to her, and indicating the time of this event. These words were overheard by many, but were not understood in their true signification, for they began to apprehend the approaching departure of Colomba out of this mortal life; and their regret was increased when she answered some of her devout companions who questioned her as to the time of this event, that in the coming month of September they would be deprived of her company. Her afflicted mother shed tears at these words, and imparting her grief to her daughter she received no other comfort than affectionate arguments to induce her to conform herself to the Divine Will.

The month of August in the year 1488 being come, and the festival of the Assumption of the Blessed Virgin drawing near, the parents of Colomba saw one night at sunset our crucified Lord over their daughter's chamber, dropping blood from His sacred Hands. A few evenings later a large comet appeared visibly to many over the same house, extending its rays towards the west above Perugia. These unaccustomed signs, joined to their previous suspicions, giving rise to many reflections, increased the affliction of the inhabitants and the grief of Colomba's family, all being in expectation of soon losing the Saint, without knowing in what manner.

The twenty-first of August, which was Thursday, being arrived, Colomba asked her father to procure a lamb for her, as she desired to give a supper to twelve of her friends and connexions. Her father immediately granted this favour, but not without great surprise, contemplating within himself the mysterious novelty of the request. Supper, which was passed in devout conversation, being over, Colomba entreated these twelve guests to allow her to wash their feet, wishing to imitate the example of Jesus Christ; this was granted, and after the ceremony the company took leave, and she, according to her custom, retired to her room to give herself to holy prayer.

Friday morning being come, Colomba did not appear at her accustomed hour, but her parents imagining that she was immersed in profound contemplation, as it had several times happened, did not seek her till the dinner hour, when, having called her many times, and knocked at the door without success, they resolved to break open the door, which they did, but found nothing excepting her clothes on the ground in the middle of the room. The tears and cries which Colomba's afflicted parents sent forth to Heaven soon collected a crowd of people to be spectators of this unexpected affliction, which threw them into great wonder, as they could not conceive how she had passed through closed doors, not only out of the house, but out of the town also, as she was not there.

Whilst they were forming various conjectures, an unknown pilgrim suddenly presented himself to Giovanna, Colomba's mother, and whilst in the act of asking alms from her, seeing her troubled state, began to console her, assuring her that all had happened purely by the Divine Will, and thus concluded: "Know, woman, that this staff is so strong a support to thy daughter that she cannot fall; and, therefore, do thou lean upon it, and fear no danger." Having said this, Giovanna wishing to give him an alms, he disappeared, and she saw him no more.

CHAPTER VIII

EXTRAORDINARY JOURNEY OF COLOMBA TO FOLIGNO, AND SEVERAL MIRACLES WROUGHT THERE.

ON the same Thursday night, towards the dawn of Friday, Colomba found herself on the road between Spoleto and Trevi, not knowing how this happened, but recognizing it as the same road which she had seen in her vision. She could not without supernatural strength have made so long a journey in so short a space of time as two hours. She could not explain at all whether she had been brought from her room like S. Peter out of prison, or whether she had been carried out of Rieti by angels, and answered to the repeated interrogations and examinations made by her confessor and many others on this point, that she knew nothing at all about it. She said she only remembered that being in prayer in her room that night, her clothes, which are now kept in the monastery of S. Agnes at Rieti, were taken off and others put on her.

Walking afterwards during that night along the road which she recognized from her vision, she met an old man, who with a false appearance of kindness conducted her to a small house near, where some wicked young men tried to ensnare her. Our Saint, perceiving the great danger in which she was placed, for she was exceedingly acute, had recourse without delay to prayer; and invoking by her faith that Divine assistance which was granted on a similar occasion to the glorious and holy virgins Lucy and Agnes, she repelled the boldness of these impious men with so much courage, that seized with a sudden fear they all took to flight, except one bolder than the rest, who had dared to attempt to lay his sacrilegious hands on the holy virgin, and who remained stupefied. The treacherous old man, astonished at the miracle, and convinced of Colomba's sanctity, prostrating himself on the ground, humbly asked our Saint's pardon, and recommending himself to her prayers, promised to watch over her with reverence the rest of the night, and to conduct her with great care the next morning as far as Trevi. Colomba derived from this greater courage to pursue her journey, judging that what had happened had been foretold in her vision. Having arrived at Trevi, she joined several other females, and desiring to continue her journey to Foligno, she met by the way some dissolute sportsmen, who wished to follow her, but she had recourse to prayer, and became invisible to them.

Being arrived at Foligno, Colomba asked for the monastery of S. Catherine. She had the intention of going to the Dominican convent, and not knowing the designation of the monastery, she supposed it was that of S. Catherine of Siena; but she was conducted to the monastery of S. Catherine, virgin and martyr, belonging to the religious of the Order of S. Clare, and finding the door open she entered without delay. This was a dispensation of Divine Providence for the good of this convent. The nuns were much surprised at the appearance of this unknown and unexpected guest, and much more so as they knew that the door had been shut and locked, and they began to put many questions to her, to which the humble young virgin only answered that the door was open and she had entered, for she was also a religious person: but as a singular spirit of innocence and meekness in conversation was united to her holy and humble demeanour, which gave pleasure to all who conversed with her, the nuns became much attached to her and resolved to detain her.

They soon perceived the price of the treasure they had

found, and having observed her very austere mode of life, her abstinence from every kind of food, with her continual prayer and ecstasies, they entered into an engagement to watch minutely her most secret actions, and many of them deposed on oath that, filled with astonishment, they had seen her several times at night suspended in the air during prayer, raised above the earth a cubit and a half. In the daytime, when not in contemplation, she held with these nuns such devout and wise discourses on the glory of Paradise, that they could not tear themselves away from her, and drawn by her mild exhortations, and overcome by her holy example, they undertook willingly and with unanimous consent to eradicate several abuses which had been introduced amongst them. Regular observance was thus not a little advanced in this convent, and all was executed with so great union and concord, that they even came to the resolution of electing her their superior.

But Colomba could not long remain hidden here, for the light of her sanctity, already spread abroad, soon made her known. In Foligno mention was publicly made of a young and unknown woman that had appeared in the monastery of S. Catherine; and as their ignorance of her condition kept the people in suspense and made them curious to trace her origin, the fact came to the notice of the governor, who, suspecting she might be a noble young lady from Naples, whom he had orders to arrest, wished to examine, her; so she was obliged to declare herself a nun of the third Order of S. Dominic at Rieti. This news soon came to the ears of the Father Prior of S. Dominic at Foligno, who entreated that Colomba might be taken out of this convent without delay, and conducted to the monastery of Santa Maria del Popolo of his Order. The permission being obtained, the Father Prior went to the monastery of S. Catherine and severely reproved Colomba for her sudden and secret flight, and for taking up her abode there out of the Order. She said a few words humbly in excuse, saying that as to the flight, her Master, Christ, was the cause of it; and for the place, she was ready to obey wherever she might be sent. To the great regret of these nuns, who suffered this loss very unwillingly, Colomba, after begging pardon of all the inmates, left the monastery of S. Catherine, having remained there eighteen days, and was conducted to Santa Maria del Popolo.

Colomba's residence in Foligno being soon made known at Rieti, Angiolo Antonio, her father, lost no time in setting out for Foligno, accompanied by Father Tommaso, Prior of S. Dominic's at Rieti, and another religious, Colomba's cousin, to induce her to return home. When they arrived, after several conferences with the prior and other learned men on this point, they examined our Saint several times, but nothing resulted except her fervent desire to continue her journey by the road pointed out to her in the vision, though she knew not the place of destination.

These persons reflecting that her desires had been wonderfully seconded by Heaven, resolved to grant her devout petition. The Father Prior of Rieti was of opinion, that this road would lead her to Siena to visit the relics of S. Catherine, to whom she was most devout, as in her vision this Saint had appeared to her and invited her to the church, in the company of S. Dominic. Colomba's father, the Prior of Rieti, and his companion, determined to accompany her as far as Siena, taking with them a lady as companion to Colomba; and on the morning of the 16th of September, leaving the monastery of Santa Maria del Popolo, to the regret of the nuns, she set out with her companions to the Madonna degli Angeli. When she reached this place, after a long prayer in the church, she began joyfully and with great eagerness to pursue her journey; but the Father Prior noticing that Colomba, advancing quickly before them, had taken the straight road which led to Perugia, instead of the road to the left for Siena, which he had resolved to follow, called back the party, telling them to turn back, for that was not the road to Siena, but Colomba then rapidly proceeding on her road said that was the one pointed out in her vision, and therefore by that she must go. The father consented to her wishes, and all together pursued their journey towards Perugia.

At the vesper hour, arriving at the bridge of San Giovanni, over the Tiber, about three miles from the city, some millers with other idle people, suspecting that these devout travellers were vagrants, stopped their progress, and began to threaten with abuse and insults to have them arrested in order to extort money from them. Here a prophetical vision which Colomba had had was verified; it was, that above the waters of the Tiber she would imitate and follow the traces of S. Francis of Assisi, of whom it is related that in the same place he was ill-treated and insulted by some wicked persons. It is not very astonishing that Colomba should have received such affronts, and that in these times such disagreeable interruptions should have occurred; for the sanguinary contests between the Guelphs and Ghibellines were then at their height, and throughout Umbria, especially along the banks of the Tiber, both parties had stationed their guards and soldiers, so that military license and disorder reigned everywhere.

The Father Prior of Rieti having considered the danger to which they might be exposed if they continued their journey, as the night was closing in, agreed with Colomba's father that they had better first proceed to Perugia, to procure from government a safe conduct, placing Colomba for that night in a place of safety with her companion. A civil and wealthy lady, the wife of a Perugian merchant, who was living in the country, offered courteously to receive her. Her house was near an inn, and a soldier, under pretext of taking up his lodging there, tried to break through the wall near Colomba's room, to take her by surprise. He had succeeded in making a hole large enough to admit his arm, when suddenly becoming benumbed and stupefied he began to cry for assistance, and our Saint having called upon the Name of Jesus cured him and converted him to a good life.

The next morning the two travellers returning from Perugia furnished with their letters, and coming to the bridge of San Giovanni and presenting their passport, were allowed to depart in peace, and they pursued their journey to Perugia. Before they arrived in the town, another prodigy was wrought by Colomba to deliver herself from the snares of some huntsmen who intended to insult her. Our Saint went boldly to meet them, offering them her apron filled with fresh roses, which were out of season; and all being seized with compunction at this sight retired, celebrating everywhere the praises of her sanctity.

PART II

OF THE LIFE OF THE VIRGIN S. COLOMBA, WHICH CONTAINS THE ACTIONS SHE PERFORMED IN PERUGIA.

CHAPTER I

HONOURABLE RECEPTION GIVEN TO COLOMBA BY THE PERUGIANS. THE CITY OPPOSES HER DEPARTURE, AND THE INHABITANTS RESOLVE TO ERECT A MONASTERY FOR HER.—COLOMBA MAKES HER SOLEMN PROFESSION.

God is wonderful in His saints! Who would have ever thought or imagined that a simple young female, humbly clad, insulted on the road a short time previously, without human assistance, would meet in Perugia with the praises and honours which are usually reserved to great heroes? But this extraordinary homage was precisely that which Almighty God prepared for His beloved servant Colomba at her entrance into Perugia. In the year 1488, on the 17th of September, which fell on a Wednesday, as Colomba entered Perugia the citizens put themselves in motion in a moment, vying with each other in honouring her, making thus a prelude to the obligations which they were about to contract with our Saint. The name of Colomba was already in high repute in Perugia, and the people, urged by the desire of knowing her, went to meet her, coming beyond the walls for this purpose. At the first appearance of the humble servant of God the air was filled with their cries, as they exclaimed with a loud voice, "Here is the Saint!" and some tried to cut off portions of her dress.

Having visited the church of S. Dominic, Colomba at once took up her abode in a house belonging to the third Order of Dominicans, in which one sister was residing. Scarcely had she entered her room when a white dove flew towards her and settled in her lap, remaining there some time, till her hostess returning Colomba asked her with a smile if in her house or the neighbouring ones there were a dove's nest; to which she answered, No, and that the neighbours did not keep any.

More than three days had not elapsed from the arrival of Colomba in Perugia, before the citizens began to contrive how they might detain her. Her attractive manners, which proceeded from a solid virtue, and were adorned with innocence and humility, drew a numerous concourse of visitors, and especially of persons of the higher ranks; and this increased very much when a miracle worked by Colomba on her arrival in Perugia was made known throughout the city. Maria Antonio Giappesi was returning from the oven loaded with new bread, and Colomba meeting her asked for a piece in charity, and the pious woman gave her a whole loaf. On counting her bread when she reached home, she found the same quantity notwithstanding the diminution she knew she had made, and not understanding this mystery she went to ascertain if Colomba had received the loaf, and our Saint answered, "Be not astonished, for that which is given for the love of God is never diminished, but increases." After this event, which was sworn to by the woman and by others, the people ran in crowds to Colomba, not through curiosity, but to beg, exhort, and entreat her to undertake the education of children.

But as sanctity, when too much extolled by the popular voice, runs the risk of being infected with the poisonous breath of vainglory, and as applause and honours always cause pain and uneasiness to these who are truly humble, the fathers of her Order wisely showed their disapprobation of these public tokens of honour, which were too great a peril, especially for the weaker sex. They therefore judged it expedient to prohibit these frequent visits to Colomba, and also her reception of children for education. The fathers were of opinion, that at her tender age a burden ought not to be placed upon her which requires mature experience.

This prudent resolution of the Dominican fathers did not suffice to overcome the resolution of the citizens; and the Perugians suspecting from this prohibition that the fathers might intend to remove her from Perugia and send her elsewhere, lost no time in taking every precaution, even so far as to guard her, that she might not be secretly taken away. This very much displeased the Father Prior, and much more Colomba's father, who foresaw the obstacles that would be raised to her return home. In fact, both these persons having become objects of jealous suspicion to the Perugians, their access to Colomba was prevented, so that finding every attempt vain they returned home alone sad and sorrowful.

This pious robbery on the part of the city of Perugia did not meet with the approbation of the people of Rieti, who, unwilling to lose their holy fellow-citizen, through whom they had received such benefits, represented their case to Rome, and greatly urged the General of the Dominican Order to cause her to be restored to them. The Father Prior of S. Dominic in Perugia received orders therefore to oblige Colomba to return home, and in the meantime to remain enclosed in a monastery; but the efforts of the people to prevent the execution of this command were no less earnest, and formally assembling their council by the sound of a bell in the church of Sant Ercolano, at which many of the nobility and people were present, and Signor Troilo Baglioni, who a few years later was bishop of the city, presided, it was decreed, "That

Colomba should be provided for at the public expense; that every request of hers should be granted; and that a monastery should be built for her according to her own choice, in which she might receive and educate children." Rome was somewhat more satisfied with this, but not so the people of Rieti, who lost no time in offering the same advantages and even greater to their countrywoman to induce her to return, and they even sent her parents back to Perugia to give these offers greater force; but all efforts to elude the caution and vigilance of the inhabitants of Perugia were in vain.

The fathers were obliged to yield to the repeated entreaties of the town authorities, and permit Colomba to take children for education; and they gave this consent the more willingly, as they observed with astonishment that applause and honours in no way injured the humility of Colomba. The fathers rejoiced exceedingly to find in her a spirit of prompt and blind obedience, ready to obey any command, and this, joined to the example of her most innocent life and assiduous prayer, gave certain promise of the great fruits that would result from the contemplated design of founding for her a new monastery.

Colomba knew from these events that this was the will of God, and she resolved first to make publicly her solemn profession. She made before the ceremony a devout spiritual preparation, during which she had frequent ecstasies, many of them publicly in the church of S. Dominic, where she was several times seen raised from the earth in prayer. The day of Pentecost having arrived, which was the 30th May, in the year 1490, being then twenty-three years old, Colomba made her solemn profession at the hour of Vespers in the church of S. Dominic, before Father Vincenzo Da Vio her confessor, who represented the Prior, and in the presence of the Sisters of the Third Order and of a great concourse of people.

CHAPTER II

OF THE FOUNDATION AND ERECTION OF THE NEW MONASTERY, DEDICATED BY COLOMBA TO S. CATHERINE OF SIENA.—THE NUMBER OF SISTERS IS MULTIPLIED.—RULE GIVEN BY COLOMBA TO THE NEW MONASTERY.—PROPHECIES AND MIRACLES WROUGHT BY OUR SAINT.

From this same year, 1490, after Colomba's solemn profession, the original epoch of the foundation of the monastery may certainly be dated, though the new edifice was not commenced till the year 1493. In order to fix this date clearly, we must here relate what is contained in an ancient manuscript of the year 1515, which is preserved in the same monastery. In this paper, which is a register or catalogue of all the sisters first clothed, without indicating the year of their clothing, we read the following: "At the end of five years from the time that the nuns began to take the habit, we, knowing that Colomba's mother, Sister Vanna, had taken our habit, desired to have her in our community; we sent for her; she came with two children, Felice, and Brigida; Felice, a few days later took the habit in the convent of S. Dominic in Perugia, and is now Brother Giovanni; Brigida remained in the monastery to be a nun."

Now it is certain that this young Felice, Colomba's brother, took the religious habit on Easter Sunday, the 19th of April, in the year 1495, as appears in the chronicles of this convent, taking the name of Fra. Giovanni, which was the name of his brother, who had died a Dominican at the tender age of ten years. A few days only had elapsed after Sister Vanna, Colomba's mother, arrived in Perugia, and five years had already passed from the time of beginning to register the nuns who entered the new monastery, so that it clearly appears that it must have been founded in 1490. This notice is necessary to the course of the narrative, for as some writers place the beginning of the monastery in the year 1493, and others in 1490, some understand it as the foundation, others as the new building. In fact, this date corresponds perfectly with that which all writers unanimously give, saying that at the end of two years, that is, towards the end of 1492, the number of nuns having increased to fifty, and the small house not containing them comfortably, it became necessary to solicit the commencement of the new edifice, which was begun in 1493.

In this year, 1490, Colomba, having happily overcome all obstacles, made her solemn profession, and obtained the necessary permission, began immediately to assemble the sisters who lived dispersed in their own houses, and they, following Colomba's example, entered the monastery. This monastery was a house containing a few rooms, with a private chapel, which served as an oratory in which the sisters who dwelt in their own houses assembled to perform their devotions and other holy duties in common. It was then inhabited by only one sister, Lucrezia di Giuliano Casalino, and here Colomba had taken up her abode on her arrival in Perugia. She now entered into it formally to begin the community life, accompanied by three other sisters, Caterina, daughter of Giappesi, Amidea, and Giovanna, who was immediately elected prioress.

Scarcely had they thus commenced when many young ladies and widows of Perugia, admiring so fervent a beginning, came to the new monastery to take the habit. A Roman lady, hearing of the holy work undertaken by Colomba, left Rome and quitted her friends in order to take the habit from the hands of our Saint. In the meantime, rumour, which had already made known everywhere this new and holy work, moved many sisters of the same third Order, who lived in the neighbouring cities, to leave their homes, their parents, and their country, and take the road to Perugia, to embrace in the new monastery the community life which Colomba had introduced. Four came from Siena, two from Spoleto, two from Rieti, and two from Viterbo, and in the space of the two first years the monastery could count fifty nuns.

Colomba foresaw in the spirit of prophecy the arrival of these strangers, and when one of them was drawing near she used to announce it with joy to her daughters, saying, "This evening we shall have guests." It happened one day when Colomba had said this, that a sister replied that it was impossible to receive guests, for there was no bread for them; our Saint answered, that they must trust in Divine Providence, and beginning to pray before they went to table, some one knocked at the door of the monastery, and the portress opening it found a man with two great baskets full of bread, which he presented as an alms to support the community for two days.

The Blessed Caterina Lenzi, a sister of the third Order of S. Dominic, who at this time lived at Siena in the odour of sanctity desiring to become acquainted with Colomba, obtained leave this year to go with three of her companions to the Pardon of Assisi, to have an opportunity by this means of seeing her. No notice of their coming had preceded them; and this devout party had not yet arrived in Perugia, when our Saint said frankly to her sisters, " Today I expect Sister Caterina Lenzi with three companions;" and being towards evening in the Church of S. Dominic with some other sisters, rising up from prayer, she said, turning to her companions, "Let us go and meet our dear Sister Caterina." And when she came to the threshold of the church and met the guests, she knew Caterina from the others, though she had never before seen her; and after joyfully embracing her, conducted her to the monastery. These guests remained some days, and it was observed by all the sisters that Colomba had a little basket filled with fruit, which she often presented to the strangers, and distributed also to others with her own hands, and during all this time they did not see any diminution of the fruit. Sister Caterina Lenzi having returned to Siena, was after a few months called by her heavenly Spouse to her eternal repose in the year 1491. Scarcely had this happy departure taken place, when Colomba, who was praying, turned with joy to her religious, saying, " At this moment the soul of our dear Sister Caterina Lenzi is gone in glory to heaven."

These wonderful actions of Colomba induced young people to press more and more into this sacred cloister, but the smallness of the house did not allow of a great increase in the number, and these who were already there were very much crowded.

Some cities of Tuscany took occasion from this inconvenience to try to gain Colomba, making her greater and more advantageous offers. The people of Rieti, on the other hand, did not cease trying to make her leave Perugia, and even Rome had used several means to obtain her. These circumstances awakened the jealousy of the people of Perugia, and they began earnestly to solicit the commencement of the new building. What is here mentioned regarding this event is taken from the Process of her Canonization, page 405.

"On Friday the 22nd of February, 1493, in the morning, Monaldo Boncambi de Guidalotti, and Giovanni Francesco di Gregorio, being constituted by the Prior and convent of S. Dominic, commissioners and procurators for the erection of a monastery entitled of S. Catherine of Siena, in the Porta San Pietro, near to S. Mary Magdalen, as it appears by the hand and signature of Ercolano del Ranso, having for this purpose purchased certain houses; on this same day, the feast of the Chair of S. Peter, desiring to begin to build this said monastery at the request of Sister Colomba of Rieti, the promoter of this erection, the dormitory and refectory were begun in this place; and at this ceremony the Reverend Prior of S. Dominic, Father Antonio, confessor to Sister Colomba, Sister Colomba herself, Atlanta de Baglioni, Maria, wife of Signore Simonetto, and mother-in-law to Ridolfo Baglioni the Magnificent, the daughter of the said Ridolfo, the wife of Monaldo Boncambi, and many other ladies were present, and it was performed by the Prior and his companions.

"The said Sister Colomba, before she began to lay the first stone, spent half an hour in prayer, during which she was not seen by us to stir or move a limb, standing like a statue, afterwards with tears, she twice called upon S. Catherine her sister and S. Jerome, and it appeared to us that she spoke with them on heavenly things, recommending to them the city of Perugia, and for a quarter of an hour she thus conversed with her invisible companions; then she called for a blessed palm branch, and a blessed candle, made a cross with them and fixed it in the foundations, and laid the first stone with her own hands, and the other ladies who accompanied her did the same, and Colomba said that this place would be inhabited by a hundred nuns."

After having thus commenced the new building, Colomba being one day in the garden of the monastery, heard herself called by name from above, and looking up she saw S. Barbara, to whom she was very devout, as she was patroness of the city of Rieti; she stood upon the wall which surrounds the monastery on the side of Santa Maria de Fossi, now named S. Anna, and promised her special protection to the monastery, assuring her that she would guard it from the effects of lightning.

Colomba was very zealous for the good regulation of the

choir, and to have her religious well instructed in singing and in chanting the psalms, and for this purpose she wished very much to have in her new community some experienced religious person fit and capable to undertake this office. Having manifested this excellent thought to her superiors, she obtained from the Father General of her Order the assignment of Sister Tita, a professed choir nun of the monastery of Pistoja, who, to Colomba's great delight, instructed her in a short time in the good regulation of the choir. The sisters joyfully and happily blessed Almighty God, who had made them daughters of so holy a mother, in whom they continually discovered wonderful signs of sanctity.

The new monastery being now placed on so good a system, Colomba found a vast field for the extension of her charity, and she soon began to show that superior degree of active love which inflamed her. She was always the first at the labours and most abject employments of the monastery, and she was the last to seek quiet and repose. In the distribution of the cells she tried with admirable patience to contrive to satisfy every one, and for her own habitation she chose a dark, damp, and narrow place between two walls on the ground floor, with a table for her bed. In the poverty of furniture she did not allow anyone to want what was necessary, but she did not keep even that for herself. The alms and presents which she received from devout people, and especially sweetmeats and fruit, she took with pleasure, thanking God, but put everything in common for the comfort of her daughters, without allowing the least satisfaction to her eyes or to her taste. She did not fail before night advanced to visit every sister, and patiently interrogate them concerning their wants, animating them to holy perseverance. To the sick she would not only be the first assistant, but also the fixed and perpetual servant, and she often cured them by her prayers.

Her great charity extended itself to people of every rank who had recourse to her, lending them her assistance immediately in every calamity, and Heaven often wrought miracles at her intercession. Signora Atlanta Baglioni, who had a great veneration for Colomba, having given birth to a living creature which had no shape or human appearance, full of affliction, yet confiding in the assistance of our Saint, sent it to her wrapped up. Colomba took it, and disposing all its disarranged limbs in their proper places, formed a vigorous and robust baby, which she sent back to the impatient and afflicted lady.

The son lived, and when he grew up, acknowledging that he owed his life to Colomba, he took the religious habit of S. Dominic, with the name of Father Dominic Baglioni, and became a friar of great merit. The wife of Francesco Gregorio, a Perugian merchant, the same lady who courteously received Colomba at the Ponte S. Giovanni, having a child nearly dead, despaired of by the physicians, deprived of the use of its limbs, and unable to take nourishment, carried in grief and tears this breathing skeleton to Colomba. The holy virgin was in S. Dominic's, in the chapel of S. Catherine; moved with tender compassion, she immediately took it, and placing it in her lap, she signed it with the sign of the cross, anointing it with oil from the lamp which burned in the chapel. She then placed her beads round its neck, and in the mouth of the dying babe she put a lozenge, which she had first masticated, and which the infant soon swallowed as a liquid. Finally, she placed him on the altar of S. Catherine, and after a short prayer restored him to his mother perfectly cured.

There were present at this miracle, among others, Grifone Baglioni and Caesar Borgia, who was afterwards made a cardinal, and not being able to contain themselves through wonder and delight, they would have had the bells rung to publish the miracle if the prudent efforts and entreaties of Father Sebastiano had not prevented them.

In the same year another wonderful event happened, which

clearly proved how carefully Heaven protected this its beloved servant. A dissolute youth, though of illustrious birth, tried to make by night a secret and sacrilegious entrance into the new monastery. He had succeeded in introducing part of his body through a window which looked into the room where Colomba was praying, and behold the posts and architraves of the window moved from their places, and squeezed him with so much force that he was obliged to cry for help. Colomba ran thither, and at the sign of the cross the stones returned to their places, and the youth departed humble and contrite.

CHAPTER III

SUFFERING LOVE OF COLOMBA.—SHE TAKES UPON HERSELF THE SCOURGE OF THE PLAGUE TO DELIVER THE CITY OF PERUGIA.—PERSECUTIONS AND GRIEVOUS CALUMNIES ENDURED BY OUR SAINT.—HER FIRST PUBLIC ECSTASY.

However frightful may be a torture, an affliction, or a peril of death, which presents itself to the loving soul, it is not capable of moderating its ardour. The spouse of the sacred canticles, who is a figure of this soul, even when struck and wounded in the midst of the enemy's guards, could not contain herself, and asked them where she could find her Beloved. There are indeed but few souls who mount to this degree of suffering love, to the force of which every great fear yields, but amongst these few, the pure, generous, and inflamed heart of Colomba is eminently distinguished, for she would choose no other path to walk than the bloody path of Calvary to find her Beloved.

The terrible scourge of the plague fell upon Perugia in 1494, and in spite of every possible precaution, joined with the most powerful remedies science could furnish, the contagious disease spread in a short time through the whole territory, of which it threatened to make an unhappy desert without inhabitants. At so mournful a sight the citizens, pale and trembling, unanimously resolved to implore the aid of Colomba.

THE PLAGUE AND PERSECUTIONS

The city had already experienced three years previously the fruit of her powerful intercession; when troubled with civil wars the people had recourse to her, and were delivered from them.

The faction of the Guelphs was in these times very powerful in Perugia, nor would they admit into the city the adverse party of the Ghibellines, who had been long banished. They several times came to a bloody engagement, the Guelphs always remaining victorious. One night, the 6th of June, 1491, the Ghibellines made a sudden assault on the city, and had already scaled the walls, which terrified the citizens so much that they thought more of flight than of defence, but, encouraged by the prayers of Colomba, whom they all boldly called upon, they attacked the enemy, whom they observed to be retiring, with so much vigour, that they pursued them as far as Corciano, which town was on that occasion recovered by the Guelphs. Great was the confidence which the Perugians placed in the prayers of Colomba, and therefore they had recourse in this new tribulation to their consoler. Here we may observe that in this or any other calamitous circumstances, the ignorant opposition which worldly policy is accustomed to make to the solitaries and these who live in contemplation, calling them idle and useless to human society, is always convicted of falsehood; for these censors do not reflect how necessary to the world are their prayers, and how pure and agreeable to Almighty God their state renders them.

This was easily perceived by the sad and afflicted people of Perugia, when they did not in vain implore the help of the servant of God, who, making herself like another Moses, mediatrix between God and His chastised people, supplicated and obtained from the Divine Judge, that the blows of the Divine wrath should be all discharged on her body, and that the city should be freed. She advised that a banner or sacred standard should be made, in which Christ should be depicted as a Judge irritated by the sins of the people, with the patriarch S. Dominic, S. Catherine of Siena, and the Saints, Protectors of the city, as intercessors,, and at the foot of the picture the whole city prostrate in a penitential and supplicating attitude, and that it should be carried processionally for three days.

This project of Colomba did not at first meet with entire approbation; for the government foreseeing the great necessity which exists on these occasions of preventing any popular meeting, on account of the danger of mixing the infected with these in health, and thus causing a greater spread of the disease, made great opposition to the execution of her plan; but, on the other side, that great confidence which they placed in Colomba, the efficacy of whose prayers they had several times experienced, prevailed, and overcoming every other fear and obstacle, the execution of what the servant of God proposed was accomplished without delay. In fact, their expectation was not frustrated, for scarcely were the processions ended, than the scythe of death was broken, which had mown down its victims without regarding age, and these sick of the disease recovered when only anointed by the oil of the lamp which burned at the altar of S. Catherine, where Colomba was accustomed to pray.

That which appeared most wonderful during this sorrowful time was Colomba's incomparable charity; for, fearless and indefatigable in nursing the sick, she ceased not day and night to give them spiritual and corporal assistance, consoling them with holy conversation, and dressing their wounds with her own hands. Her confessor fell seriously ill of the contagious disease, and our Saint, moved with compassion, obtained that the sick man should be removed to an oratory in the neighbourhood, where, giving him herself proper remedies, he was cured in a few days. The Benedictine monks of S. Peter's, terrified by the danger of the plague, after losing one of their religious who died of it in the monastery, implored Colomba's assistance, and were all preserved.

When the severe scourge was becoming more gentle in its effects, and brighter hopes were dawning, the indignation of the Divine wrath seemed to discharge itself upon His servant. The patient virgin suddenly saw herself covered from head to foot with black spots, which gave her such torture that her approaching death was universally expected. In the paroxysms of her burning fever, when out of her senses, her countenance was observed to be smiling; for she enjoyed a fixed contemplation of God. The Saint had requested her sisters not to apply to her any human remedy, desiring to fulfil entirely the holy will of God; but the nuns, observing that a wound in the patient's foot threatened inflammation, took the opportunity when she was out of her senses to apply a caustic remedy. When Colomba's senses returned, she who never had allowed a word of complaint to escape her, merely said that she suffered very much from that part. On the ninth day of her suffering, her love being perhaps sufficiently purified in the eyes of God, Heaven vouchsafed to console her with a vision, and at the same time to cure her. Colomba sent for the mother prioress, to whom she related that the patriarch S. Dominic and the seraphic Catherine of Siena having appeared to her, she had been cured by these saints in a moment.

But while the nuns and citizens were rejoicing, and rendering thanks to Almighty God for Colomba's recovery, the devil, enraged at the invincible constancy of the servant of God, tried to attack her honour, exciting against her a violent persecution raised by odious calumnies. There were two religious, boarders in the monastery, of a different institute, but received by Colomba through pure charity and mercy; these persons, displeased with some resolutions that had been taken for the good regulation of the rising monastery, contrived various impostures against our Saint, hoping thus to succeed in their evil intention; and in order that the diabolical mine, which they tried to set on fire against the monastery, might be sure to explode, they attacked Colomba on various sides.

They first endeavoured through pretext of zeal to insinuate themselves into weak and wicked minds, both within and without the monastery, cunningly painting the innocent Colomba with dark colours, as in a state of deplorable illusion and affected piety. All the charitable offices exercised by Colomba towards her confessor in his illness, were taxed by them as suspicious symptoms of a secret understanding in her affections. They then declared her wonderful abstinence from all food to be false and only apparent, accusing her of having secretly taken food when supposed to be in prayer; and, finally, that her published prophesies were inventions, or mere suggestions of her partial confessor.

These venomous calumnies being passed from tongue to tongue, as human malice is of its own nature ever prone to evil, a sinister and diabolical party was formed against Colomba without much difficulty, and giving themselves by little and little more liberty of speech in conversation, they began to answer all objections raised in her defence, interpreting as evil all the heroic actions of our Saint. Father Sebastiano degli Angeli was her confessor, a master and a very learned man, not only in theology but also in mathematics and astronomical sciences. This circumstance, heightened by their malice, served wonderfully well to give colour to the calumny against Colomba's prophecies, making them appear to be astronomical knowledge suggested by her confessor; such was the ignorance and also the malice of that unhappy age. The visits paid by Colomba to her sick confessor, an old man of sixty, were made to appear unbecoming, as they maliciously concealed the fundamental circumstance of her defence, which was the company she had always had with her in these visits, namely, two of the oldest sisters in the monastery. And, in fine, impiously turning to abuse a common saying of our Saint, who when often asked if she eat, replied that she ate of every thing, meaning the relish of every delight contained in the Eucharistic Food, they published that she was convicted of deception and falsehood in her abstinence.

These accusations being arranged with the greatest care that cunning envy against our Saint could suggest, were sent to Rome with a memorial begging for redress. By a commission from Rome the superiors in Perugia made a juridical and exact examination into the points of accusation, by which not only their unsubstantial nature was discovered, but also the origin of the whole diabolical plot was found out; and to make reparation to the innocence of the Saint, they decreed that the two wicked inventors of it should be driven from the monastery and severely punished. But as it is easier to create an evil impression than to efface it, this favourable sentence on Colomba served indeed to confirm good and upright minds in their opinion of her sanctity, but did not succeed in entirely eradicating suspicion from the minds of the malignant and perverse. Troubled and afflicted, the innocent virgin poured forth tears at the feet of her crucified Spouse, lamenting not for her losses, her affronts, or her perils, in which her love of suffering for Christ exulted, but for the many sins committed in this infernal conspiracy, and for the leading astray of the children under education in her new monastery. But Almighty God, who from above was pleased to exercise and refine in the love of the cross the spirit of His servant, deigned to honour and exalt her on this occasion by publicly raising her into an ecstasy, to beat down and confound the strong.

On the day consecrated to the honour of the glorious patriarch S. Dominic, to whose church the governor with the magistrates had come to hear Mass at the high altar, Colomba was on her knees with the other sisters, in the presence of this Divine Sacrifice, when, at the elevation of the sacred Host, she was ravished into an ecstasy and raised from the earth before eyes of the people, and remained there a long time till after Mass was finished. This wonderful sight, on so solemn and public an occasion, in presence of a numerous assemblage, in such difficult circumstances, owing to the free and various discussions which were made upon her honour, put a stop to detraction, and raised her in public opinion. The governor and magistrates departed filled with consolation, and declaring that they would be constant defenders of Colomba in every misfortune which might happen to her.

CHAPTER IV

THE LIFE AND SPIRIT OF COLOMBA ARE, BY AN ORDER FROM ROME, MADE THE SUBJECT OF SECRET RESEARCH, AND FORMALLY EXAMINED.—THE LOVE OF COLOMBA NOW APPEARS, ASPIRING TO THE POSSESSION OF GOD.— HER SPIRIT OF PROPHECY.—SHE FORETELLS THE TIME OF HER DEATH.

Though sanctity derives its origin from the assemblage and union of all Christian virtues, by a wonderful effect of Divine grace, nevertheless that virtue which occupies the first place, and manifests the others, as a burning lamp affords to others oil and light, is charity alone. This virtue melts away, as it were, all that is evil in man, and gives a relish for eternal happiness alone. It had been already proved several years before that this virtue shone forth in Colomba, when by order of Innocent VIII all the great opposition offered to her wonderful abstinence from all earthly food was entirely overcome, as it appeared from the evidence that Colomba's stomach did not abhor food through any natural indisposition, but that by the work of Divine grace she derived strength and vigour from the pure Eucharistic Food. If it happened that the time of communion was delayed for an hour, she could not support her body through weakness, and fell into swoons and fainting fits; but scarcely had she been refreshed with this heavenly Food, than to the astonishment of all an unusual vigour was infused into her frame, which, spreading itself over her, coloured her lips and cheeks with a vermilion hue that remained some time.

This point had been already cleared up at Rome, and these facts had been made known to the Pope, Alexander VI who had also received from his relation, Don Caesar Borgia who was dwelling in Perugia, an account of the miracle wrought by Colomba in the public and instantaneous cure of the dying infant, in the church of S. Dominic, and who felt for all these reasons great esteem and veneration for the servant of God. The envy of others not ceasing, however to tear in pieces Colomba's reputation with sinister interpretations, and the subject being one so delicate, the Pope ordered a new and rigorous examination into the spirit of Colomba.

A process had just been undertaken in France against the deluded spirit of some cloistered nuns condemned for obreptitious proceedings in matters of a similar description; and the delegate, who was a Dominican, a Doctor of Sorbonne, and an Inquisitor of France, had gone to Rome on affairs relating to this business. To this priest, who was very learned and skilful in such affairs, was entrusted the commission of examining into the spirit of Colomba; and he went for that purpose to Perugia, with the Father General of the same Order. Having used all that skilfulness in the examination which science suggested, they were both comforted to find great innocence, humility, and meekness in Colomba; and filled with admiration at the plenitude of the Spirit of God which dwelt within her, they would not leave Perugia without taking with them some relic of the Saint. The Sovereign Pontiff felt great satisfaction in this result, which confirmed more and more the good opinion he had already conceived of Colomba.

After this formal proceeding there were other secret researches made in Perugia by order from Rome into the actions of the servant of God. Two acute women were sent from Rome to Perugia under the pretended habit of religion to watch her; but they had not yet arrived when Colomba, foreseeing all this in the spirit of prophecy, made her confessor acquainted with it. Our Saint received them with great charity, and after a diligent observation made by these examiners for some days of all her actions, they returned to their destination edified with their agreeable reception, and giving testimony of Colomba's holiness to the whole of Rome.

A young person presented herself to our Saint, who had been sent to try to tempt her to work miracles, and feigning to be ill she entreated her to cure a cancer in her breast. Colomba answered with profound humility, that her intercession could not avail to procure what she requested, but that she would pray that this disease might not infect her soul. A Spanish father, who was, like S. Dominic, of the Guzman family, and of the same Order, came from Rome to Perugia for the same cause, and he had the happiness to see and admire Colomba in an ecstasy in the Church of S. Dominic, trying on that occasion every experiment to make the truth clear. After this the Spaniard desired to converse at length with our Saint, and beginning to speak of his convent at Valencia, he was astonished by Colomba's interrupting him, and giving him a minute and exact description of his convent, of its situation, and finally of the number of religious, and the rules they observed. This father was another ocular witness, who made known in Rome and in Spain the fame and sanctity of Colomba.

Amidst these examinations and opinions given of our Saint's sanctity, Heaven seemed to defend Colomba particularly, and keep her under its jealous custody and protection; for at this very time, when the spirit of Colomba was attacked by suspicion, her gift of prophecy appeared more wonderfully. Many were the future events foretold by our Saint: things at a distance were seen as actually present, and even the secrets of hearts penetrated. She predicted to several married women, her friends, that they should bring forth children, as it happened. She foretold to Sister Cecilia, the second daughter she had clothed, a long tribulation and illness, and she was ill during a whole year and confined to her bed. A person named Barnabea Massoleni was going to take the habit in her monastery when Colomba approaching her, said secretly and candidly to her, that she would not be a nun at all, but would be married and lead a life full of misfortunes and tribulations, as it actually happened, and as she deposed on oath in the process of canonization. Our Saint foretold that the reigning faction in Viterbo would be banished with great slaughter, and that the opposite faction would assume the government, which occurred as she said.

While she was praying in the church of S. Dominic, before the altar of S. Catherine, the son of Benedetto Guidelotti fell from a high window into the street, and Colomba seeing him in spirit, cried out aloud with extended arms, "Help him! O Lord, help him!" and the boy was taken up from the ground safe and sound without any hurt, and he asserted that he had seen Colomba supporting him. The same thing happened another day when Colomba was praying in her monastery: many of the sisters hearing her cry aloud to God for help, went to her with the prioress, to whom Colomba said, "Your brother Camillo has been in imminent danger of shipwreck; let us thank God that he is now safe." When Camillo reached Perugia, he related the great danger of shipwreck in which he had been at the very time the Saint saw him. Colomba told her confessor, who was seriously ill of pleurisy, to take courage, for in five days he would be perfectly well, which was the case.

In this year, 1495, Colomba's widowed mother, Sister Vanna, who was also a nun of the third Order of S. Dominic, in Rieti, resolved to leave her country, and go to Perugia, to live in the monastery with her daughter, in compliance with the repeated entreaties of the sisters. She had not yet reached Perugia, where she intended to arrive unexpectedly, when

Colomba said to the nuns that she expected her mother that day with her brother and sister.

She sent word to a gentleman of Perugia, who nourished a secret hatred against an enemy, designing to take away his life, that he had better take care not to put his design into execution, for it would certainly cause his ruin; and this gentleman knowing that it could only be the Spirit of God which had penetrated into his heart, as he had never outwardly manifested his wicked thought, became changed all at once, and thanked the Saint for what she had done.

While Colomba thus wonderfully gave evidence of the true Spirit of God with which she abounded, she at the same time gave many clear signs of her aspiring love and longing for the possession of God. She gave a great proof of this love on the Feast of the Ascension in this year. After having heard Mass, during which was read at that time the Sequence composed by Blessed Albertus Magnus, beginning, "Omnes gentes plaudite," she entreated her confessor to explain the meaning of it in her own language, and when he came to the happy passage of Rachel, Colomba interrupted him, and, changing colour, she eagerly and joyfully foretold her death, saying, " Ah! Thus it will happen to me when I am thirty-three years old! Ah! how long have I yet to wait!"

CHAPTER V.

COLOMBA'S LOVE INCESSANTLY TENDS TOWARDS ALMIGHTY GOD.—WONDERFUL EVENTS WHICH OCCURRED DURING THE TIME ALEXANDER VI. REMAINED IN PERUGIA.

Love never allows of any limit, nor can it repress its ardour. The great contemplative Colomba tended rapidly towards the Fountain of life, and meeting with creatures on her way she regarded them as so many little streams, from the waters of which she tasted in passing to satisfy her thirst as far as it was necessary, without stopping in her progress towards the Source. Having thus fixed her course, she was never seen to stop at anything which afforded pleasure, however innocent, that she might not turn away from God. Thus, like a timid stag which flees from every breath that blows, she did not even regard her own necessity.

Through fear of Charles VIII, King of France, who after taking Naples, was passing on his return through Rome with a large suite, the Pope Alexander VI left Rome with his court, and determined to retire to Perugia. Joy and delight at this unexpected honour beamed in the hearts and on the countenances of all the citizens, who were intent

Charles VIII

AUDIENCE WITH THE POPE

on preparing a reception which might be suitable to the Vicar of Jesus Christ. Colomba rejoiced on this occasion, but as she sought God alone, and tended only towards Him, she was not seen to make the least alteration in her words, thoughts, or desires, which were all for God alone. In fact, on the  6th of June, which was in 1495 the Feast of Pentecost, Pope Alexander VI entered Perugia, accompanied by the College of Cardinals, with a number of prelates and troops. All the nuns with Colomba were ranged on their knees at the gate of the monastery to receive the Pope's Apostolical Benediction, as he was to pass by their monastery. Scarcely had Colomba received this benediction, than she retired with her sisters to their usual functions in the house, without saying one word about this solemn entrance.

The Pope, who had heard such wonderful things of Colomba, wished to see her and speak with her. Having gone solemnly to the church of S. Dominic on the Feast of Corpus Christi, being seated on the throne placed in the centre of the choir, he ordered that the celebrated Colomba should come thither. The humble virgin came accompanied by several sisters, amongst whom was her mother, Sister Vanna, and a considerable number of ladies and gentlemen. The church was filled with a crowd of people pushing one another, and to make way for the Saint, whose clothes they cut through indiscreet devotion, the pontifical guards were obliged to escort her as far as the Pope's throne.

The Pope allowing her to kiss his foot, she knelt with her head bent down and her arms stretched out, and she fell into so profound an ecstasy that she became immoveable as a stone, and elevated a little above the earth. In vain was every effort put forth to raise her up. The ambassador of Spain, who was present, earnestly begged that by a pious robbery a little rosary which she held between her fingers might be taken from her, as he wished to keep it for a relic; but it was not possible to take it out of her hand.

The Pope was extremely astonished, but in the meantime allowed the other nuns to kiss his foot, and interrogated Sister Vanna, Colomba's mother, on the whole life of her daughter. After a little delay, coming to herself, she rose of her own accord, and answered the Pope's questions with admirable modesty and simplicity; but when the Pontiff began to interrogate her of heavenly things, she fell again into an ecstasy, and remained so a long time.

Cesare Borgia

The Pope then turning to Padre Maestro Sebastiano, who was present, ordered him to relate his true opinion regarding Colomba. The old religious obeyed, and while he was making known to the Sovereign Pontiff the many virtues and heavenly gifts with which the Saint had been enriched by Heaven, Cardinal Caesar Borgia, named the Cardinal of Valencia, who was one of these present at the throne, interrupted his discourse, beginning himself to praise Colomba's virtues, and asserting that he had been an ocular witness with the noble Grifone Baglioni of the miracles that had occurred in that very church, when she restored life and health to the dying babe.

To these encomiums succeeded the confirmation of the same with great praise of Colomba from Cardinal Piccolomini of Siena, afterwards Pius III, who, setting forth the solid doctrine of the Angelical Doctor S. Thomas, taken from the Areopagite, showed wonderfully well that all the actions of this contemplative were pure effects of Divine Love. He finally added to his discourse the testimony of Siena, his own country, where Colomba was held in great veneration, and where the people wished to have her for their fellow-citizen. The Pope applauded these testimonies, which confirmed still more his good opinion of the excellent spirit of Colomba, when Cardinal Oliverio Caraffa, a Neapolitan, protector of the Dominican Order, a man of powerful mind, who was shedding tears on this occasion through joy and consolation, assured the Sovereign Pontiff that the greatest care should be used in examining the spirit of Colomba.

Pius III

The Saint being come to herself from her ecstatic sleep, had more conversation with the Pope, received many praises, and was presented with many spiritual graces, and he enriched her new altar of S. Catherine with many indulgences. He granted the Papal Benediction to her brother, the Dominican novice Fra. Giovanni. He assigned a sum of money for the completion of her new monastery then building, and dismissed her with many demonstrations of honour and esteem. This event, which made so much noise, and was calculated to form in the eyes of the world a glorious epoch for Colomba, was regarded by the humble virgin merely as a shadow which passes, and neither the splendour of the Pope's tiara, nor the majestic court in attendance at the throne, nor the applause of the numerous assemblage, could distract her; for Divine love tending towards God possessing alone her soul, she enjoyed as soon as she returned to her cell her accustomed contemplation with God.

The demonstration of great esteem shown by the Roman court to Colomba did not cease here; for during the time of the Pope's stay in Perugia, there was not a cardinal, prince, or prelate who was not moved by devout curiosity to speak with Colomba. The above-mentioned cardinal, protector of the

Dominican Order, wishing to keep the promise he had made to the Pope of investigating Colomba's spirit, joined to himself the Cardinal di Santa Croce, and Lorenzo Cibo Cardinal of Benevento, and together with Mgr. Lopez, the Bishop of Perugia, they often went to visit Colomba, and held frequent and long conferences in the oratory of her monastery. These princes and prelates caused some iced drinks to be brought one day to the monastery, and offered them to Colomba, who took one without the slightest affectation. The Cardinal of Benevento would not lose sight of this glass which had approached Colomba's lips, but kept it as a relic.

These prelates easily discovered her sanctity in conversing with her, and finding in her a spirit of prophecy regarding the great calamities which were at that period lacerating Europe, and furnishing motives for tears, they made their conferences more frequent with the Saint, to beg her intercession with Almighty God, and to understand the meaning of her answers, by which they became possessed of secrets of the greatest importance. The Spanish ambassador obtained from Colomba, by means of a Spanish prelate, two little white scapulars worked with her own hands, and blessed in honour of S. Catherine of Siena, which were sent by him into Spain; he presented one to Ferdinand King of Spain, the other to Queen Isabella, his consort, and the gift was very pleasing to these monarchs, who had already been informed of Colomba's sanctity by that Spanish bishop who had examined her spirit in Rieti.

All these great personages, in fine, who had conversed with Colomba, departed filled with admiration and veneration for this servant of God; and though some went thither on purpose to try her, they were so consoled, and formed so high opinion of her sanctity, that they could not go away without taking something from her to keep as a relic. Her conversation was the same with every one, without affectation or artifice in words, so that her simplicity and humility, and the singular innocence of her pure actions, which had no care for earthly things, no thought of her own perfections, showed clearly and brightly that attraction which led her spirit to seek God and tend to Him alone.

CHAPTER VI

VARIOUS MIRACLES WROUGHT BY COLOMBA. PROPHECIES, REVELATIONS, AND AN ECSTASY, WHICH SHE HAS IN PUBLIC.

After such glorious proofs of Colomba's sanctity had been given in the sight of the Pontifical court, the fame of our Saint and the devotion of the people towards her increased very much, and spread over the whole of Italy, and still more did they increase when it was found by experience that it sufficed to ask a grace from Heaven in Colomba's name to obtain it. Thus God willed to glorify His servant, whom He had given to the world purposely to be a comfort to the faithful in that unhappy age. The people of Rieti, who often went to Perugia to obtain relief in their tribulations through their countrywoman, found means to spare themselves the journey and still obtain their requests. Their devotion suggested to them to make the chamber of Colomba an object of veneration, and by this means they obtained many graces and miracles. In the year 1496 a possessed man was carried thither, and being placed upon our Saint's little bed, he was delivered from the devil. This miracle induced many lame and sick persons to have themselves carried into this bed, which became a pool of Bethsaida, from which they departed cured.

The nuns of S. Agnes, who lived at that time outside the walls of the city, finding themselves exposed to the danger of incursions through the war in the kingdom of Naples, resolved to retire into the town, and having heard that Colomba's apartment had been changed into a sanctuary, they wished to take Colomba's house for their habitation, and in the year 1499 they removed thither, beginning the erection of their new monastery.

A young son of Basilio di Deruta, having lost his eye, it was restored to its proper place, and healed by the touch of a piece of her chain, which is preserved by the Dominican fathers of S. Martino, in Gubbio. A lady of Orvieto, dangerously ill, and despaired of by the physicians, begged health of Almighty God through the merits of Colomba, and scarcely was her prayer ended than she was cured, and she published the praises of her benefactress, and divulged everywhere this miracle, which was registered as having taken place on the 24th of August, 1496, at four o'clock. Soon after, a similar miracle of instantaneous cure was wrought in favour of a lady of Viterbo, who invoked Colomba.

By these unaccustomed favours, which Heaven dispensed through Colomba's merits, the devout faithful perceived how dear to Almighty God was this His beloved servant; and on this account she received frequent messages from distant countries, seeking advice or decision, and imploring favours. The Saint felt much regret at the interruption which these visits caused in her manner of life, but her charity prevailing, she was ready to console every one, always showing herself in her discourse full of the unction of the Spirit of God.

A gentleman, named Carletti di Corbara, went to Colomba in this year, being sent from Viterbo, to question her and ascertain the truth relative to the Stigmata which had recently made their appearance in Blessed Lucia di Narni, a nun of the third Order of Dominicans, who was then living, and at that time dwelling in Viterbo; and though Father Sebastiano tried to dissuade the stranger from making such inquiries of Colomba, he still found means to execute his design, and confer with her, and Colomba answered him, "I rejoice and am consoled at the honour conferred on my sister in religion; for the Stigmata are signs of the charity of God, bright and shining through the innocence of virginity and the candour of sincerity; bloody, through the rigour of penance; deep, and pierced with the nail, by the firm affection and compassion rooted in the Crucified." The messenger entreated that she would give her opinion, but Colomba interrupted him, replying, "What you have narrated, I believe, nor is it permitted me to think otherwise." The stranger then taking leave, asked her to give him at least a letter of admonition or exhortation to her Sister Lucia di Narni, but Colomba refused this request, answering, "May Heaven preserve me from such a thing, as that I, an unworthy servant, should dare to presume to instruct with my foolish words the servant of Christ who is enriched with such heavenly gifts. Here is the letter in two words, 'I recommend myself to her prayers.'"

United with this profound humility, there also appeared in her a lively and strong confidence in God, by which without any injury to humility she was always ready to afford help to the needy, even by miracles.

She gave a truly excellent proof of this in the year 1497. There was a scarcity of corn this year in Perugia, and the two sisters who went to beg alms, being returned home at the dinner hour, had only seven loaves, which were not sufficient to feed the number of mouths in the monastery, exceeding fifty, and they did not know how to remedy this necessity. Colomba then made them all go to table, and calling upon the holy Name of God, with confidence she took the seven loaves, and breaking them in pieces distributed them to the nuns, who, when they were satisfied, filled two baskets with the fragments, by means of which, when carried to the sick, Almighty God dispensed many favours. Atlanta Baglioni, who had a very great veneration for Colomba, procured immediately a large provision of these fragments, and she attested on oath that she had cured with them many sick people in the town of Santa Fiora; and wishing one day to break off a particle to give to a person sick of pleurisy, she saw with astonishment several crosses of gold appear on the bread.

But we now come again to the arrival of princes and prelates in Perugia who wish to consult Colomba. The disturbances in this year very much afflicted the mind of the Pope, who feared for the safety of his own person even in Rome, on account of the seditions and scandals which everywhere prevailed. In these great dangers the Pontiff had no comfort but in recurring to the prayers of Colomba, whose prophetic spirit he had already witnessed. Cardinal Giovanni Borgia, Legato of Umbria, was the medium through which the Pope held correspondence and communication with our Saint; but several events which were adverse to the Pope and to Rome having followed each other, the Cardinal Legate determined to go without delay to Perugia, and hold a long conference with the Saint.

The legate would not enter the town for political reasons, but having taken up his abode in the Benedictine monastery of S. Peter, outside the walls, he sent for Colomba thither. The people of Perugia were fearful at this time of difficulty, that there might be some intention of removing Colomba, and they reluctantly granted her permission to go beyond the walls; but the Cardinal Legate, to remove every shadow of fear, allowed the audience to take place in the public church of S. Peter. This news greatly afflicted the humble virgin, who with tears complaining to her spiritual father said, "That the graces and gifts of God ought to be kept secret and hidden, and that these frequent visits were robberies of the heavenly treasure which she desired to keep with jealousy; that instead of bringing her thus into public, they ought to impose on her severe flagellations, penances, and prayers, to appease the Divine wrath."

She could not, however, exempt herself from this mortification, and obedience prevailing, she went accompanied by several ladies and many gentlemen; and as any object which struck her senses was sufficient to raise her to the contemplation of heavenly things, it happened that soon after leaving the city gate the mountains appeared in her view, and in a moment stopping and becoming abstracted she cried out, " Mount Sion! Mount Calvary!" Being come to the church, and kneeling before the crucifix, she fell into a profound ecstasy, in which she became immoveable as a statue. To recall her to herself the cardinal ordered the organ to be very loudly played, but remaining fixed and immoveable in the same manner, she was seen by the astonished observers to keep her eyes open and fixed, and frequently to change colour, becoming first red, then pale, and neither her limbs nor her pulse gave the least movement or sign of life. Being at last come to herself, the Cardinal Legate held with her alone at the right side of the altar a long conversation, in which she manifested her usual humility and meekness. So great was the satisfaction received by the cardinal, that being afterwards in the company of persons of consideration, he pronounced a public *eulogium* on the prophetic spirit of the virgin, attesting that he had several times experienced it himself. There was present among other persons of consideration Mgr. Bartolommeo Torrelli, Bishop of Cagli, the intimate friend and confessor of Pope Alexander VI; this ecclesiastic had a short private conversation with our Saint, after which he was commissioned by her to warn the Pontiff to keep himself in readiness, because the vengeance of Heaven was about to manifest itself, and he would be exposed to great peril, as it actually happened; for not long after, that is, in the year of the Jubilee, during a thunderstorm in the night, a whirlwind blew down the chimney of that apartment of the Apostolic Palace in which the Pope slept, and the Pope was found under the ruins in great fear, but only slightly hurt, having been wonderfully protected by a large beam, one end of which remained fixed in the wall, while the other was broken. Before Colomba left the church of S. Peter she performed a miracle in favour of the monks. The abbot of the monastery, Don Erasmo of Genoa, presented himself to her, recommending himself to her prayers, that he might be freed from a disease in the eye which had long troubled him. Colomba made the sign of the cross on it, and the Father Abbot was cured at that moment. Being returned to her monastery, she saw in spirit when in prayer, the imminent danger of drowning in the Tiber which, that same day, threatened Padre Maestro Fra. Tommaso of Rieti, giving him assistance with her prayers.

CHAPTER VII

COLOMBA ACCEPTS THE POST OF PRIORESS THROUGH OBEDIENCE.—GREAT CALUMNIES AND PERSECUTIONS WHICH ARE PATIENTLY ENDURED BY OUR SAINT. HER SELF-ABASEMENT AND HUMILITY.

Though the sanctity and heroic actions of Colomba, joined with the great zeal for regular observance she had shown in the foundation and extension of her monastery, had justly acquired for her the title of Mother of all the Sisters, and though they acknowledged and venerated her as such, still they had never been able to induce her to accept the office of Prioress, as they yielded too easily to her humble but earnest reasons founded on her great youth. But scarcely had she completed the ago of thirty than the desire of having her for Superioress again awoke in the sisters, and being now experienced and mature in the exercise of virtues, she was obliged by obedience to submit to the burden.

Admirable in this post were her charity and prudence, and truly wonderful were her constancy and patience, by which her love attained to the degree of true humiliation and abasement. Her meekness and the amiable sweetness of her manners attracted the hearts of the sisters to a ready and exact obedience, even in the most arduous and difficult things; and as she was accustomed to do penance for the faults of others, she corrected with extreme compassion the failings of her subjects, but discharged upon herself with severe flagellations the punishment due to them. In the correction of defects she was never seen to show the slightest anger in voice, manner, or looks, but was moved only by an affectionate energy, which soon drew tears from the person who was listening to her.

This mild system caused young girls to flock to the cloister during her government, like bees to the hive. But infernal envy, enraged at so much good, without losing time began to discharge all its fury upon our Saint. Murmuring sacrilegious tongues began to spread with greater diligence the old and already refuted calumnies, accusing and condemning Colomba as a hypocrite and a witch, through the use of astrology taught her by her confessor.

Memorials filled with these accusations circulated in Rome through the hands of many prelates of rank, and though the previous judgments in this cause inclined good and upright minds in Colomba's favour, it was necessary to make some resistance to this wicked persecution. Father Sebastiano set to work in good earnest, and in a learned and well reasoned apologetic letter confuted all these calumnies, and made all the daily devout occupations of the Saint, the rigours of her continual penance, the fervour of her charity, her profound humility, and the innocence of her life, shine forth brightly. But the good father not being satisfied with this, took the opportunity, when the Cardinal Legate of Umbria was returning to Rome, to join him in the journey; and he obtained by this means an audience of the Pontiff, to whom he presented his valid justifications.

While Colomba was under this trial, like gold in the crucible in the midst of the fire, Heaven, who protected her under its wings, willed that she should be glorified on this occasion. Father Sebastiano had taken with him to Rome some relics of the bread multiplied by the servant of God, and having gone to visit the Master of the holy Apostolic Palace,

Brother Giovanni Manni, who had been for some time seriously ill, he gave him one of the pieces of this bread, exhorting him to ask for health by the intercession of Colomba. The sick man followed this advice, and immediately regained his health, testifying throughout Rome the signal grace which he had received. The truth of the cause being thus put in a clear light, and all the contrary memorials rejected as false, Father Sebastiano returned home victorious and triumphant over the perfidy of Colomba's enemies.

Lucrezia Borgia

This peace however did not last long; for a new and very strong cause arose suddenly to embitter the persecution against the innocent nun. The Duchess Lucrezia Borgia, who then governed Spoleto and Foligno, desirous through devotion to confer with Colomba, caused her to be invited to go to Spoleto; but the people of Perugia, who always suspected some design of removing her, opposing this strongly, the duchess sought to colour this departure by causing Colomba to be invited to Montefalco, under the pretext of visiting the celebrated body of S. Clare; and for this purpose she sent pressing letters to Perugia through her private treasurer. These new attempts only served to increase the suspicion of the Perugians, and put them more on their guard that the Saint might not go beyond the city walls. The duchess being then angrily determined not to be disappointed, changed her plan, and taking advantage of these who calumniated our Saint, she affected to join this party, and gave them her protection in order to overcome Colomba's constancy by this means; flattering herself that fatigued with the long continuance of these insults she would resolve of her own accord to abandon Perugia.

The efforts of this lady were very powerful; for before long orders from Rome arrived in Perugia, by which Colomba was deposed from her government, deprived of her ordinary confessor, and forbidden to have any conversation with the fathers of her Order under pain of censure. Before these orders reached Perugia, while everything was in perfect calmness, after the defence made by Father Sebastiano, and no one thought of this new affliction, Colomba went one day to her spiritual father, begging him to explain to her this text of the Passion of our Lord: " My God! My God! why hast Thou forsaken Me?" Father Sebastiano began to explain to her the dereliction by His Heavenly Father, which Jesus suffered when dying on the cross; but knowing by experience that the servant of God never spoke without some meaning, he asked her why she came to request this exposition; and she replied, "You will know later."

These orders from Rome being presented to Colomba, like a meek lamb silent under the sharp knife, she was seen to bow her head, and with tears in her eyes declare herself deserving of greater punishment, for she was anxious only to preserve the grace and friendship of God. Persons were secretly sent to her, exhorting her to fly from the city to avoid persecution, and suggesting to her that in this case it was necessary to have recourse to Rome, to be heard again and give weight to her defence; that if she went to Rome persons of influence would not be wanting to protect her, and that if she remained in Perugia she would be continually derided as a foolish and deluded person. But not all these fierce storms of calumnies, of contempt, scoffs, menaces, and punishment, were able to overcome Colomba's constancy or even to alter the serenity of her countenance, which was the reflection of her innocence; and though she suffered from great pain in her teeth, which was habitual to the servant of God, and almost continual during the course of her life, yet being accustomed to rejoice in suffering, she was never seen discomposed or disturbed.

The heroic virgin remained as a rock in the midst of the waves, copying in herself that Calvary which had been ever the object of her desires. She had always on her lips her favourite

Psalm, "Qui habitat," with which she loved to unite these two verses of the 137th Psalm, *"In conspectu Angelorum psallam tibi"* and this, *"In quacumque die invocavero te, exaudi me; multiplicabis in anima mea virtutem."*

The martyrdom endured by Colomba at this time did not terminate here, and whether Almighty God designed to preserve His servant from pride, or to render her conformable to Jesus in His abandonment, He presented before her a more terrible Calvary, in which she displayed her humble love, her respectful fear, and the lowliness of her soul. Oppressed by these calumnies and severe prohibitions, recalling herself to the consideration of her whole life, which reminded her of her own incapacity, and reproached her with her sinfulness, in presence of that infinite Majesty before which all the seraphim of heaven tremble, she fell into so great an abasement of soul, that she suffered as it were the pains of hell. In this state the goodness of God being hidden from her mind, from which she formerly drew so sweetly her delightful contemplations, and His Majesty and infinite greatness alone appearing to her eyes, the afflicted and trembling Colomba found herself in a deep and dark abyss of her own nothingness, misery, and impotence. She armed her hand more strongly against herself with scourges, but this seemed to bring more clearly to her memory, and to reproach her with her tepidity and ingratitude, which might be the cause of Almighty God's retiring thus from her. The devil did not fail to increase her affliction in this state, and assailing her by night at her prayers with ghosts and horrid spectres, threatened to strangle her, and bruised her face with severe blows. For the space of nearly a year our Saint endured this martyrdom with heroic patience and profound humility; and it was observed by every one, that her face, which had before always appeared cheerful in combats, in this trial exhibited continually the paleness of death.

The solemnity of Easter, which fell on the 19th of April in

the year 1500, being arrived, when our Saint was occupied in prayer in her cell, the patriarch S. Dominic appeared to her, and showing her a beautiful garland and inviting her to the glory of Paradise, said to her, " Come, beloved daughter, come, for now the time is arrived, when the Bridegroom will unite Himself in a holy manner to His spouse." Overcome with consolation Colomba fell into a fainting fit, but the superabundant spiritual joy which inundated her, circulating through her veins, so bright a rainbow of peace, if we may so speak, appeared in her countenance, that it astonished the eyes of all who saw her. Being asked the cause of her excessive joy, she answered merely by these words, "We have good news, and you will soon know it."

S. Dominic

CHAPTER VIII

CONSTANT AND COURAGEOUS LOVE OF COLOMBA. THE ORDERS FROM ROME WHICH GAVE HER PAIN ARE RESCINDED.—SHE OBTAINS A NEW CONFESSOR. SHE IS AGAIN WARNED BY HEAVEN OF THE TIME OF HER DEATH.

After the darkness of night dawns the beauty of day, and after tempests, lightning, and thunder, tranquillity returns, and the sun with its brilliant light restores cheerfulness to these who have been in fear. Thus, after Almighty God has overwhelmed a soul with the splendour of His majesty, He communicates to it a more distinct knowledge, and shows Himself to it under the amiable qualities of Friend, Brother, and Spouse, which cause it to rise from fear and begin to hope for all things. These were precisely the sweet impressions which God made on the soul of Colomba after she had suffered these great tribulations. Scarcely had the spouse of Christ received the happy announcement from Heaven, that the time was certainly drawing near when she would enjoy her Divine Spouse for ever in Paradise, than, like a slave who at the joyful news of his freedom feels no longer the pain of his hard fetters, she seemed to have passed completely from Calvary to Thabor.

This was the good news she had heard, for no other news but this would have been capable of satisfying her desires. In effect, the rigorous and afflicting orders from Rome against the innocent virgin had not yet been relaxed, when to the great admiration of every one she showed what blessed repose she enjoyed in the bosom of God. Forgetting herself entirely, and creatures disappearing from her sight, her soul was nourished by continual flames of light, intelligence, and charity, and her time passed in continual ecstasies of mind, rapture of soul, and ardent love; thus showing that she had already a happy foretaste of the approach of Paradise. Would to God that the memorial of these delights had not been entirely lost to posterity; but through the privation of her spiritual Director from which she then suffered, they remained almost all sealed up in the bosom of God, and in the happy heart of our Saint who experienced them, and are entirely concealed from us. We may, however, judge, from a public ecstasy which she had in the church of S. Dominic at this time, to what a great degree of confidence and familiarity with God she had attained. In this ecstasy she was heard to discourse with her heavenly Spouse as with a person present and speaking to her, and with great familiarity to make an agreement with Him, uttering these words: "Suspend, O my merciful Lord, the punishment of the sins of this people till the coming Easter, for I promise Thee that they will repent."

And as to complete Colomba's victory nothing was wanting except that her innocence should be acknowledged by men, our Lord vouchsafed also in this manner to console His beloved spouse, who sang with so much confidence in God, *"Ipse liberavit me de laqueo venantium."* In the same month of April the severe orders against the servant of God were rescinded; and further, the privilege of the Jubilee was granted to her for her monastery, and a new confessor of her Order was granted. In order to cut off any further motive for slanderous tongues to speak against our Saint, Father Sebastiano with great wisdom and prudence had contrived that a new confessor should be assigned to her, for he preferred to bear patiently this loss, rather than to bring any fresh insults upon the innocent. This father interested himself with Cardinal Raimondo Perualdi, Bishop of Gorizia, and Legate in Perugia, who, having a great veneration for Colomba, warmly undertook to procure that Father Michael of Genoa, a man renowned for sanctity and learning, and a celebrated preacher, should be assigned to Colomba for confessor.

This priest, in the very beginning, that he might not be deceived in understanding Colomba's spirit, had recourse to the Crucifix to obtain sufficient light, adding to his prayer the maceration of his body with severe and indiscreet penances; but he soon changed his plan, for this austere tenor of life was revealed in spirit to Colomba, who secretly persuaded him to moderate it. Some months having elapsed after this event, and the time of Advent drawing near, her confessor assailed her with this dilemma, "I do not know what I ought to believe of you, daughter; for it is said of you, that you do not eat nor taste food, whilst you often tell me and others that you eat of every thing; I do not understand this enigma of yours. There is some deception here." "I said truly to you, father," replied Colomba with holy intrepidity, " I said truly, that I eat of every thing, for in feeding on the Sacred Body of Jesus Christ I feel all the relish and perceive the taste of all earthly nourishment, and I will make you also experience it before the new year arrives." In effect, on Christmas Eve, Colomba being with her sisters in the church of S. Dominic at matins, was raised into an ecstasy, which continued even after matins, and when her senses returned, turning to her confessor who was present, she said, " To-day, father, you will have it." The good priest then disposed himself with the greatest possible recollection and fervour, to render himself worthy to receive the graces which our Saint had obtained for him, and going to celebrate mass on the night of the Holy Nativity, he tasted in the Communion that ineffable sweetness which contained every relish, as Colomba had promised him; and meeting him during the day she said, "May it be of great benefit to you, father; I rejoice greatly that you have tasted the Food which possesses every relish."

This facility with which Colomba dispensed graces to others from the Divine Treasury, clearly showed the increased strength which her love had acquired. Finally, as the Divine Goodness, for the greater consolation of His servants, is wont in this state to conceal all the infinite greatness of His Majesty, and to take pleasure in willing to be equal with them, so Colomba showed that she had attained to this special degree of love, when under the impulse of a holy confidence she dared to aim at and to ask that which it would have been temerity to hope for, if everything were not permitted to love.

On the feast of the Epiphany, in the year 1501, our Saint being in an ecstasy at prayer in the church of S. Dominic, was heard by her confessor to utter distinctly these words, "Lord, since it is Thy will to defer it till the Ascension, may Thy will be done." These words, " to defer it till the Ascension," were immediately, with good foundation, interpreted by her confessor, as referring to her approaching death, according to the previous words of our Saint. They also imply a secret conversation of Colomba with Jesus Christ on this hidden and uncertain subject of death; and as this could not occur to a servant in regard of his master, without his incurring the blame of boldness, it discovers sufficiently the intimate confidence with which Colomba acted towards her heavenly Bridegroom in the quality of His spouse.

CHAPTER IX

UNITIVE LOVE OF COLOMBA, WHICH IS AT THE SAME TIME ARDENT AND INFLAMED–SHE PREPARES HERSELF FOR DEATH.—SHE RECEIVES A CELESTIAL GIFT— WONDERFUL ECSTASY—MIRACULOUS COMMUNION.

The last end and the sole aim of Colomba's love was to unite herself to God. All her endeavours, her desires, and her sighs, were directed towards seeking, running after, and uniting herself to the Object of her love. Scarcely had the holy virgin received that wonderful favour from Heaven, which invited her to her approaching passage out of this life, than, like a heavy weight which seeks to fall towards its centre, she resolved to abandon all action, to give herself purely to contemplation, and to fix her mind and heart with all their powers on God. And as the universal esteem of her sanctity had obliged her often to receive letters from princes and prelates, and frequent visits for the discussion of spiritual and sublime things, she began from this time to free herself from all. In the second place, she asked pardon with great humility of the citizens and ladies of Perugia, especially of these who had been her calumniators, and of all the fathers of her Order; then, going into chapter with her nuns for this purpose, after asking pardon of all, she made them most fervent exhortations to persevere in holy observance, giving each of them the holy kiss of peace. Being asked the cause of this unusual ceremony, she evaded the question by saying, that perhaps she would not be able to do it another time.

Having thus freed herself from creatures, she resolved to retire into holy solitude, beginning from Septuagesima Sunday till Easter, that is, from the 7th of February till the 11th of April, choosing her cell in the monastery for the place of her retirement, naming it the Desert, and observing a continual and uninterrupted silence till Holy Saturday. She also practised during this time a more rigorous abstinence, which consisted in taking no other nourishment than the Blessed Eucharist alone. A bare table was her bed, and adding to the chains and hair-shirts she already wore, she applied her mind entirely and solely to a very high and pure contemplation. Deeply penetrated with Divine love, she was every day favoured by Heaven in her Desert with most joyful heavenly visions, which gave her a foretaste of the glory after which she sighed; but as her confessor was occupied in preaching at the cathedral in the city, he did not record them, so we have no information respecting them.

During this time of her retreat an unknown pilgrim came to the monastery, earnestly asking for Sister Colomba; and the portress answering that she was in retreat and could not come, and that she was indisposed, the pilgrim renewed his entreaties that at least Sister Colomba might be informed he was there, as she would come. This request being granted by the portress, Colomba received notice of his coming, and going to the turn she found no one there, but seeing inside it a folded cloth, she took it and carried it with her to her cell. Here, untying it, and opening the roll, she found a beautiful picture of Jesus Christ drawn upon it, which admirably represented Him in the act of walking towards Calvary, carrying the cross on His shoulders, and panting for breath. It was the universal opinion that this was a gift from Heaven, as they could never find out who brought it, so that in a short time this holy picture became famous.

The Mother Sister Maria Vincenza Danzetti, deposed on oath in the process of our Saint, that one day some young girls speaking irreverently in presence of this holy representation, Christ was seen to extend His right hand from this picture, and give a blow to one of them. This fact was also attested by Sister Maria Angelica Meniconi. This holy picture is still kept with the greatest veneration in the cell of our Saint.

Of the many other favours communicated by Heaven to our Saint, one only is recorded, which was seen by all the sisters in the monastery; and from this, which is truly wonderful, we may judge how many others our Saint received in secret. A whole day having elapsed without any of the nuns seeing Colomba, some of them went to her cell to observe her; but finding her in an ecstasy they did not dare to enter, all retiring for fear of disturbing her. Part of the second day being past, and the spouse of Christ still remaining immoveable in the same manner and place, fear obliged the sisters to visit her. The Mother Prioress, Sister Caterina di Jacopo, having entered her little room in company with others, saw with surprise the holy virgin immoveable on her knees, holding in her left hand a crucifix and in the right an open book, with her eyes open and fixed upon it without motion. They placed there a continual guard to prevent any unfortunate accident, for so long a rapture seemed very extraordinary; nevertheless, Colomba passed the second day in the same state. But when the third day had arrived, and the Mother Prioress, Sister Caterina di Jacopo, was on guard, she saw Colomba rise to her feet, and, with her hands joined and her mouth open, go forwards to her little altar and receive a Sacred Host, which in a wonderful manner descending from above, placed Itself on her lips, and after being communicated she returned to the place from whence she had arisen. Returning to her senses the same day towards evening, Colomba was so weak that she could not support herself on her feet, but in a few days, having a little recovered her strength, she resumed all her accustomed offices till Holy Saturday. On this day she went to the church of S. Dominic, and, having communicated, assisted at all the holy functions; then returning to the monastery she predicted that she should never again go out of it alive.

In fact, scarcely had she reached it than being attacked with fever and great exhaustion of strength she was obliged to lie down on her little bed made of tables. On the three festival days of Easter she heard mass celebrated in the Oratory of the monastery, and received Holy Communion. On this occasion they observed in her cell a globe of cloth and paper, which Colomba had made during her retreat, modelled after the likeness of Mount Calvary, on which she had clearly printed the Meditations on the Passion of our Saviour, which work is still kept in the little chapel of our Saint. In the meantime feeling a great increase of bodily weakness, and knowing that the time of her much-desired heavenly nuptials was drawing near, Colomba earnestly entreated her confessor constantly to suggest heavenly mysteries to her, in order to keep her mind in continual contemplation.

CHAPTER X

TRANSFORMING LOVE OF COLOMBA.—HER LAST SICKNESS.—HEAVENLY VISIONS.—HER LAST INSTRUCTIONS AND HAPPY PASSAGE.

Transforming love causes the soul to exclaim with the Apostle, "I live, now not I, but Christ liveth in me." This holy love reigned wonderfully in the heart of the seraphic Catherine of Siena, whose portrait Colomba with delicate strokes perfectly copied in herself. In her long illness, in the midst of dreadful pains in the head and teeth, and violent fever, she showed the plenitude of God in her spirit, thinking only of Him. Amidst a thousand offers made to afford her relief and remedy her wants in her sickness, she evinced His full possession of her will, desiring nothing but Him; and finally, in her exhaustion and weakness she gave proof of the plenitude of God in her heart, which rejoiced in suffering for Him alone. Thus our Saint manifested in this state that transforming love which causes God alone to live in the soul, and the soul to live only in God.

The third day of Easter week being past, on the Wednesday, which was the 14th of April, Colomba's weakness showed itself by a mortal sickness. Towards the hour of two in the night she was seized with so copious a vomiting of blood, that the nuns amidst tears and sobs feared to lose her. The night being past, and having been refreshed the following morning by the Holy Communion, she afterwards predicted that very great calamities were ready to fall upon the city, the States of the Church, and the head of the Church; and the melancholy prophecies of the virgin were sadly verified, as during sixteen years the Pontifical States experienced the greatest calamities that history records, as anyone will perceive who reads the account of that sorrowful time. For thirty-three days Colomba's tender body was tormented by burning fever, with severe pain in the head and teeth, without her adding to the comfort of her bed, without relaxing the austerity of mortification, without ever uttering a sigh of complaint, manifesting, on the contrary, and expressing always in her countenance a joyful contentment, as if she were reposing in a garden of flowers. A little water was her usual refreshment, and once only through obedience she tasted the julep which her father confessor offered to her, begging him to dispense her from it. The prioress, moved with compassion to see the invalid so much extenuated, prepared a glass of water, with which julep had been mixed, but in the act of offering it to the servant of God, the vessel broke, spilling all the liquid.

The most Holy Communion alone, in her long illness, was not only the comfort of her soul, but also the remedy for every one of her pains. Scarcely had she communicated, than to the great wonder of every one her countenance lost its emaciation, roses again bloomed on her cheeks, and her lips became tinged with vermilion; and free from pain or fever, she appeared perfectly well. After a little time a mortal pain returned to attack the invalid, which she bore with heroic patience and fortitude. No day passed, however, in which she was not consoled by her celestial Spouse with some heavenly vision; and enjoying a foretaste of the delights of Paradise, her heart burst forth into most lively expressions of joy, to give vent to the happiness which inundated her soul.

Of these visions, which were very numerous, the principal alone are related, which were made known by our Saint herself. She saw one day a large and majestic street, filled with beautiful youths, some of whom adorned it with flowers, while others were preparing for a concert of instruments, and a majestic Pilgrim clothed in purple, passing in the midst of them, presented himself to Colomba, telling her to put herself in order, and keep herself prepared, for she would be soon invited by Him to rejoice eternally. The heavenly beauty of this Pilgrim so ravished the heart of Colomba, that during the whole day she kept from time to time exclaiming with exultation, "Oh, how beautiful is this Pilgrim! Oh, how beautiful!" The seraphic S. Catherine of Siena appeared to her with a numerous troop of young virgin queens, all adorned with bright stars interwoven with gold, and rejoicing with her, they seemed to wait to accompany her to heaven. After this troop arrived the glorious S. Peter Martyr, followed by a number of soldiers of Christ. The vision being ended, Colomba turned to her confessor, and relating it to him, added that her departure was near, but that she expected two sisters to accompany her. These two companions, who were not named, but were seen by the Saint, were of the same institute, of no less merit, and whose names Almighty God concealed to make them known more gloriously in heaven.

On the Sunday preceding the Rogation Days, which was the 17th of May, the innocent virgin had another special and very joyful vision. Our Saviour appeared to her in triumph and glory, surrounded by angels, in the act of ascending to heaven, with an innumerable crowd of holy patriarchs, prophets, martyrs, confessors, and virgins following Him. The patriarch S. Dominic, and S. Catherine of Siena, took Colomba and conducted her to heaven by a ladder, presenting her before the throne of God and to the Blessed Virgin. The invalid repeatedly related this vision to her confessor and to her sisters, with signs expressive of superabundant joy.

The whole city, and especially the nuns, were inconsolable at the thought of their approaching loss, which they saw to be irreparable and the more bitter, because Colomba was in the prime and vigour of her age. Some of the nuns, oppressed by grief, and giving themselves up to excessive melancholy, thinking they could not remain in the monastery without their dear Mother Colomba, had resolved to go out and leave it after her death. But our Saint, who with a joyful and serene countenance already enjoyed the foretaste of approaching beatitude, and by her spirit of prophecy had foreseen all this, called, all the religious to her, and with unaccustomed energy of voice began in the presence of her confessor and others thus to speak to them and console them: " Dear sisters and beloved daughters, I thank you for your charity and for the prayers which you offer to our Lord for me, that He may grant me a happy passage; but cease, I entreat you, to pray to God for the health of my body, for I have already with my whole heart made the sacrifice of my life. Yes, O death, precious in the sight of the Lord, come, and no longer delay. Come, my only comfort, after the storms of this miserable life, since thou alone canst eternally unite me to my sweet Spouse Jesus. Ah, sweet death! why dost thou delay longer, since every delay is a torment to me? Ah, dear sisters, raise your eyes to Paradise and see how lovely it is! There is our heavenly Spouse, who is the splendour of the Eternal Father, who having overcome death and shut up hell has ascended in triumph to heaven. Look how beautiful He is! Never are the angels satiated with admiring Him. He is our Portion, our Treasure, the Eternal Reward, the Prize and the Crown of our labours; therefore rejoice, and do not regret that I am approaching that blessed and much desired country. Be you constant, and persevere in the holy bond of charity and union amongst yourselves in the course you have undertaken; and He will help you, He will defend you, and conduct you to heaven. Remember that our Spouse is beautiful everywhere, but He is most beautiful on the wood of the cross; He is strong everywhere, but on the cross He is strongest; He is everywhere amiable, but on the cross He compels us to love Him. He says to us, 'Let him who will come after Me, take up his cross and follow Me.' Courage, then, daughters, make haste and come, for 1 am already going to follow my heavenly Spouse. You know how many labours, obstacles, and difficulties we have overcome in the Name of the Lord to found this new holy monastery, which is entirely the work of our heavenly Spouse; and therefore the devil, our mortal enemy, trembles with rage, and tries to destroy this new plant that it may not be fervently cultivated by you; but, my beloved, let not the diabolical suggestions stop you and draw you back from so sweet a yoke. In spite of every obstacle, and scorning the attempts of hell, this place will prosper more and more if you are strong and constant, and let not any sinister event terrify you. It is true that I am leaving you, but I can help you better in heaven, and I will always ask our dear Jesus to give you strength, constancy, and perseverance in His holy love, and always to keep you in peace. But woe to anyone who should attempt to disturb the good order of observance, or should be the cause of division; for I shall assail her with the avenging wrath of God."

This discourse was so sweet, so tender, and so expressive, that the spectators shed floods of tears, and Father Sebastiano, who knew the holy life of Colomba, being present, felt his heart so burn within him that he could not repress his sighs and sobs of tenderness. This discourse being ended, Colomba asked her confessor to prevent persons from coming to her cell to visit her, desiring to remain in recollection and readiness to receive her heavenly Spouse. The holy invalid passed the whole of Rogation Tuesday in continual and long discourses on Paradise, which were so eloquent that she seemed to be already enjoying that happy mansion, and exulting in the contemplation of the various hierarchies of saints. She described the various choirs of angelic spirits with admirable observations, which penetrated the depths of the heavenly secrets; then she descended with surprising clearness to unfold minutely the glory of the patriarchs, prophets, and all the other blessed, showing forth in her mind an infused supernatural theology.

Wednesday, the 19th of May, Ascension Eve, being come, Colomba asked her confessor to perfume her room with incense, as she expected that day her beloved Spouse Jesus Christ; and at midday her confessor administered to her the Holy Viaticum. Not long after she experienced several violent assaults from the infernal enemy, who tried to terrify her; but the prudent warrior holding fast the crucifix in her hands, cried out, "O holy cross! O holy crown! O holy nails of my good Jesus, obtain for me mercy and pardon!" She then asked that the passion of our Lord might be read to her, and when these words, "*tradidit spiritum*" were read, she repeated, "*In manus tuas, Domine, commendo spiritum meum.*"

At the hour of Vespers, Father Sebastiano gave her Extreme Unction, all the sisters assisting at it, after which followed the recommendation of the soul, to which Colomba attentively answered with a tranquil countenance. After this, the priest, to encourage her, made her a short discourse on eternal felicity, to which Colomba replied, "I swim, father, I swim in an ocean of spiritual sweetness and, raising her eyes to heaven with a sigh, she spoke thus: "O Mary, Queen of Angels, Mother of my dear Jesus! O great Patriarch S. Dominic! O my seraphic mother, S. Catherine! behold I recommend my soul to your patronage." Having said this, the strength of voice with which she had begun to speak failed her, and in a low voice she continued to recommend the Catholic Church, her Order, her monastery, the city of Perugia, and especially her benefactors and friends. The hour of midnight, which preceded Ascension Day, being at length arrived, and all the nuns in prayer on their knees, her confessor being present, the face of Colomba became suddenly all inflamed like fire, and with a joyful and smiling countenance she exclaimed, " O my sweet Spouse, Thou art welcome! Thou art come, O my Jesus! Take this Thy servant, O take—And in the act of speaking she breathed out her happy soul in the hands of her heavenly Spouse, on the 20th of May, 1501, the night preceding Ascension Day, aged thirty-three years, three months, and eighteen days, remaining with her eyes open, and her face coloured and rosy as if she were sleeping.

Thus did this innocent virgin gloriously end her days, a true daughter of the patriarch S. Dominic in mortification and austerity of life, a true follower of S. Catherine of Siena in the elevation of her prayer, a true rival of angels in the whiteness of her purity; a true dove, which, attracted by love, taking its flight towards Calvary, placed her nest securely there, and being enriched with heavenly gifts, triumphed magnanimously over the frightful shadow of the infernal vulture, and with its plumage of silver and gold mounted victoriously to heaven.

CHAPTER XI

SOLEMN OBSEQUIES RENDERED TO COLOMBA.—MIRACLES WHICH TOOK PLACE, AND HER BURIAL.

As the death of the Saints is glorious and immortal before men, because it is precious in the sight of the Lord, the inhabitants of Perugia were never satisfied or fatigued with celebrating the goodness of God, who had enriched the city with so noble a treasure, some praising her innocence and charity amidst tears of joy, others her sweetness and humility, others her patience and prudence, with all her other virtues. Scarcely had the happy passage of our Saint taken place, than the whole city put itself in motion to prepare for her a funeral service in the best manner that their gratitude and devotion could suggest.

This holy body, which was found covered with iron circlets, chains, and hair-shirts, and reduced to a mere skeleton, being decently clothed, was deposited for the solemn feast of the Ascension in the Oratory of the monastery, whither flocked a continual and numerous crowd of people to venerate it. The following day, the clergy being assembled with the magistrates, it was carried in procession to the church of S. Dominic, with a magnificent quantity of lights. The bier, which was covered with purple laced with gold, and was encircled by the sisters of the monastery, was carried by the nobility under a canopy from the College of Doctors, and was afterwards followed by the magistrates with the crowd from the city. Our Saint had said two days before her death, "You will celebrate the feast with water." The bystanders did not then understand this prophetic phrase of our Saint, which was verified; for when the procession was going to enter the church a heavy shower came on. Father Sebastiano had the honour of singing the solemn Requiem Mass, after which a learned funeral oration was pronounced in praise of our Saint.

A truly wonderful phenomenon occurred here, registered with the oaths of witnesses, and similar to that which happened at our Saint's baptism. Scarcely had the solemn mass commenced, than a white dove was seen to fly into the church, which immediately placed itself on the coffin containing the holy body, and remained there till the end of the sacred function. The strength of the guards who had the custody of the holy corpse could not repress the great violence of the crowd, who advanced to cut in pieces the clothing of the Saint's body; and to satisfy the entreaties of the inhabitants, and the devotion of the neighbouring countries, from which the people flocked in troops to visit it, it was necessary to leave it exposed for three successive days, that is, till the 23rd of May.

Many were the miracles and great graces which Heaven vouchsafed to grant to the devout people who came to visit the Saint during these three days. Oppressed with fever and severe pain in the head, Signor Ludovico d' Orlandino had himself conveyed to the church before the body of Colomba, and in an instant he felt himself free from every pain, walking back to his house cured. Signor Bernardino di Cola, who was sick, and had been for several years a sufferer, received his cure in a moment, recommending himself before our Saint's body. The same thing happened to Bartolommeo di Francesco, of Perugia. Two women, who were reduced to the last extremity by pleurisy, having recommended themselves to Colomba while the corpse was exposed, rose up miraculously from bed, finding themselves cured, and went to the church of S. Dominic to return thanks to the Saint. We should lengthen our narrative too much if we were to insert a catalogue of all the Perugians and strangers who were freed from various evils on this occasion. After the third day, which was the 24th of May, though the devotion of the people was not yet satisfied, Father Sebastiano ordered that decent interment should be given to the holy corpse. When her body was opened to be embalmed, though it was the fifth day from her death, the bystanders saw with great wonder and admiration blood flow from her heart as liquid and florid as if she were alive. The holy corpse was then placed embalmed in a chest of deal well closed up, and in an earthen vessel were placed her heart with her entrails on the same chest, which was buried as Colomba had requested, under the predella of the altar of S. Catherine of Siena, where Alexander VI had knelt, and above which was placed the picture of our Saint with suitable inscriptions. Some Italian verses were also written in her praise by Signor Loreto Mattei, a gentleman of Rieti.

CHAPTER XII

BLESSED COLOMBA APPEARS TO SEVERAL PERSONS, AND REVELATIONS OF HER GLORY ARE MADE IN DIFFERENT PLACES.—VENERATION IS IMMEDIATELY SHOWN TO HER SEPULCHRE, AND CONTINUED.

DIVINE Providence, which is sometimes pleased to hide from the eyes of the world the sanctity of great souls, that He may render them glorious only in heaven, as He had given Colomba for the benefit of the faithful, and had made her glorious during life, willed also that her name should be immortal after her death by revealing her glory. Blessed Lucia di Narni, a virgin of the third Order of Dominicans, foundress of the monastery of S. Catherine of Siena in Ferrara, was there at that time, and was protected in this holy work by the Duke of Ferrara Ercole d' Este, who through the great opinion he entertained of her holiness often went to visit and hold long conferences with her. It happened on the Feast of the Ascension, in the same year, 1501, that the duke, having gone to hear mass in the church of S. Catherine, wishing afterwards to visit Sister Lucia, saw this servant of God run forward to meet him with unusual joy, and before she had come up to him she exclaimed in a voice full of delight,

Erccole d'Este, The Duke of Ferrara

"Good news, O Prince, good news! Know, your Highness, that this morning at dawn of day I saw mount to heaven, in the company of my most sweet Spouse Jesus Christ, the soul of my Sister Colomba of Rieti, foundress of the monastery of S. Catherine of Siena in Perugia." The duke was astonished at the frankness of this account, called his secretary to him without delay, ordering him to write immediately to Perugia to know the truth, and he found the answers uniform in attesting Colomba's precious death that same day.

The Blessed Osanna di Andreassi, a noble lady of Mantua, and a virgin of the third Order of S. Dominic, being at prayer on the Feast of Pentecost in the same year, saw the Blessed Colomba in glory, with two brilliant crowns of glory on her head, attended by a numerous troop of holy prelates, who turning towards her told her smiling to keep herself in readiness, for she would soon follow her to glory. This servant of God died in 1505; and the Father Fra. Girolamo Olivetano, who wrote the Life of this religious, as her adopted son, in 1507, attests that S. Colomba twice appeared to Sister Osanna Andreassi.

Bl. Osanna di Andreassi

One day, after the interment of the holy body, Colomba appeared to her mother, Sister Vanna, reproving her because she had prevented the clothing of her sister Brigida, who had earnestly and repeatedly requested it, and she exhorted her to oppose this holy vocation no longer. Colomba's mother profited by this advice, and she not only ceased all opposition, but endeavoured to hasten the clothing, so that on the eighth day from Colomba's death it was resolved to give the holy habit to her sister Brigida, who was of the age of fourteen. And on the last day of May, the Mother Sister Cecilia being Prioress, she was solemnly clothed at the altar of B. Catherine of Siena, by the hands of the Father Fra. Girolamo da Pistoja, taking the name of Sister Magdalen, a saint to whom Colomba was very devout. The holy fervour of severe mortification with which this innocent young girl immediately undertook, her course of life soon confined her to a bed of sickness, when her blessed sister Colomba appeared to console her, telling her that after two years of suffering she should become her companion in heaven; and her death took place two years after. The Father Fra. Domenico Baglioni above mentioned, attested on oath in the Process, that he had been visited and favoured by our Saint, who appearing to him when he was seriously ill, consoled him and told him to take courage, for he would soon be cured.

For a long space of years the event continued to correspond to the promise made by Colomba, of giving special attention and assistance to her new monastery; for her apparitions to her nuns were very numerous and frequent, sometimes to correct abuses, sometimes to console them and cure the sick, and sometimes to bless their cells. This protection helped much to keep the monastery flourishing in regular observance; for the good religious perceiving by the powerful patronage of Colomba how acceptable her holy actions had been to Almighty God, entered into a devout emulation to imitate her example minutely. Being even too much inflamed with the desire of practising rigorous penance, and having armed themselves indiscreetly with instruments of mortification, it was necessary to stop them and put them under control.

The protection of Colomba did not confine itself solely to the limits of the monastery; it extended itself farther for the benefit of the faithful who sought favours from her, for which reason the devout people were assiduous in frequenting her holy sepulchre. There were seen at this holy place all sorts of votive offerings, lamps, and burning candles. The images of our Saint were spread in various places, both prints and pictures with rays, with the title of Blessed, and even in the churches. Her cell in Perugia was converted into a devout oratory with her altar, on which her relics were venerated. Innumerable were the sick persons cured with the oil of her lamp, and as the monastery was not then obliged to enclosure, more than forty persons troubled with incurable diseases being carried to the little room of our Saint, and laid on the table which served her for a bed, rose up and returned to their houses cured. That wonderful representation of our Blessed Saviour carrying His cross, drawn on the cloth which was given to Colomba by the unknown pilgrim, shows by the number of silver offerings with which it is covered and adorned, how favourable it was to the supplications of the faithful who had recourse to it.

Her cell at Rieti, under the care of the nuns of S. Agnes, became a sanctuary for the satisfaction of the faithful; and the relics of her clothes, with her instruments of penance, were always passing from hand to hand to be applied to the sick. In Rieti the pious custom of blessing water in honour of our Saint was introduced, and a little chain which had belonged to her being immersed therein, the water was carried in procession and swallowed by the sick, and it cured them. Eighteen years after Colomba's death the great bell of S. Dominic at Perugia was repaired, and it was consecrated in honour of our Saint, her image in the act of flying to heaven being impressed upon it, with this motto, "*Patriae liberationem.*"

The graces and benefits gained by the faithful through Colomba's intercession increased in their hearts the pious desire of seeing greater veneration shown to her; and, therefore, in the year 1566, at the entreaty of Mgr. Ercolani, a Dominican and Bishop of Perugia, the pontifical leave was obtained, "*vivae vocis oraculo,*" of Pius V to

S. Pius V

make a commemoration of B. Colomba in the Office and in the Mass, on the day of her happy passage, which grant was afterwards confirmed by the same holy Pontiff in the year 1571, and permission was also given to keep lamps burning at her sepulchre, to exhibit her pictures with rays of glory, to hang votive offerings before them, and for every other public act of veneration.

But in the year 1625, the decree of Pope Urban VIII having gone forth, by which every sort of public veneration was prohibited to be given previous to solemn canonization to any of those who had passed out of this life in the odour of sanctity, it was necessary again to prove the lawfulness of this veneration, and to examine it in the juridical form of a Process. This was done by Cardinal di Torres, Bishop of Perugia, and it was found deserving to be confirmed by the Sacred Congregation of Rites in 1627, and declared lawful, and not opposed to the decree of Urban VIII.

This success greatly increased the devotion towards B. Colomba, and Heaven, which favoured the increase of her glory, multiplied its signal graces for the benefit of these who had recourse to her in every place, so that a new register of the miracles and graces obtained through our Saint's intercession, in Rieti as well as in Perugia, was made after this new approbation of the devotion towards her. It was judged that it would be very proper to submit an entreaty to His Holiness, for the formal Process of the canonization and beatification. In effect, when the earnest entreaties of the people of Rieti and Perugia were presented in Rome, the cause was happily taken up again, and in the Process a hundred and sixty-seven witnesses were examined on twenty-four articles, of which a summary was made and proved in Rome; and a favourable decree was issued in 1647, the Father Lodovico Allegrini, who belonged to the Order of Preachers, a native of Perugia, and a man of great virtue in regular observance, being the promoter of this pious cause.

After this immortal triumph of greater accidental glory had been gained, our Saint, as if wishing in gratitude to reward these who were devout to her, obtained for her country a signal and memorable benefit, by which the magnificence of her annual feast was increased. In the year of our Lord, 1656, during the month of October, the city of Rieti was suddenly attacked by a raging pestilence, which obliged them to shut up communication, and to live in confusion and terror. Remembering, however, the powerful intercession of their blessed fellow citizen, which the people of Perugia had experienced on a similar sorrowful occasion, they lost no time in having recourse to their protectress by public prayers, by which they soon obtained a deliverance from it. The relics of our Saint were the best remedy to restore health to the sick, and it was seen with astonishment that death, which had begun its slaughter with great fury, was stopped in its course, and though the contagious disease remained for two months longer, the sick improved, and every house resounded with the glorious name of our Saint; so that after performing a rigorous quarantine for security, the usual commerce was re-opened in the month of April, 1657. In thanksgiving for so great and signal a benefit, they celebrated a solemn feast that year in honour of our Saint; and to make the remembrance of it descend to posterity, a confraternity was erected, under the title of the Blessed Colomba, in the parochial church of S. Donato, in 1661, the picture of our Saint was painted, and the anniversary of it celebrated every year.

CHAPTER XIII

OF THE TRANSLATION OF THE BODY AND HOLY RELICS OF THE BLESSED COLOMBA.

This chapter will, without doubt, appear strange to the common opinion of the people, who still preserve the idea, that in time they will be able to find our Saint's body, to make a solemn translation of it. But the truth of this history being clear and evident, it may avail not only to remove every vain imagination, but also to satisfy the desire of anyone who wishes to know where the relics of S. Colomba are. No solemn and public translation of this holy body was ever, or could be ever made, and still the pious desire which for two centuries past has existed in the hearts of the devout, to see and venerate with solemn pomp these holy relics, is still alive in all its vigour.

This was the cause of the expensive excavations made in the church of S. Dominic in the past century, which were renewed in this one, although fruitlessly; for the relics of the Saint are all preserved not in S. Dominic's, but in the monastery "*delle Colombe*," in the interior chapel of the Saint. In order to prove the truth of this assertion, it will be necessary to recall to mind what was observed above regarding the burial given to the Saint, and the veneration offered at her sepulchre. The manuscript of Father Sebastiano, an eye-witness, attests, "That the holy body being embalmed, was put into a chest of fir, carefully locked, and was buried under the predella of the altar of S. Catherine of Siena, and above the chest was placed the earthen vessel containing her heart and entrails." It has been observed in the  preceding chapter, that immediately after our Saint's death, the faithful began to offer public veneration at her tomb.

Now, to proceed in the clearest manner with the thread of our narrative, it is necessary to investigate at what time this veneration at the sepulchre ceased, and why it ceased. This will also serve to point out without a doubt the situation of the sepulchre of our Saint, about which many devout persons have puzzled themselves, setting to work in the vain hope of finding it by digging up the earth in various parts of the church. There will be no longer room to doubt that this veneration at the sepulchre of our Saint continued more than a century, if we reflect on what has been said in the preceding chapter. For, if in the year 1571, Pope Pius V gave permission to hang votive offerings at this sepulchre, and to burn wax lights there as was the custom, and if, in 1625, when this doubt was proposed in the Sacred Congregation, "Whether this veneration were comprised in the prohibition of Urban VIII," a negative answer was given, it appears clearly that up to this time the sepulchre must have been constantly honoured. In fact, it is registered in the archives of the Convent of S. Dominic, that in 1629, the people rejoicing in the approbation of the devotion which they had obtained from the Sacred Congregation, came to the determination of providing a more decent place for these holy relics, and of making a public translation of them. In the month of May, in the same year, no doubt having been raised as to the situation of the sepulchre, the work was begun, and the vault was made under the predella of the altar of S. Catherine of Siena, where our Saint was buried, and where she had been venerated by the people up to this time; but this undertaking was unsuccessful, and their pious hopes were disappointed, for they  could find no vestige of the holy remains. Astonished and perplexed, they gave themselves up to imaginary conjectures and arbitrary interpretations, in consequence of which, for four successive months, that is, May, June, July, and August, they continued to make various excavations in different parts of the church, which were expensive but perfectly useless, for they were made without any good reason. Here then is clearly laid open the reason and the time of the cessation of this veneration. The Saint's sepulchre being thus laid waste, and these excavations still going on, it is no wonder if an epoch full of obscurity and doubt now began; but, from the body's not being found in the sepulchre, which had been pointed out for a century to the veneration of the faithful, we cannot come to the conclusion that she was buried in another place, but we must rather infer with greater clearness and probability, that before this excavation these holy relics were removed elsewhere by other hands, which inference gives us the certainty of a previous translation, though this fact still remains obscure and unknown.

We, then, leaving this epoch enveloped in obscurity, will turn to search among the ancient writings of the archives of the Convent of S. Dominic, from which we shall draw light enough to discover this hidden and previous translation; and the proposition assumed in the beginning of this chapter will be evidently demonstrated. In the year 1640, that is, ten years after this public excavation had been made, the Father Ignazio Fantozzi, Preacher General, and at this time Prior of the Convent of S. Dominic in Perugia, a very careful man who without sparing labour, put in good order all the archives of this convent, by chance reading a book in the said archives, found registered the whole authentic fact of this previous secret translation for which we are seeking; and, moreover, written by the hand of the very author of the deed, who was the Padre Maestro Serafino Razzi.

The narration is as follows: "As in the year 1571, the permission of Pope Pius V of glorious memory had been already obtained for the public devotion, from that time the desire of the faithful to make a public translation of the Saint's body began to exist. A memorial was at length presented to His Holiness about the year 1582, that this public translation might be made, and leave also obtained to celebrate the solemn feast of it in the whole diocese of Perugia. While waiting for the answer, which was quite expected to be favourable, it occurred to the prior of the Convent of S. Dominic, who was the above-mentioned Padre Maestro Razzi, that it would be a prudent thing to make a private examination of the said relics, by secretly opening the sepulchre to see them, and thus insure the decorum of the public ceremony that was to take place."

"In the evening, therefore, of the 25th of July, in the year 1582, about one o'clock in the morning, the above-named Father Prior, with the Padre Maestro Niccolo Alessi, inquisitor of Perugia, eight other principal religious of the convent, and two seculars, entered the church, and having offered up some prayers, the excavation was made under the predella of the altar of S. Catherine of Siena, the doors being closed; and a little beneath the surface of the earth was found first an earthen vessel, in which the entrails of the Saint had been placed. At a little distance was found the fir chest, which was nearly rotten, and through the negligence and inadvertence of these employed, the lid fell in, carrying with it a quantity of earth, with bricks and stones, which crumbled in pieces the whole of this holy body. Frightened at this unfortunate accident, and a stop being put to the work, the Prior, Padre Maestro Serafino Razzi, descended into the place of burial with surplice and stole and lighted torches, and began with diligence to separate these holy relics from the rubbish, but he was not able to dig out anything but the skull, with the upper part of the head and some bits of bone, all the rest being mixed with dust, rubbish, and earth. Being filled with confusion, and perceiving their error too late, in spoiling the authenticity of the holy relics by disturbing the remains and fearing, on one hand, that the necessary decorum, in the public function would be lost, and, on the other hand, not being willing that this unlucky event should be discovered, they took the expedient of replacing in the same vessel the few bones they had found, keeping it out together with- the fir boards; and they began to fill up the excavation, and arrange it so that it should not appear to have been touched, that the devotion at the sepulchre might not cease; and having imposed a rigorous silence about this affair, the translation was no longer talked of. The Father Prior then carried privately to the monastery '*delle Colombe,*' all these relics, consisting of the earthen vessel with the entrails, and the bones, with the fir planks, recommending the nuns to keep them in the little interior chapel, or chamber of B. Colomba, as they were her relics."

Returning now to the Father Ignazio Fantozzi, the discoverer in 1640 of this registered fact, he himself attests that he afterwards used still farther diligence, and succeeded in finding a letter written by the same Padre Maestro Serafino Razzi, to the Padre Maestro Bottonio, in Rome, then Vicar General of the whole Order, in which he gave him a distinct account of the excavation and of the whole event, which letter agreed with the record left in the archives. In the same year, 1640, the Very Reverend Padre Maestro Ridolfi, General of the Order, came to Perugia, to whom Father Fantozzi imparted the discovery of this account, and he was charged by the General with the care of making a diligent search to discover from the nuns whether these relics really existed, described by Padre Maestro Serafino Razzi in his register. In effect, Father Fantozzi, the Prior, found in the interior chapel of the monastery the half rotten fir planks of the chest, the vessel which contained the entrails of the Saint, and some vessels of crystal, in which the entrails had been put; he also found the greater part of the head, and some little bones of the arms and legs. After this discovery the oldest nuns were examined juridically before the Bishop's Vicar, and they attested on oath that they well remembered these relics to be the same which Padre Maestro Serafino Razzi had brought to them, telling them "to keep them in the Saint's chapel, as things which belonged to their blessed Colomba." This deed was drawn up and attested by Ser Francesco Riccordi, a notary of Perugia, in the month of August of this same year, 1640, the above named Father Fantozzi, the Prior, and the Padre Maestro Ludovico Allegrini, or Pellegrini, Prior of Rieti, being present. All these little bones, with the half of the head, were wrapped up and put in a box, sealed with the seal of the monastery. These relics, and especially the crystal vases containing the entrails, were afterwards exposed for several years for public veneration in the church of the nuns, on the feast of S. Catherine of Siena, as we read in the Process made for the beatification in the year 1647, which confirms the truth of the present narration; for as the Padre Maestro Sebastiano de Angelis assures us, that the entrails of the Saint being placed in a vessel were buried in the sepulchre, and, as it appears otherwise certain, on the testimony of the nuns above cited, that before the year 1582 there were not in the monastery these entrails enclosed in the said crystal vases brought to them by Father Razzi, the whole occurrence of the private translation of these holy relics is clearly confirmed.

We cannot pass over a difficulty which opposes itself to this story. How is it that in the face of such clear and strong evidence the old opinion of the people, who were always trying to seek these holy relics, was not extinguished, and that, on the contrary, it appears that little account was made afterwards of all these records, which have been buried in oblivion? But this difficulty will fall to the ground of itself if we reflect on the want which unfortunately exists of a full authentication of the relics found in the monastery. And we must also take notice of the method observed by Padre Maestro Razzi in consigning to the nuns the excavated relics. This father, being frightened after the first mistake, wishing to hide from the nuns the spoliation of the Saint's sepulchre, fell into another error. He carried these relics privately to the monastery, and in giving them he told them " to keep them with very great care, as they belonged to B. Colomba;" but he concealed the place whence they had been removed. In effect, when the older nuns were interrogated in presence of the Vicar, they answered that they remembered very well that these relics were the same that Padre Maestro Razzi had brought to them as relics of B. Colomba, but as they were ignorant of the excavation made by Father Razzi they could say no more. Now although, with the testimony of the nuns verifying the first part of the question which concerns what Father Razzi said, there may be sufficient evidence of the second part, which regards the action of Father Razzi registered by him; still the testimony is wanting to us which relates to the indication of the place whence the relics were taken, which information was necessary to prove their identity in a public, juridical and authentic manner. The authentication, then, regarding the place whence they were taken being wanting, and it being impossible to obtain it, we need not be surprised if the above-mentioned authentic and historical monuments, though strong in themselves, and capable of persuading any of the truth of this narrative, have never met with this good fortune with the whole of the people, and therefore the old opinion, which hoped to discover these holy relics by digging, was not abandoned.

The authentication of the place whence the relics were taken being held back, liberty of opinion remained amongst the people, who are very tenacious of the traditions of their country, be they true or false, when they are not overcome by evidence to the contrary, as we see in many similar cases which history furnishes. For this reason there is foundation for believing, that through this vain notion of the people arose that indifference which was unfortunately witnessed, in continuing the annual exposition of some of the relics existing in the monastery, which had received veneration for some time, and are still preserved in the same place.

This narration is not confined within the limits of mere probability, but may enjoy the certainty which is necessary to every accredited history, because the want of authentication for the identity of the relics which are preserved in the monastery may indeed deprive us of evidence, but not of the certainty of the truth of the fact. Still, however this be, no damage can happen from it to the propagation of the devotion towards our Saint, for that God who was pleased to glorify His beloved spouse, raising her after death to veneration on the holy altars, has always granted in every age new graces and miracles by the Saint's intercession, so that there is every reason to hope that her glory will be in future still farther extended by her solemn canonisation among the Saints.

CHAPTER XIV

SPIRIT OF B. COLOMBA, DRAWN FROM THE VIRTUES SHE PRACTISED.

Since the Author of grace, Jesus Christ, has commanded all Christians to be holy, as His heavenly Father is holy, every Christian soul, whoever it be, may by the help of this grace, dying indeed to all worldly things and to the desires of nature, arrive at this perfection, or at least advance in the road towards it. But as this happy state, which has so great a similarity and connexion with the sanctity of the blessed in heaven, properly belongs to the state of innocence in which sanctity, keeping man superior to his passions, united him to God as the Eternal Truth, by which he perceived the nothingness of all creatures; so there are very few souls here on earth who enjoy this blessed state, for small indeed is the number of these who have not tarnished the beautiful whiteness of innocence given back to them with the white robe of baptism. The strong and violent assaults of the passions, which develop themselves in man as he advances in years, frequently darkening reason, render the straight road of virtue so difficult that not to swerve from the path may be called a miracle of grace.

Now this miracle is precisely that which is the most valuable ornament of the spirit of Colomba. She was taught in her assiduous prayer that true purity of heart and mind cannot be maintained without solid mortification, which bridles the passions and repels their boldness, and eradicates every guilty inclination; and so by the austerity of her life she obtained not only the preservation of her innocence, but even an insensibility to all earthly things, and an ardour only for these belonging to heaven.

She acquired so great a command over her passions that she was not merely without the impulse to evil, but seemed incapable of committing it. So great was her hatred of any offence against God, that the name alone of sin was sufficient to make her turn pale, tremble, weep, and fall fainting to the ground. It seemed to her a horrible thing that a Christian should be found who would commit sin.

She had a great contempt for all earthly thoughts, to which she could not apply herself without suffering great torment. Being sometimes obliged to hear necessary things spoken of which did not regard Almighty God, she was obliged on these occasions to do herself great violence. This system of virtue had taken, firm and entire possession of her heart, and thus it was not only the spirit of Colomba which panted after heaven, but her whole body was also continually and indefatigably labouring for spiritual things, so that she could say with David, "My heart and my flesh rejoice in the true God alone." From thence proceeded her great fervour of spirit and zeal for the honour of God. Her love, which as a fire was capable only of ascending without stopping, never allowed her to fear difficulties in anything which occurred; for whether they presented themselves to her under an aspect of sweetness or bitterness, she considered in these which were agreeable the sweetness of Divine love, and in these which were painful the bitterness of the bloody Calvary. She forgot every good action she performed, it appearing always to her that she had not yet begun to do good, and therefore she poured forth daily and almost continually inflamed sighs towards Almighty God, lamenting her misery in being so far removed from Him, nor could she find any comfort but in her long and fervent prayer.

Zeal for the glory of God caused Colomba to spare herself in nothing which it was in her power to do to augment it, labouring continually for this purpose; and that God might be praised in the best manner that it is possible on earth she magnanimously undertook the foundation of her monastery, which she was accustomed to call the Paradise of the Earth, happily overcoming on this occasion the most violent persecutions, like a rock in the midst of the waves. She manifested on this occasion her singular simplicity of heart, which was candid and innocent as a dove, never using words that had regard to self-interest or human respect, but having a pure intention of pleasing God alone, without caring for the praises of men. Her zeal extended itself still farther; for considering the infinite price at which souls have been redeemed, she united her wishes with the desires of her Celestial Spouse, labouring to contribute to the return of souls to the grace of God. She applied with this intention her prayers, her communions, the indulgences which she was able to gain, her macerations, her severe nightly disciplines, for the conversion of sinners and the relief of the souls in purgatory; and she visited the sick, assisted the agonizing, instructed the ignorant, and prayed for them.

But all these cares; and the various solicitudes of her great zeal for the salvation of souls, never diverted her from that lively desire to which alone her heart was entirely abandoned, of keeping herself closely united to God. This was the centre around which her charity revolved, so that she often returned and ran to the retirement of her solitude; and in this careful manner she always kept her heart pure; and her mind free from a thousand importunate ideas, which usually hinder the knowledge of God and of ourselves.

Her mind, reposing in the presence of God, and conversing interiorly with Him, soon recovered that true tranquillity and peace which is a fruit of the Holy Ghost; and as the presence of the sun disperses the clouds, this sight of God always present, joined to a movement of the heart which sweetly carried her towards Him, drove away every perturbation and kept her in perfect tranquillity. So happy a tranquillity was this that it kept her senses in continual obedience, so that even in visible and created things she could with great facility elevate her mind to God.

In fact, if she were in action, this virgin passed in an instant without perceiving it to the highest contemplation. She had no occasion to make use of reasoning to warm her heart; one word that she heard of truth, of God, of goodness, of love, sufficed to transport her to God in a moment, better than by the most sublime discourses which could be made on these matters; and in these happy moments she sometimes appeared ecstatic and motionless, sometimes extended on the ground in holy insensibility, like a cold corpse, and sometimes in holy repose. The continuation and familiarity of these ecstasies show us clearly how bright was Divine light in the breast of Colomba. Because if the Eternal Truth representing Himself to her mind filled it so completely that she could neither see nor hear other objects, it was a manifest sign that her lovely soul being clothed with the gift of intelligence, immediately penetrated and joyfully embraced eternal truths, with the same facility with which first principles are embraced; and of this it is impossible to doubt, for the gifts of the Holy Ghost working wonderfully in her, her understanding saw that which eye hath not seen.

The contemplation of Colomba was not, therefore, an idle amusement or curious speculation, but an active and penetrating operation of her love; and as the eye naturally turns whither the affections of the heart are placed, thus, the experience and delight which the holy virgin had in heavenly things, excited her to attain more than the highest knowledge could reach, and employing love instead of the lights of reason, she became an admirable mistress, not only in sanctity, but even in learning. For this reason princes, prelates of rank, cardinals, and even the Pope, had recourse to her, to consult her and discourse on affairs of great consequence and importance, discovering in the spouse of Christ a profound wisdom, which was yet more wonderful from its not being adapted to the capacity of her sex, of her age, or her condition. Her lights being drawn from pure love, made her mistress of the secrets and mysteries of God; and adding to these Divine communications the love which she conceived, and the transports which she experienced, she became a lively image of a blessed soul, for she already enjoyed a participation of eternal felicity. This caused her to feel great sorrow and torment every time she was obliged to go out or leave her contemplation. The desire for heavenly sweetness which inundated her breast moved her violently to resume her contemplation, which she would never have been willing to interrupt if nature could have borne it. Days and whole nights passed in this union with God seemed a single moment to her. Hunger, thirst, sleep, and every other action necessary to nature, not only never tormented her, but were never felt by her; for love, which made her a martyr of spiritual hunger and thirst, and repose in God alone, overcame all these things in her; thus the most painful death to Colomba was not to die; and being entirely swallowed up in divine fire, and feeling herself often melt away and liquefy like wax, she incessantly repeated, "O how beautiful is Paradise! how beautiful! I burn with love!"

    The spirit of Colomba then was a spirit entirely transformed into the spirit of God, of whom alone she thought, whom alone she loved, in whom alone she rejoiced and breathed; and therefore it is no wonder that being thus caressed by Divine love she was admitted into its secrets, predicted future things with so much facility, saw distant events as if they were present, penetrated into the secrets of hearts, arrested the stroke of death, obtained what she requested, and was in continual ecstasies and raptures. She lived in God and God lived in her, participating as far as she was capable in the beatitude of heaven. And from this blessed transformation we see the reason why Colomba lived so short a time, and why in the flower of her years she took her flight to heaven. Her actions had attained the highest degree of perfection, and therefore, according to the condition of human weakness, she could not remain long on earth in this state, but must in a short time become incapable of every action which appertained to earth. Submerged in this ocean of delights, and consumed with the ardour and flames of Divine love, she took her flight like an eagle, still higher, to contemplate more nearly the Divine Sun.

THE LIFE

OF

S. JULIANA FALCONIERI

A FLORENTINE LADY, AND FOUNDRESS OF THE THIRD ORDER OF SERVANTS OF MARY, CALLED "MANTELLATE."

BY

FRANCESCO LORENZINI

The Seven Holy Founders of the Servites

THE LIFE

OF

S. JULIANA FALCONIERI.
(1270-June 19, 1341)

CHAPTER I

WHICH SERVES AS A PREFACE TO THE LIFE.

The illustrious city of Florence was a fertile mother, not only of the sciences and liberal arts, but of the most holy souls, who, abounding in heroic virtue, are seen to shine among the first luminaries of the Catholic religion and of the Church.

This glorious city reckoned among her most illustrious families in the year 1200, that of the Falconieri, one of these who, having escaped from the ruin of the ancient Fiesole, descended to live on the banks of the Arno.

Historians relate that this family had the honourable distinction of being known in Florence by the title of *Famiglia Popolana*. And this happened, I believe, because the greater part of the people were its adherents, and were ready to act at the smallest sign from it; so that it gave great weight to the side towards which it turned; and I see no other reason why we cannot discover with any certainty from history the party to which it belonged, whether Guelph or Ghibelline, it having sometimes adhered to the one faction, and sometimes to the other; except that with its number of followers among the people, it formed, as it were, an intermediate party, which, when joined to either, made that one superior to the other. That it was so, is evident from the fact that, when wishing to appease the civil discords of the city which had arisen from the new factions of the Bianchi and Neri, it was found necessary to unite and reconcile together first some few families, and in particular the Falconieri with the Visdomini; as if the Republic were divided between these two families, and nothing could be done unless they were agreed in desiring it; thus, we read that to reconcile them it was necessary to interpose the authority of the Pope, who gave orders to Francesco de Monaldeschi, then Bishop of Florence, to negotiate the peace in the city, where, with great labour, he succeeded in establishing peace between the Falconieri and the Visdomini, as is related by l'Ammirato.

I might say a great deal of the honours enjoyed by this family in Florence, calling to mind their many respectable connexions, the duties of magistrate worthily exercised by them; and afterwards in Rome, the rank of prelates and of the grand priorships of Malta bestowed upon them. The dignity of cardinal was also well supported by Cardinal Lelio; and in our times we have seen with what untarnished justice Cardinal Alessandro behaved in the unpopular and difficult charge of governor of Rome, and with how much rectitude he exercised it, insomuch that being attacked by a serious illness while he was governor, the people flocked to his palace, grieved at the danger of losing him; and what is more surprising still, some criminals whom he had visited with salutary punishment, as he was accustomed to do, caused many masses to be

PREFACE

Bl. Alessio Falconieri (1200 – 17 February 1310),

celebrated, and visited the churches, imploring the Divine aid for their judge. But it is not my intention to relate the history of this family, the curious reader may refer to what grave authors have written regarding it; and following out my intention, I will confine myself to speak of S. Juliana's illustrious father, and of his brother the Blessed Alessio, who must be noticed to make the Life complete.

While they lived in the world, they were employed in the public affairs of their city, on account of the reputation they had gained for sense, prudence, and great dexterity in conducting business. But it is of greater consequence to know that they were both highly adorned with moral virtues, and with so much Christian piety, that one employed the greater part of his large fortune in founding churches and building monasteries, and the other attained to so great

The Santissima Annunziata

sanctity of life and manners, that with six other noble Florentines he founded the illustrious religious Order of the Servites.

There is no occasion to search for witnesses to prove the truth of what I say, for the magnificence of the church of the Santissima Annunziata, in Florence, raised from the foundations to complete perfection by her illustrious father, with the Convent, the Piazza, and all necessary ornaments, visible to every one, and praised by all, confirm the truth of my assertion.

I must briefly mention the Blessed Alessio, his brother, that I may not be induced through the interest of the subject, to pass the limits which I have prescribed to myself, on account of the short time I have had in which to put together these few papers.

I will confine myself to that which will be the most to our purpose, and it is, that the sanctity and heroic virtues of the Blessed Alessio served as an example to our Saint, to detach herself from the world and to run with rapid steps towards heaven, so that Divine Providence willed that we should see her before him honoured as a Saint on our altars, as the devotion to her was published to the Catholic Church by His Holiness Clement XII who was himself an honour to the city of Florence, and belonged to one of these families who are illustrious for antiquity and for great men, and celebrated for arms, learning, and for Saints given to the Church.

While the Blessed Alessio lived he was so much beloved and venerated by the Florentines, on account of the mild and sweet manner in which he exercised all Christian virtues, that he was considered as a father by all, and held in his hands the affections of all, and could turn their minds which way he pleased. Through his example and exhortations the city of Florence became quite changed, and almost turned into a monastery of religious men; for his virtues not only engaged, together with S. Juliana, many others of his own family to take the religious habit and to follow the path of Christ, but numbers of others besides. Amongst these we must specially remember S. Philip Benizi, who, attracted by the sweetness of his manners and by his prayers, disengaged himself completely from the world, and, assuming the religious habit of the Servites, became the first luminary of his Order, and was remarkable for so great sanctity, prudence, and learning, that he was not only raised to the dignity of General of the same, but was on the point of being raised to the chief priesthood and the headship of the universal Church, if his humility had not, by a firm, yet rare refusal, opposed itself to the wishes of the electors.

Almighty God permitted the same S. Philip Benizi to give testimony, while yet an infant in swaddling clothes, to the sanctity of the Blessed Alessio; for while Alessio was walking through Florence begging alms for the support of his religious, that Florence where, a short time before, he had been seen in the dress of his equals, exercising the first offices of the republic, the infant Philip in the arms of his nurse, hitherto unable to pronounce any word, was heard clearly and distinctly to say, "Here is the servant of Mary," and turning to his mother he added, "Give him an alms."

This greatly raised Alessio and his religious companions in the opinion of the whole city, as we may see by the pleasure which every one took in lodging them in their houses and in striving with on another to assist them by alms; but the holy man, who wished for no more from the world than would suffice to enable him to live as a servant of Jesus Christ, thanking them all, took shelter in a small house in a retired part of the city which was called Cafaggio.

Here he caused the Holy Annunciation to be painted by Bartolomeo, a foreign painter, who being perplexed at not being able to find any idea which would represent our Blessed Lady as he desired, had recourse to the Saint's prayers, that he

S. Philip Benizi (August 15, 1233 – August 22, 1285)

would obtain from God that he might be able to complete it in a worthy manner; and it is related as certain that Heaven favoured the desire of the devout painter and the prayers of the Saint, for having fallen asleep on the bridge through fatigue, he found on awaking that the picture was finished, and in such a manner that a superior Hand seemed to have brought it to perfection, as every one judges who fixes his eyes attentively upon it, for he feels himself obliged through a holy awe to restrain his too curious looks and to cast his eyes down. In the same place and in honour of the same picture Juliana's illustrious father afterwards erected that famous church which we have mentioned above, within which the little chapel which was the first abode of the founders of the Order of the Servites was enclosed.

To the testimony already adduced of the sanctity of the Blessed Alessio I will add that of one of the greatest saints of the illustrious Dominican Order, to whom the glorious grace was granted of shedding his blood in martyrdom for the Catholic faith: I mean S. Peter Martyr, to whom, when in Florence, whither he had been sent to purge it from the evil seed of heresy, at that time infesting the whole of Italy, our Blessed Lady showed the seven founders sheltered and protected under her mantle, amongst whom he clearly recognised the Blessed Alessio.

In order to give a striking proof of his gentleness and holiness, I will bring an example which is nearer to our own times, and well known to all, and it is the sweet and amiable sanctity of the great S. Philip Neri, who was also a Florentine citizen, to whom, as he was a diligent examiner and imitator of the lives of saints, the courteous and gentle manner in which Alessio recalled to the love of God souls that had gone astray in the path of the world could not be unknown; and being himself equally inflamed with the love of God and zeal for the conversion of others, we may believe that he copied in himself whatever is recorded of Alessio by historians and still more by tradition.

Now, such a man as this was the spiritual father of Juliana, and under the influence of her father's piety, who spent so much for the honour and glory of the house of God, and the admirable instructions of her uncle, a sublime master in the spiritual life, what progress would she not make, being thus stimulated and conducted on every side by example and exhortations! And certainly in the complication of so many wonders, the governing and regulating hand of the grace of God clearly appears, which besides the example of men was pleased to choose an innocent virgin to awaken piety amongst all ranks of the people, and to add to the crowd of men who in numbers received the religious habit, the concourse of women to take the same habit, moved by the example and under the guidance of Juliana, the foundress of the Order of the Mantellate. And in order to give value to this narration, let a special remembrance amongst others be given to the estimable Giovanna Corsini, who through her illustrious birth and rare virtues increased not a little the veneration of the people for the new Order.

The death of Bl. Alessio

Our Lady Queen of Martyrs, the principal devotion of the Servites

CHAPTER II

BIRTH OF S. JULIANA, AND HER MANNER OF LIFE TILL THE AGE OF FOURTEEN.

The way for the birth of our Saint having been prepared by Divine Providence in so particular and wonderful a manner, she came into the world in the year 1270, precisely at the time when her illustrious father was piously occupied in erecting the above-mentioned church. He and his wife Riguardata were advanced in years, and past the hope of having children; and it was evidently shown by the quality of the gift, that it came from heaven as a reward for the prayers and virtuous actions of the aged parents, as in one daughter was included all the good which they could desire from a numerous family of children; in the same manner as it happened to the happy parents of Samuel and S. John Baptist, who being also old and barren, became the fathers of sons, that the wonderful effects of the grace of God might be declared in them, to the great glory of the Giver and particular benefit of the world.

In her first tender years she gave signs of her future heroic virtue; and her uncle, B. Alessio, whose mind Heaven enlightened with superior discernment, foreseeing what would happen, used to tell her mother that she should continually thank God, for she had not brought forth a baby, but a pure Angel of Paradise, and that by the wonderful actions which as she increased in years she would perform, the truth of his words would be known. In fact, Juliana herself caused great surprise and confirmed our Saint's prediction; for the first words which issued from her mouth while she was yet an infant, and had never before uttered any distinct word, were the most sweet names of Jesus and Mary, articulated with so devout an expression, that it was commonly said that she must be dedicated to God.

All the actions which she performed in the years of innocence had no other end but piety and devotion, and her childish amusements were confined to building little altars with her own hands to our Blessed Lady, adorning them with flowers, in imitation of these which her father erected to the holy Virgin with extraordinary magnificence. Being come to the use of reason, she always had her holy uncle at her side, who, in exhorting her to virtue and to evangelical perfection, recalled to her continually the counsels of Christ, and inspired her soul, which was obedient to his every sign, with these salutary maxims which conduct to the height of perfect sanctity.

He wondered at the rapidity with which she brought to maturity these fruits which were not to be expected from so tender a plant, and he thanked the infinite goodness of God, who deigned to raise her to that which surpassed the strength of her youthful years. She was always far from any feminine levity; she never used any ornament that was at all vain or pompous, and her dress was regulated only by decency, not by vanity; she never in her life looked at herself in the glass, a very remarkable thing in one of her sex; and if she modestly dressed her hair, as it was proper for her to do, she concealed pins in the midst in such a manner that they pricked and tormented her head; and all the time which she took from vanity she spent in very fervent prayers, in reading spiritual books, and in singing psalms to the praise of God and of His Virgin Mother.

CHAPTER III

OF S. JULIANA'S LIFE, FROM HER FOURTEENTH YEAR TO HER DEATH.

In these, and similar exercises, having reached her fourteenth year, a dangerous age, in which natural impulses have the greatest power in us, she appeared so highly adorned with gifts of mind and body, that many noble youths desired to marry her; and her mother also, as is the custom with women, revolved in her thoughts to which of the suitors she should allot her, weighing the possessions and merits of each, and reflecting on the greater profit which would result to her house if she granted her to one rather than to another; and having fixed her mind on a rich and noble youth, of high birth, and nearly connected with her by blood, who showed greater affection for the young girl than the others, she began to try to win her daughter's consent to conclude as soon as possible her nuptials with Falco, which was the young gentleman's name. But, to her displeasure, she discovered in her daughter's mind a very different desire from that of a worldly settlement; so that, vexed by the repulse, which she did not expect, she passed from coaxing to endeavouring to compel her by these marks of tenderness which loving mothers are accustomed to use. These had only the same effect on the constancy of Juliana, who being resolved to have no other Spouse but Jesus, would not give ear to any discourse of the world, and did not

VESTIZIONE DI
S.ta GIULIANA FALCONIERI
IMMAGINE CHE SI VENERA NELLA CAPPELLA

become terrified nor yield to the tears or the violence of her mother. Riguardata being tired with her efforts, reluctantly yielded to the advice of Alessio, who persuaded her not to use force; she consented, though unwillingly, to the desires of her daughter, and allowed her to live according to her holy resolution. Seeing herself to have escaped greater snares, Juliana resolved to consecrate by vow her virginity to her celestial Spouse, which she did, and kept so well her promise, that fearing every slight fault she was never seen while she lived to look at any man in the face.

Her mind being strengthened by this generous refusal, she meditated greater things within herself; and not content with having in this manner separated herself from the world, she desired to unite herself more closely to her Spouse, and having consulted the Blessed Alessio on what she should do, she was persuaded by him to take the habit of the Servites.

No devout woman had yet taken this habit, and as it seemed that if this were done, it would tend to the glory and service of God, the Blessed Founder, in imitation of S. Francis, who a short time before had admitted S. Clare, afterwards

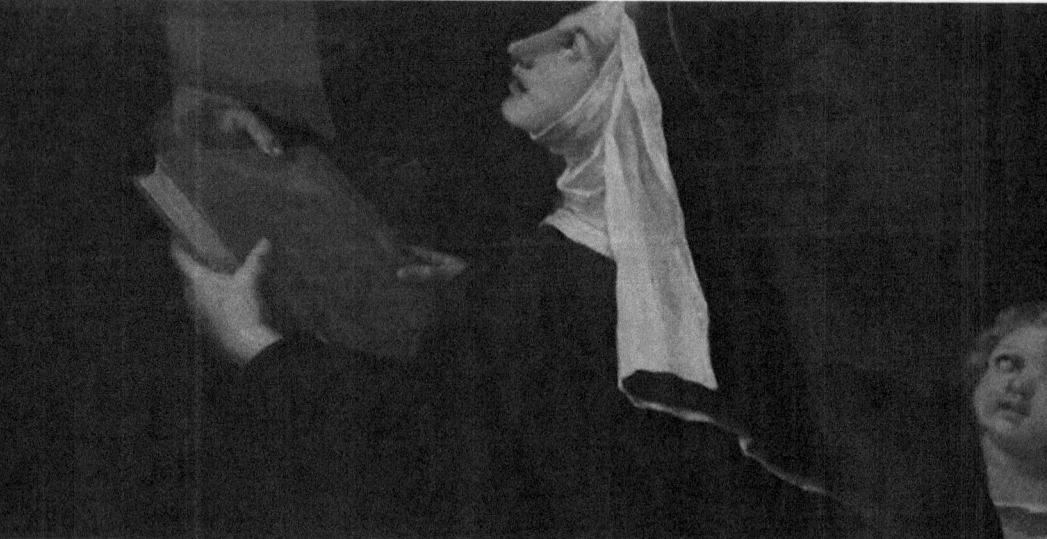

foundress of the Franciscan Nuns, into his seraphic Order, earnestly advised his niece to take it, having a firm hope that many ladies would follow her example, and by her sanctity and virtue would be perfectly taught and instructed in religious exercises. Nor was he deceived; for our Saint, inflamed with this pious desire, caused her supplications to be presented by him to S. Philip Benizi, then General of the Order, who, recognising her merit and vocation, though she was yet young, being only about fourteen, gave his consent, and in 1284 clothed her with the habit of the third Order in the Chapter which he was come to hold that year in Florence.

It would be impossible to express the joy which she felt when she saw herself clothed with this holy habit. Being made of wool, it caused sensations of pain, and reminded her of the sufferings of Christ, and of His Virgin Mother, which had always been deeply impressed on her heart, and were so identified with her soul that she seemed not to meditate on the Passion of our crucified Lord, but to carry it about with her and to be herself crucified with Him.

During the year of her novitiate, these virtues which before by a profound sense of humility she had been accustomed to hide, appeared more outwardly; for she knew that in the state wherein she was she owed much to God and to men, and that these who assume the religious habit ought, so to speak, to make a show of these virtues which others should hide; for the world expects much more from these who withdraw from its laws, than it requires from its followers.

She added very much to her usual prayers, she redoubled her fasts, disciplines, and every other sort of penance which she had formerly practised, exercising religious modesty in walking and speaking, staying little at home and much in the church, where so absorbed in pious meditations before the images of our crucified Lord and His Blessed Mother, she dissolved into tears of loving sorrow. With such exercises our Saint prepared herself in the year of her novitiate for her profession, which she was to make at its termination, and which she did make in the hands of S. Philip Benizi.

This profession, which she was the first to make, was, I believe, similar to that made by the Friars, as the third order of nuns which began with her could not yet have any formula or institute to follow, as it had after she gave rules to her nuns and founded and instituted the said Order perfectly. That she was the first to make it, is proved by the decree of the Sacred Congregation of Rites, given on the 10th September, 1718, in which we read, that the Sacred Congregation of Rites having heard, as well by word as by writing, the Reverend Father Prospero Lambertini, Promoter of the Faith, decreed that the office and mass of S. Juliana, Foundress of the Sisters of the Blessed Virgin Mary, might be granted to the whole Order of Servites of both sexes, if it seemed good to the Pope; who benignantly assented to the petition on the 24th day of the same month and year.

And here it may be of use to relate a fact which ought to place in high esteem the virtue of our Saint, through the great opinion which the same S. Philip Benizi had of her, who being one of the most conspicuous luminaries of the Church, very prudent, wise, full of learning, and glorious in his miracles, is a very worthy witness, to whom we cannot, without temerity, refuse our belief.

During the short time in which, after receiving our Saint's profession, he dwelt in Florence, he often conversed with her, giving her many spiritual instructions, and one day particularly predicting his own approaching death, he recommended to our Saint's prayers, with very earnest words, not only his spiritual daughters, but the whole Order of Servites, who were at that time in great affliction, a rumour having been spread that the Pope wished to suppress them, and that the Order of Servites was not included amongst those which had been approved; and as this oppressed the Saint very much

Bologna antica
Ritratto di Benedetto XIV - Papa Lambertini (1675-1758)

he committed the affair to her known sanctity, and to her prayers, which he knew to be very acceptable to God.

It is certainly credible, that her intercession availed with her Spouse Jesus to calm so furious a tempest, as it happened that under the government of Fra Lotaringo Stufa, successor of S. Philip, privileges and pontifical bulls were obtained, and the Servites were received among the other approved Orders, and restored to their first splendour. It appears to me without doubt, as I said above, that from thence we may draw authoritative testimony of her sanctity, greater than that which may be had elsewhere; and here it will be useful to relate the words of the Processes printed in Rome, which are, "Hence it was that S. Philip Benizi, when near his death, considering her excellent virtues and sanctity, which he also foresaw would increase more and more every day, commended to her care, not the third Order only, but the whole flourishing family of the Servites; for the man of God knew that Juliana would govern his family well, both by word and by example, and would ennoble it by her virginity." And this must appear yet more surprising to us if we reflect on the virtue and age of S. Philip, who, ripe in years, was already near death, and on the other side consider the youthful age of Juliana, still a young and tender virgin; yet so great a man recognised in her such sublime and mature virtue, that he could recommend to her a whole Order of men of holiness, learning, and tried prudence.

The holy General having taken his departure for Todi, Juliana began with great care to reduce to practice his instructions, which she had treasured up in her heart. And to speak truly, there was no sort of penance or devout exercise which she did not put in execution, nor any example of a virtuous and heroic action which she did not imitate. All that had been foretold of her, in the prophetic words of her uncle the B. Alessio, and of S. Philip Benizi, was fulfilled in her, as is expressly asserted in the first chapter of the processes.

On account of the advice given her, that she ought to

form in herself a living example of religious piety, so that her spiritual daughters might have a model to follow and imitate, she neglected no occasion of practising virtue, for "her virginity was as a garden bringing forth many fruits of sweet odour, which allured many to dedicate themselves to God in the Order of the Servites, and to become her followers amidst the lilies of purity and the mournful dolours of the Queen of virgins; and they too brought forth like fruits as obedient disciples of so accomplished a mistress." Amongst these were particularly distinguished the Blessed Giovanna Sodrini, the Blessed Francesca Cammilli, the Blessed Subilia Palmieri and Giovanna Macigni, the Blessed Agnesa and Angela Uguccioni, the Blessed Rosa of Siena, Agnesa de Vanni, Angela Tolomei, Lisabetta de' Varj, Margherita and Clara of Montepulciano, to whom we must add for her greater glory her own mother, who became her spiritual daughter, with Bilia and Guiduccia of the same family, and Francesca also of the house of Falconieri, a lady of great piety, who was so inflamed through Juliana's means by the love of God, that she gave in large alms and to benefit the poor almost all her possessions. All these, copying her examples of rare virtues and the precepts of most singular perfection, merited particular esteem and veneration from these who knew them.

In the meantime our Saint went from virtue to virtue, and added every day some new ornament to her soul: thus she was seen to pass whole days in continual prayer without growing weary, to punish her body with severe and continual disciplines, scourging herself to blood so that she fainted on the pavement; to allow but a short and painful sleep to her eyes, taking her rest on the bare ground, or at best on a rough mat; to tie tight little cords round her legs and arms, and to wear iron chains round her with sharp points turned towards the naked flesh. Her food was so sparing, that it seemed impossible it could suffice to nourish her, and she often passed two days of the Week, Wednesday and Friday, without any sort of refreshment but the Eucharistic Food, for which her appetite was insatiable, and on Saturday she only took a little bread and water; her clothes were of rough coarse cloth, even in the greatest heat of summer, and she always went barefoot in the midst of the coldest winter.

Many devout women had for some years, as we have said, lived together under the care of their mistress Juliana, and they were so numerous that they might now be gathered under closer and more regular discipline, and be formed into a very numerous monastery. It seemed that this might be successfully done at this time, for the opposition against the Order of Servites had ceased in great part, and it had been approved by an express Bull of Benedict XI, and put into good order by the General Andrea del Borgo S. Sepolcro, successor to Lotaringo; for it had been put before this in confusion, and almost scattered by the slanders of others; and, besides this, our Saint's mother, with whom she had lived till this time, had been removed by Heaven, so that she thought she could now give herself up more entirely to the good of her neighbour and the government of her disciples. All the nuns of the third Order being, therefore, called together in chapter by the General Andrea del Borgo, he made known to them the necessity which existed, in order to prevent their being dispersed, of choosing a person out of their number, whom they would recognise as their head and guide, who should have authority to add to the holy customs they had hitherto practised new ones which should be for the good of their souls, and to form laws and rules to which all should be subject who wished to live with them; and though, as superior of the Order, he might have done this himself, he nevertheless left it to their choice and judgment.

While the General spoke to this effect, the holy Juliana, though she had first taken the habit and had governed her companions till now, sat in the last place, recollected in herself, with her eyes cast down, esteeming herself the lowest and the

SANTA GIULIANA DE' FALCONIERI
VERGINE FIORENTINA.

most incapable of all. Scarcely had this proposal been heard by the devout congregation of religious women, than they cried out with one accord, without a moment's hesitation, "Let Juliana be our guide, Juliana our mistress, and we desire to obey expressly as our Prioress Juliana, whom we have hitherto by tacit consent obeyed."

It would be difficult to imagine the confusion of the humble Juliana's heart, which showed itself in her countenance when she heard these words. She changed colour, and when she could command her voice, prostrating herself on the ground before the General, with tears and sighs she endeavoured to make known her insufficiency, entreating him not to load her with a burden which she knew she had not strength enough to support: but the reasons she brought forward did not avail her at all; for the General, who had the same desire as the sisters, remembering what S. Philip Benizi had already predicted of her, obliged her to undertake the charge, and she, knowing this to be the will of God, yielded to obedience, and was elected Prioress.

When she had assumed the government in the thirty-sixth year of her age, she devoted herself entirely, with the advice of the Blessed Alessio, who was still living, to forming the rules of the Third Order, which, being afterwards collected together, were approved with Pontifical authority by Martin V; and we cannot do otherwise than piously believe, that S. Philip Benizi, who composed the Constitutions of the Friars, would, without fail, regulate the Third Order of the Sisters, for he knew that Heaven had chosen Juliana for this office of foundress.

When she had formed the rules, she began to try with all diligence to observe them rigorously, imitating Christ in this, who began to do and to teach; and on this account there was no one who had difficulty in observing them, but all strove with one another in fulfilling their common obligations with so much religious exactness, that they made the city of

Florence, which was then full of quarrels and scandals, and occupied with anything but religion, stand in astonishment, looking on them with horror and remorse of conscience, so that the most vicious, comparing their irregular manner of life with the piety of the sisters began to detest their corrupt habits.

The great prudence with which she exercised her government, and the love which her companions had for her, are clearly apparent from the increase of the Third Order under her guidance, and from her having remained in the office of Prioress till near the end of her life, when she was obliged by grievous infirmity to relinquish her charge; nor could we expect otherwise from a soul in which all virtues jointly were enthroned. This will be easily proved if we consider the ardent zeal with which she instructed her subjects, exhorting them to the exact observance of the laws of God and the Church; and also the devotion and veneration which she had herself persuaded others to bear towards all the mysteries of the Christian religion, and in particular to the Incarnation, the Birth of Christ, and His most Sacred Passion, on which she meditated continually with great tenderness. This was manifested at the end of her life, when with burning desire she sought to be united to Jesus in His Divine Sacrament, and by the figure of the crucifix which was found imprinted on her breast after death, from which circumstances we perceive her heroic faith; and also her firm hope of receiving these rewards promised by God through His infinite mercy, shown by her contempt for earthly alliances, for riches, and for everything prized by the world; her courage in embracing arduous and difficult undertakings, such as the foundation of religious orders, with great generosity and constancy in conducting them to the desired end; supporting with humility, patience, and equal resignation of mind, labours, sickness, and in particular the very painful infirmity which accompanied her to her death; her austere manner of life and the severe penances by which she afflicted her body, fasting, disciplining herself, and wearing continually besides the hair-shirt, pricking chains on her bare flesh, as we have already said, her body being found after death quite livid and marked with the strokes she every day gave herself.

Her hope having reached this heroic degree, could not be separated from charity, by which she loved God so intensely that she was never seen to desire anything but His glory, often turning towards Him with words of tenderness, and these prayers that are called "ejaculatory," being often accustomed to repeat, "No one shall take from my heart my crucified Love" and in the disputes which she had with the devil, she was sometimes heard to say, "Lord, Satisfy this fierce enemy, and throw me into hell; if I perish, at least I shall not have offended Thee." Through this ardent love she was often raised while meditating and praying into very sweet and wonderful ecstasies, by which her loving God consoled her, giving her a foretaste of that delight which the blessed experience in heaven.

This charity appeared very perfect in her through the promptitude and cheerfulness with which she always laboured in the service of God, and for the assistance and love of her neighbour employed every means to bring souls to God and convert sinners. Who, and how many they were, I will not now mention; I will only speak of the great pleasure she felt when it was related to her that S. Philip Benizi had converted two well-known public sinners in Todi, and induced them to take the habit of the Third Order of Servites; and also of the consolation she experienced in hearing other conversions of sinners wrought by the same Saint spoken of by her blessed uncle, when she melted into tears of tenderness and joy; and, on the other hand, her grief and affliction at the death of S. Philip, because he was so useful and profitable for the salvation of souls, the preservation of which in innocence, and purity she desired above all things; and of whose falling

into sin she had so great a hatred and horror, that hearing an offence against Almighty God once related, she fell down suddenly and fainted; indeed, she shuddered and trembled every time she heard the name only of sin. She added to this solicitude and desire for the spiritual good of her neighbours, an ardent wish to succour them in their temporal wants, and therefore she spent all she had in giving large alms to help the poor, and she even took off her own clothes to give them to poor girls who through want were in danger of losing their virtue.

She visited and served the sick in the hospitals, and to overcome the disgust which one usually feels on these occasions, she ate the miserable fragments of their scanty meal, and what is more surprising, and will perhaps disgust the too delicate, she was sometimes seen to suck the putrid blood from the wounds of the sick, and Almighty God showed how pleasing this action was to Him by the cure which these soon received to whose wounds her lips had been applied. We read similar examples of other saints nearer to our times, which are much thought of and esteemed; it will be sufficient to cite the admirable S. Mary Magdalen of Pazzi, also the glory of Florence and country-woman of our Saint, and whose sublime actions we may say have been modeled upon the pattern of Juliana, who had long before sown the illustrious seeds of true sanctity in the hearts of the Florentine women, which being successively propagated from one to another have rendered Florence at all times fertile in holy souls.

Besides these virtues a singular prudence appeared in her, by which she regulated her whole life, choosing in her tender years the state of virginity, which she kept untarnished to her death, and poverty, with all other works appertaining to the service of God. This prudence was very well known to all, and was the cause of her being elected Prioress and appointed to form the rules of her Order, and rendered her worthy to have the whole Order of Servites recommended to her by S. Philip Benizi, and to be persuaded by him to accept in his time the superintendence, and after Father Andrea del Borgo was made General, the government of the Sisters, in which she was confirmed till near her death with universal satisfaction, and by which as many beautiful fruits were yielded to the Catholic religion as there were souls who by following her maxims and advice lived and died holily.

What shall we say of the justice with which she most vigilantly watched over the observance of the Divine precepts, avoiding even the least occasion of sin, an evident sign of great interior piety, which produced in her fervent devotion towards God, the Blessed Virgin, and the Saints, and caused her to assist at the Divine Office, and to recite the Canonical Hours carefully, occupying herself in the intervals in contemplation of the Divine Mysteries. By this she was moved to show reverence to all these to whom the Church commands us to pay reverence and obedience; maintaining unspotted chastity, poverty, and obedience, and being most zealous that every one else should embrace these virtues; desiring the sisters to wear the sleeves of the habit covering their hands, so careful was she regarding purity. Poverty was so dear to her, that being very rich she refused to receive her paternal inheritance or even enough for her necessary subsistence, which she procured by the labour of her hands, dividing it with the other sisters; and she loved obedience so much, that when she reluctantly undertook the office of Superior, as well as after she renounced the charge, she showed herself in all things submissive and obedient to others.

Nor was her heroic fortitude less than the above-named virtues, for with invincible courage she "gained always a victory and glorious triumph over the flesh, the world, and the devil," supporting generously and with great joy and content the painful infirmities which she suffered continually, and the poor, austere, and rigorous manner of life which she had chosen, keeping her soul and her countenance in great tranquillity; and this virtue was confirmed in her by a singular temperance, by which she had imposed a restraint on her passions. There shone forth wonderfully in her an angelical purity, an admirable modesty, a rare sobriety, and a singular humility, which is sufficiently proved by what we have already said.

CHAPTER IV

OF S. JULIANA'S HAPPY DEATH.

It remains now for me to speak of her most happy death. She had attained the age of seventy-four, in the year of our Lord 1341. By her continual penances and fasts she had brought her stomach to such a state that through great weakness and nausea it could not retain food, and if she did digest a little, it became converted into bad and hurtful nourishment; so that the physicians, knowing her illness to be mortal, despaired of every human remedy, pronouncing her already near death. Juliana at this news, losing nothing of her accustomed cheerfulness, but on the contrary becoming more joyous, as if she did not feel her weakness, rejoiced greatly, and could truly say, *"Laetata sum in his, qua dicta sunt mihi in domum Domini ibimus,"* hearing, as it were, the walls of the prison which kept her soul in confinement and prevented it from taking flight towards God, cracking and breaking down around her.

Her companions were sad and sorrowful to see themselves so near losing their mother; but she, who sighed for the embraces of her Divine Spouse, consoled them, and entreated them to rejoice with her at her approaching departure, by means of which she hoped to be eternally united to God. The malady increased so exceedingly, that few minutes longer of life could be promised. She kept herself most closely united to her Crucified Love, and to our Blessed Lady of Dolours,

and moderated her own pains with the remembrance of the most bitter agony of our Saviour on the cross, keeping her eyes fixed and immoveable on His image.

On one account she was inconsolable, and this was, that being in the habit of refreshing herself several times in the week with the Eucharistic Food, it was not granted to her in the last moments of her life, on account of her continual nausea, to receive Jesus in His Divine Sacrament: her confessor, and these who surrounded her bed, comforted her, and told her to remember the dereliction of which the same Divine Jesus complained on the cross, when He exclaimed, "*Deus meus, Deus meus, ut quid dereliquisti me,*" entreating her to acquiesce in the Divine Will, and to offer these same desires to our Lord, by which she might in part satisfy her mind, as she could do no more. The Saint being tranquilized by their words, and having received with signs of humility and resignation the Sacrament of Extreme Unction, turned, as it is related, to the other side of her little bed; and overcoming with great delight the torments of her agony, she began to entertain herself in sweet colloquies with her guardian angel, begging his assistance; and to call to mind the sorrows of our Blessed Lady, in memory of which she wore the habit of the Servites; remembering also the precious and happy death of the Blessed Alessio her uncle; who was visited at this last hour by angels in the form of white doves, and by Jesus Himself under the appearance of a very beautiful Infant, who crowned him with a charming odoriferous garland of flowers of Paradise; and dwelling a little on this last thought, she again broke out into sighs and sobs, grieving that she could not at least satisfy her eyes, since nothing more was allowed her, with the sight of Jesus in His Adorable Sacrament; she was afflicted, and earnestly begged to see Him, saying that death would be very bitter to her, if the Sacred Host were not first brought near her bed.

The wish of our Saint appeared good to Father Giacomo; director of the nuns, and to the others, and wishing to give her this last spiritual consolation, they caused the Sacred Host to be brought into her presence, in looking at which, all on fire with a most ardent love, she several times tried to leap from her bed and to prostrate herself before It, but her weakness did not allow it, to her great sorrow. She however gained sufficient strength,—for what cannot an ardent love effect?—to succeed in throwing herself out of bed and stretching herself on the floor in the form of a cross humbly adoring her God. At that moment her pallid countenance, emaciated by her long and painful sickness, recovered its colour and beauty, so that her face seemed like that of an angel, and on it was expressed that intense desire which she had to feed upon this Heavenly Bread, not being allowed to partake of it; but as it is the property of love not to be satisfied till it attains the full possession of the beloved object, she began to think of all the means by which she might satisfy her desires, and she entreated the minister of God to bring the Divine Jesus so near that she might at least gratify herself by giving Him a most humble kiss, but the Priest would not allow it; she begged him again to place for a short time the Sacred Particle on her breast, that her heart might receive some refreshment from its vicinity to Jesus, with whom it earnestly desired to unite itself. Her tears, and the affecting manner in which she asked this favour, and above all things, the knowledge of her many virtues, and of the love which inflamed her, which caused him to esteem her a living temple of the Holy Ghost, induced the good priest to grant her this last favour; and having washed her breast, she caused a veil to be placed upon it, and over that the corporal on which the priest placed the Sacred Host. Scarcely had he placed It on the chaste breast of the loving virgin, than languishing with love, and collecting, the small remains of her strength to speak, she exclaimed, " O my sweet Jesus!" and in saying this she sweetly and quietly expired. But O wonder! in drawing

her last breath the most Sacred Host disappeared from her breast, and could no more be seen by the bystanders, so that they fully believed that as Jesus under the veil of the Host had comforted her in her passage, and defended her against the assaults of the enemy, so He accompanied her to heaven, to reward her with the two crowns of virginity and martyrdom, for what she had suffered in her long and painful illness.

When the surprise had passed away a little, which for a long time held the bystanders in astonishment at the wonderful passage of our Saint, and the sighs and tears had partially ceased, with which, prostrate on the ground around the holy corpse, they bathed its hands and feet, grieving that they had lost their mother, their mistress, the support and the guide of their Order, they began to lay out and wash the body according to custom. When they took off the habit, and came to the sharp hair-shirt which even in dying she would not lay aside, their wonder increased on seeing a severe and heavy iron girdle, which from having been long tightly drawn round her sides had gone so deeply into her flesh that it scarcely showed to others what it was. All redoubled their tears in considering

Her relics as venerated in Santissima Annunziata in Florence

Juliana's severity towards herself, but more than the others her beloved disciple, Giovanna Soderini, a perfect imitator of her virtues, not being able to bear her inward distress threw herself in tears with her face on the breast of the corpse, and, O new wonder! which seemed to exceed all preceding ones, she saw in the very place where the Sacred Host had been placed a little before, a sign in the form of a seal, on which was represented to the life a crucifix, which seemed to resemble the Host, a very evident proof how dear to the Saint while living was the memory of the Passion of Jesus, as she merited by her deep contemplations to have her body signed even after death with the sign of man's redemption.

These two wonderful miracles of the Blessed Sacrament and the crucifix, which occurred almost together, being made known, brought all Florence to see and venerate the holy corpse, which wrought many wonders through the merits of the blessed soul, curing of many infirmities those who touched it with faith and recommended themselves to her intercession. It was afterwards accompanied with pomp to the Church of the Annunziata, and placed after the accustomed Offices in the chapel belonging to her family, and her grave being afterwards venerated, many prodigies wrought by Almighty God were seen, and may yet be witnessed.

The reader will remember that as in the famous instances of S. Bernard interrupting his mass to work a miracle, and of S. Clare of Assisi carrying the monstrance, so in this of S. Juliana, both the priest and the Saint were acting under a special motion of the Holy Ghost, as is plain from the miracle which followed in all the three cases.

F.W.F.

CHAPTER V

OF THE MIRACLES AND GRACES GRANTED BY GOD, THROUGH THE INTERCESSION OF S. JULIANA.

Much would remain to be related if I wished to enumerate one by one the miracles and graces which Almighty God has been pleased to grant to these who have invoked and still invoke in their necessities the intercession of S. Juliana; but to avoid prolixity I will only mention a few, just as they come before me, collected from the processes and the Statements of the witnesses; and we will begin by several which happened in the ancient city of Pisa, whose citizens were very devout to our Saint, and in order to experience continually the good effects of her protection, chose her for one of their holy protectors.

On the 7th of December, 1715, in Pisa, Father Orazio Fortunato Riminaldi, of the Order of Servites, returning towards dusk with the other fathers from the Exposition of the most Blessed Sacrament in the church of their Order, was seized at a few steps' distance from the altar with a violent fit of apoplexy, which depriving him of his strength and the use of his senses, left him as a dead man. He was carried by the fathers who were with him into the nearest room, where a vein was opened by order of the physicians, by which remedy his head being relieved he opened his eyes, which he had kept closed, and astonished to find himself in this room with so many religious and physicians round him, not remembering what had happened, he tried to rise from bed, but could not succeed, for his left side still remained paralysed, and though the remedies were again applied he gained nothing more than we have said already, and continued thus for six months, until the skill of the medical men was exhausted.

Despairing at last of all human remedies, he had recourse to these of Heaven, and the festival of S. Juliana, to whom he was very devout, being at hand, he resolved to implore her intercession. "On the morning of our Saint's feast I went to her altar with great difficulty," these are his own words, "leaning on a stick, to celebrate mass, the chalice having been brought for me to the altar; and when I came to the first memento, I asked, with great faith, through the merits of our S, Juliana, this favour of God, that He would vouchsafe to help me; and in a moment I felt my left side, which had been, as it were, bound, set at liberty, and I immediately set my foot to the ground, which I had not been able to do before, and after feeling a little pain from this disengagement, I found myself perfectly cured."

In 1711, Maria Maddalena Cittadelli, wife of Doctor Benedetto Spina, in Pisa, who had been five months in the state of pregnancy, hearing that her mother was dying, felt excessive grief, which had a very bad effect upon her in that state, and not being able to eat or sleep, she became so weak that she could not support herself on her feet, and was obliged to lie in bed the greater part of the time. Besides this, losing the warmth of her body, she continually felt an icy coldness, which made her fear that she would die in childbirth. In the midst of this affliction she recollected the many miracles which she had heard that Almighty God had wrought at S. Juliana's intercession, and, taking courage, she strongly recommended herself to her; and if she would obtain this favour for her from God, she made a vow to wear for a year the habit of the Servites, and to make the Seven Fridays in her honour, a devotion which women in this situation are accustomed to practise. Her strength continued to diminish till she arrived at the eighth month, and on S. Andrew's day she felt new pains, which gave reason to believe that she was near bringing forth her child.

The nurse, seeing she had not strength to bring it into the world, already despaired of her life and that of the child, and the more so because, as she did not feel the usual pains of childbirth, it was a sign that the infant was already dead. She remained in this state two hours; at last she fainted, and returning to herself from her swoon, she said, "If God and S. Juliana do not assist me, all is over," and she extended her arms in the attitude of prayer, recommending herself to the Saint. A quarter of an hour had not elapsed from the time of her making this prayer, when, without feeling any pain, she was suddenly delivered, to the astonishment of the nurse, who, taking up the infant, found it had been dead some days.

After her delivery, when fears were justly entertained for her life, before an hour had passed she recovered her colour and her strength, and became quite well without any human remedy, declaring that she had never had an easier delivery than this; for on the other occasions when she had happily brought forth her children, she had felt pain for some days after, and in this case, which was thought fatal, no sooner was she delivered than she was well, which was judged to have happened miraculously by the intercession of S. Juliana, as the physicians attested in the Process.

In 1712, Sister Angela Gattai, a lay sister in the monastery of S. Giovannino at Pisa, who had been ill for about six weeks of a very severe and incurable asthma, came on the 31st of March to the wicket for communion, where the father confessor, who was waiting for her, touched her head with the relic of S. Juliana, while she invoked her protection, and after a short prayer she was entirely cured, and never has felt any return of the malady up to the time when I write. This was attested by Dr. Pabretti, the physician, to have happened miraculously, and he gave as his reason that it took place in the greatest height of the disease, and when every medicine used to cure her had been fruitless, and even hurtful to the invalid.

In January 1712, Sister Angela Teresa Fabbroni, a nun in the monastery of S. Benedict, at Pisa, who had suffered for twenty months from a cough, convulsions, and other most violent symptoms, had recourse to S. Juliana's assistance; and Sister Cherubina Bocca, at that time Abbess, applying to her forehead the relic of the Saint, she was entirely cured, and was never afterwards subject to this disease.

In the same monastery of S. Benedict, Sister Felice Fortunate Sardi, having two large wounds in her left side, occasioned by the long disciplines she gave herself, concealed them through modesty, and at last by the remedies she secretly adopted they healed, and when they were closed the good religious resumed her usual exercises of penance; but one day disciplining herself to blood with a scourge full of sharp iron points, she again tore open these scars, which caused her very great pain, and she derived no help from her usual remedies. One night, about five months after, she began to feel so much pain that she thought she was going into convulsions, and not being willing to make it known, she had recourse to S. Juliana, and having placed upon her side a little cotton in which one of her relics had been wrapped, she fell asleep; on awaking in the morning she felt no pain, and examining the wounds found them dry and clean, as also the cotton, which bore no appearance of having been placed over putrid wounds, and these were so perfectly closed that even the scars did not appear.

The same religious in 1712, having attained the age of forty, had been ill for fifteen years, seven of which she had spent in bed with fever, convulsions, contraction of the nerves, and bleeding from the mouth about twice a week. On the 16th of

January she felt herself worse than usual, so that she moved to compassion all the nuns in the convent, who despaired of her life; and having sent to call the Father Confessor, Fra Luigi Maria Garbi, of the Order of Servites, that he might come and bring with him the relic of S. Juliana, as he had promised to do when she should be taken with very dangerous symptoms. The good religious hurried thither; and scarcely had he touched with the relic of the Saint the forehead and throat of the sick person, than the severe convulsions which agitated her ceased, and at the same moment she felt her soul filled with interior joy, and rising immediately with vigour, she sat up in bed, and joyfully cried out, " I am cured!" and she would have quitted it if the Abbess had not forbidden it; and, causing the relic to be left in her room, she occupied herself for a long time during the following night in thanking the Saint for the favour received. Towards the break of day, beginning to meditate on the benefits of God and her own ingratitude in not corresponding to them, a lady appeared to her brilliantly shining from the breast upwards, so that confused by fear and dazzled by the brightness, she could not discern the lineaments of the face. She saw, however, that she was invested with a black scapular, and being afraid, she was going to make the sign of the cross, fearing it was some diabolical illusion; but at the same time the lady spoke, telling her not to fear, for it was she who the evening before had cured her of her obstinate and incurable sickness, and had appeared to her for her greater consolation, and to exhort her to be fervent in the service of God, and to spend some time every day in meditating on the Passion of Jesus Christ; having thus spoken, while the good religious prostrate on the ground extended her hand to take hold of and kiss her habit, she disappeared; and she, consoled and perfectly cured, went the next morning to the choir to perform her devotions, to the astonishment of all the nuns.

Another wonderful miracle happened to the same person;

for she perceived that a very sweet smell issued from the relic left in her room, which not only strengthened her body, but seemed to give interior pleasure to her soul, and the same odour was perceived by the Abbess and the other nuns. The confessor being informed of it, caused the relic to be brought to him, and, surprised at the odour which issued from it, and not certain whether it was supernatural or not, placed it for a trial in another box, which had rather a disagreeable smell than otherwise, nevertheless, the smell increased very much; still not satisfied, he plunged it into water and washed it, but, instead of diminishing, it increased so much that it became spread over the monastery, a miracle worthy of more than ordinary consideration.

Francesco Parabosco, a surgeon in the city of Pisa, in 1711, having been seriously ill for twenty-six successive days, till near the 26th of July, of a sore throat, which prevented him from taking any food but a little broth, and the malady increasing one day so as to cause his life to be despaired of, as he could no longer swallow anything, he had recourse to S. Juliana, and having received from the Servite Fathers some water in which her relic had been infused, he drank it, and, turning to his wife, exclaimed, "I am cured!" and after that time he ate very well, being freed in a moment from his malady.

Maria Maddalena, named dell'Uomo dell'Armi, in Pisa, on the 2nd of April, 1711, caused herself to be conducted to church, not being able to go alone on account of several very severe and incurable wounds in her legs and knees, and being exhorted by her confessor to recommend herself to S. Juliana, she invoked her protection, and returned home alone after a few minutes, cured and healed, without requiring anyone to support her.

Maria Maddalena Tartini, a girl of twelve years of age, had her eye swollen to the size of an orange, and through the sharpness of the pain which tormented her day and night she lost her sight; and the physician Chelluzzi having used every means to cure her, left her as being incurable. Her mother, who was singularly devout to S. Juliana, had recourse to her protection, and at the same time that she was praying before the altar, her daughter was perfectly cured to the wonder of every one.

Maria Elisabetta, daughter of Paolo Ricci, who was ill of a violent fever at the age of five years, taking some powdered rose leaves which had touched the relics of S. Juliana, was instantly cured. Caterina Angela, another daughter of Paolo Ricci, having been eight months pregnant, weakened by a long fever to the last extremity, after having tried many remedies, and been bled several times without fruit, having at last taken a little of the powder, recommended herself to the Saint, and found herself immediately cured. Another Caterina, wife of the coachman of Leone Strozzi, by taking a little of the same powder, was happily delivered, after having been two days in severe pains of labour, insomuch that there were no more hopes for her or the child.

In the year 1678, on the 23rd of December, Maria, daughter of Giovanni Rossi, being in the garden of Boboli, a villa of the Duke of Tuscany, and suffering from a painful infirmity in one of her feet, which had caused her severe pain for twelve years, without any hope of remedy, being given up by the physicians and surgeons, who had abandoned her, turned with her whole heart to pray to S. Juliana, that she would obtain her the favour of her cure, and at the same time that she sent forth her prayer the pains ceased, and she found herself completely cured.

Annibale Orsi da Guistello, anointing his neck with oil from the lamp which burned before the image of S. Juliana, was freed from a painful infirmity which tormented and disfigured it, and returned so perfectly cured that no vestige of this painful affliction remained. The same Annibale having a dangerous flow of blood from his nostrils, which continued for two hours, having used without success the most powerful remedies which were judged proper for his cure, at last, anointing his nostrils with the same oil, and invoking the Saint's protection, the bleeding stopped immediately, and he was freed from it then and for the rest of his life.

Giuseppe, the son of Francesco Fornici, was at the age of thirteen brought to the last extremity by a very violent fever, and having received the Holy Viaticum and Extreme Unction, and nearly lost the use of his senses, he was already at the point of death, when his mother, who tenderly loved him, was persuaded by two religious of the Order of Servites, who were present, to have recourse to S. Juliana's intercession; and scarcely were a few prayers recited before the dying youth suddenly opened his eyes, and he was heard to speak as a man in health; this happened in Rome on the 6th August, 1692; and on the 15th of the same month, having relapsed into a worse state, he was again cured by the application of the relics of the Saint; on the 18th he was a third time seized by the same illness, to which were added two malignant swellings, which nearly suffocated him and prevented him from taking the least portion of food, so that he was declared incurable by the physicians, who quite despaired of his life. His mother, who had twice experienced the value of superhuman remedies, had again recourse with firm confidence to S. Juliana for the third time, and imploring her assistance received the favour of her son's life, whose cure was attested on oath by Signor Angelo Modio, the physician in attendance, to be miraculous.

Giovan Battista Berlicioni of Pontedera in the Sanese, about the year 1711, not being able to eat for severe pains in the stomach, which had afflicted him for some years, invoked the help of the Saint, and causing his breast to be touched by her relic, was instantly cured. The same person in the year 1714, being seized with a long vomiting of blood which issued abundantly from his mouth, and with a severe pain in his chest, having thrown up at last blood to the weight of thirteen pounds, was given over by the physicians, and having received the Sacraments of the Church, with the exception of the Blessed Eucharist, on account of this vomiting, he prepared himself for death. In the meantime, a Servite Father arrived with the relic of S. Juliana, which being placed on his breast, while he invoked her help, he suddenly felt the internal pain of his chest cease, and having taken a mouthful of food at the same time, not being able to swallow it he was obliged, with great difficulty and with severe convulsions of the stomach, which were calculated to provoke the vomiting of blood, to throw it up again, with a mouthful of pure water without any mixture of blood, seeing which he began to cry out, " A miracle! a miracle!' and it was also believed by all to be a miracle, for from that moment the vomiting ceased, the blood stopped, and the invalid was immediately cured; and he would have gone out to his business at the very time, as he attests, feeling himself strong, if the physician, who took leave of him the following day, had not advised him to keep quiet for a few days out of precaution.

I must not omit to relate one very remarkable instance, as it happened to a person very worthy of belief, much thought of and esteemed for his exemplary life and his sanctity, and this was Padre Fra Tommaso of Spoleto, a priest and religious of the Reformed Observantines in the Convent of S. Francesco a Ripa in Rome, and who passed to a better life only a few years ago. The following is drawn from the account which the same father published on oath and deposed in the Process, quoted almost in his own words:

He had been troubled by a long infirmity, declared by the physicians to be consumption, which, after some time reduced him to the last extremity, and resigned to the will of God he expected nothing but death. He had a great devotion to S. Juliana, and being exhorted at this time to recommend himself to God, that through the merits of this Saint He would vouchsafe to cure him, he felt a lively confidence arise in his heart that he should be cured by means of her intercession. He desired therefore to see his confessor, Father Fra Daddiodato, a religious of the same Order, of whom he requested something to drink, and his confessor took to him some iced barley-water, into which he had grated a little of the relic of the Saint, and he drank it with devotion and an assured hope of recovering his health. Although his stomach had been so irritated that it could no longer retain anything, he however kept this down with a little difficulty, and towards midnight drank a similar draught from the hands of the same Father Daddiodato, which he also retained.

Father Daddiodato then leaving him he fell asleep, and in a dream saw before him for the third time a lady dressed in a black monastic habit, whom he had seen at two other times during the course of his illness, and whom he believed to be S. Juliana herself; she made the sign of the cross on him with her hand, on the breast near the heart, from which touch he felt very great pain, and at the same time heard her tell him that he should not be so incredulous, or so reluctant to do the will of God, which words aroused in him the feeling already imprinted by what the same lady had said in a previous vision, that the will of God was not contrary to that of the Blessed, nor that of the Blessed to the will of God.

The pain caused by this touch awoke him from sleep before day, and he found himself cured, thanking God and S. Juliana for the benefit received, and grieving not a little for his past incredulity and diffidence. When day was come he asked the religious who was present in his room for his Breviary, and rising to sit on his bed began to say the Divine Office, free from all disease, a great weakness alone remaining. Father Daddiodato soon arrived, to whom he related all that had happened to him in his dream, and the pain which the touch of the hand had left, affirming that excepting this pain he found himself free from fever and from all the pains he had previously suffered. Then Father Daddiodato uncovering his chest, and not finding any vestige of a swelling, said that the pain might easily proceed from an internal cause; but diminishing by little and little it ceased entirely towards mid-day.

Father Daddiodato had not left his room when the physician Lopez arrived, who seeing him thus sitting on the bed, made a gesture of astonishment, and said to him, "I find you alive when I expected to find you dead.' adding that he had found him the preceding day with the remains of life centred in his breast, and already expiring, the other parts of the body being cold and no hope of life remaining; then feeling his pulse and his head, he asserted that the patient was in better health than the physician. When he was gone Fra Tommaso asked to communicate again, first making his confession to Father Daddiodato, and when the most Blessed Sacrament was brought, he rose from his bed and went to the door of his cell, where on his knees he received it. He would have gone to church had not obedience prohibited it. For the three following days, according to the order of his superiors, he remained part of the time up and part in bed, to regain his strength. On the Sunday morning he went to the church of S. Marcello, and said Mass there in thanksgiving to Almighty God and to S. Juliana, and from the time when, as we have said, he was cured, he continued long in good health, through the help given him by his Great Benefactress.

THE LAST CHAPTER

WHICH SERVES AS AN EPILOGUE.

From the few things briefly related above regarding the life of S. Juliana Falconieri, there is no doubt that whoever attentively considers their substance can do no less than humble himself before the Divine Goodness and say aloud, *"Mirabilis Deus in Sanctis suis;"* and we shall again repeat *"Mirabilis Deus,"* if we turn to the consideration of the unhappy state of the times, which, particularly in 1270, when our Saint was born, and in 1341, when she passed to our Lord, disturbed Italy, and especially Florence, rent on all sides by civil discord, ambition, envy, and finally heresy, with its proud ignorance and false doctrines; at which time the Divine Mercy caused this lily of purity to spring up amidst the thick thorns of the world, to recall by her example to the hearts of men that virtue which they had banished, that religion which they had blotted out, and that God whom they had little less than forgotten.

A beautiful spectacle certainly it is to see at that time almost a whole family separate itself from the commerce of universal wickedness, renouncing hopes, pleasures, riches, and the world, and devoted entirely to God, following virtue in the face of vice and triumphant error, and this not merely for their own good and utility, but for the salvation of their neighbour, suffering a thousand vexations to save the souls of others, spending whole fortunes in founding religious orders and monasteries and churches for them, and calling back from the way of perdition deluded souls, collecting them in monasteries to do penance, renewing to them all the most lively and admirable examples of perfection which the greatest saints of the Church have left us, and which after them hundreds of other holy souls have perfectly copied, by whom our true Faith has been so greatly adorned in the last ages.

Anna Caterina Gonzaga

And in order to know that such was the perfection of our Saint, it is only necessary to consider her great contempt for herself, and the ardent love of God and her neighbour which inflamed her, two things which when they exist without obstacle in a soul, raise her to that height beyond which the limit of circumscribed human power cannot mount. And what can be a greater sign of the love of God, than at the mere mention of sin, and the offence of His Divine Majesty, not only to tremble and be horrified, which would not be little, but even to lose her senses and fall fainting to the ground, as we have said it happened to Juliana at the mere mention of the word "sin"? And what greater proof of love can we have, than that which our Divine Lord vouchsafed to give her in the last moments of her life, when in His Divine Sacrament He was pleased to enter her heart in a new manner, and separating her lovely soul by a wonderful liberation from her innocent body, to take her with Him to enjoy that reward which He has prepared in Heaven for these who love Him?

If it had pleased the Almighty that their religious contemporaries should have had as much desire to register and transmit to us, for the edification of posterity, distinct memorials of the holy actions of their companions, as they had to perform their own actions well and holily, we should have found out in her the most noble and sublime examples which can be proposed for the imitation and profit of pious and devout persons. Nevertheless, the lively tradition of her merits has been kept up for little less than four whole centuries, and is increasing greatly; and the general desire of seeing her canonized on the altars has been gratified, and the monasteries of her Order multiplied, awaking to the love of her holy institute a great number of chaste virgins and respectable matrons, who have greatly advanced in the spiritual life by walking in her footsteps.

Paul V

It will not be remote from our purpose to name here the celebrated monasteries founded in Innsbruck, by the piety of the Archduchess of Austria, Anna Caterina Gonzaga, widow of the Archduke Ferdinand, who in one of the three monasteries which she caused to be sumptuously built collected the cloistered religious of the first rigid observance, in the other cloistered nuns, and in the third nuns of the Third Order. Taking the religious habit in the latter, with the name of Anna Juliana, she obtained from Paul V the Brief and Approbation of the Constitutions of her nuns, and procured from Maddalena, Archduchess of Austria and Grand Duchess of Tuscany, a relic of the Saint, which, placed in a very rich reliquary, she exposed to public veneration in the church of her monastery where she ended her life. The example of this pious mother was followed by her daughter, who renouncing with Christian fortitude not only her paternal fortune, but the hand of the King of Spain, who sought her in marriage, took also the habit of the Third Order in the above-named monastery.

In honour of the Saint, and to complete this work, it will

be necessary to make a short summary of the acts of the canonization, and I will make use of words extracted from the papers of the Congregation of Sacred Rites, which are as follows:— The fame of her sanctity and miracles increasing day by day, Pope Clement IX of holy memory, signed in 1667 the order for the introduction of the cause of her canonization,

Clement IX

in order to discover with more caution her virtues and habits, and in 1673, at the instance of Cardinal Azzolini of illustrious memory, it was discussed on the 9th and 23rd of July, whether devotion should be allowed, and a new Process being made in Florence in 1678, the devotion was confirmed. In 1698, on the 10th and 17th of October, Innocent XII granted to the whole Order of Servites and to the city of Florence leave to celebrate Mass and the common Office of virgins, " *'sub Ritu Semiduplici,'* " which afterwards in 1710, on the 8th of September, His Holiness Clement XI of holy memory, raised, "*ad Ritum duplicem,*" because he acknowledged her as the foundress of the Third Order of Servites named "Mantellate."

In the meantime the cause being maturely discussed in the Sacred Congregation of Rites, it was decreed by Benedict XIII of holy memory, in 1725, "*Ita constare de virtutibus ejus Theologalibus and*

Innocent XII

Cardinalibus ut tuto procedi possit ad discussionem miraculorum," and in 1728, on the 20th of March, the same Pontiff approved the proper lessons with the hymn and the prayer; and on the 7th of August in the same year he caused the name of the Blessed Juliana to be inserted with eulogy in the Roman Martyrology.

Clement XI

Things being by degrees subjected to examination, as is the custom, in the same Sacred Congregation, on the 8th of September, the Feast of the Nativity of the Blessed Virgin, in 1729, Benedict XIII of holy memory, approved four out of the nine miracles proposed in full congregation, and published the decree of canonization.

In conclusion, I turn towards you, O holy Virgin, who so well knew how to correspond to the inspirations of Divine Grace, and by the contempt of yourself and of fading and transitory things have merited so sublime a degree of glory in Paradise, that throughout the space of an immeasurable eternity you will enjoy in the vision of infinite Goodness that beatitude which no force can ever take from you or diminish; earnestly entreating you to receive these few lines, written, although hastily, in your honour, and in order to implore your protection that you would obtain for me, from the Giver of every good gift, that the last moments which remain of my failing years may be directed

Benedict XIII

solely to the greater glory of God, and to the salvation of my soul, and that I may not depart out of this life without being nourished by the Eucharistic Bread, which, as you eagerly desired it, you merited to receive in so extraordinary a manner; in order that each one, choosing you as protectress of the dying, may not set out on their journey towards eternity, unless accompanied by their Divine Redeemer in His Adorable Sacrament.

Clement XII

Turn also, O glorious virgin, your benevolent eyes on your beloved family the Falconieri, and guarding it from every untoward accident, be its shield and its protectress, supporting and increasing it for the love which it has shown in promoting your honour for the glory of God, by labouring here below on earth to make known what you are in heaven.

And above all things, may the welfare, the life, and the glory of the reigning Pontiff, Clement XII, who completed your canonization, and who, full of zeal and paternal love, governs the illustrious city of Rome and the whole Christian world, be dear to your heart; obtain of the Eternal God, whose sole and legitimate Vicar he is, that subduing all heresies, he may have the glory of gathering under one standard and into one fold the flock of Christ, part of which, distracted by the perversity of error, follows the path of perdition; and that in his time we may be able to say that the whole world is submissive to the Roman Catholic Faith, obeys one shepherd alone.

Saints of the Servite Order

A DEVOUT EXERCISE

In honour of S. Juliana Falconieri, foundress of the Tertiaries of the Order of the Servites of Mary, to be practised every Thursday, or any other more convenient day; and for seven days before her feast, on the 19th of June; that by the protection of this great Saint, our Lord Jesus Christ may give us the grace always to receive Him worthily in the most august Sacrament, and especially in our last illness before we die.

Antiphon. Veni Sancte Spiritus, reple tuorum corda fidelium, et tui amoris in eis ignem accende.
V. Emitte spiritum tuum et creabuntur.
R. Et renovabis faciem terrae.
V. Memento Congregationis tuae
R. Quam possedisti ab initio.
V. Domine exaudi orationem meam.
R. Et clamor meus ad te veniat

OREMUS.

Mentes nostras, quaesumus Domine, lumine tuae claritatis illustra, ut videre possimus quae agenda sunt, et quae recta sunt, agere valeamus. Per Christum Dominum nostrum. Amen.

FIRST PRAYER.

O S. Juliana, noble vanquisher of the world and all its vanities! full of confusion I humble myself in thy presence; and considering that thou didst never permit thyself to be deceived by the grandeurs and pleasures of earth, but with magnanimous and generous heart didst despise them, in order to consecrate thyself entirely to God amid the poverty and rigours of the religious state, I beseech thee to obtain for me a perfect knowledge of the frailty of these earthly things, that my heart may never be seduced by their vain appearance, and that I may neither love nor desire anything but the eternal goods of heaven.

Pater. Ave. Gloria.

SECOND PRAYER

O rare example of innocence preserved! when thou didst but hear the relation of a sin thou didst faint away through pure grief at the offence of God, and didst pray Him to consign thee to the terrible pains of hell rather than that thou shouldst commit one single sin. Ah! what confusion for me who have so often offended my God by grievous sins! Oh that I could die of sorrow for having committed them! But at least, blessed Saint, obtain for me a sincere repentance for my past faults, and the grace, which I ardently covet, never to commit them again.

Pater. Ave. Gloria.

THIRD PRAYER.

O pattern of the most heroic penance, who like a whitest lily amid the thorns didst shine forth with thine angelic purity amid the austerity of the most noted penitents of Christendom, I admire thee with all my heart. Oh let not my admiration be barren or unfruitful; but obtain for me the grace to imitate thee; if thou in all

thy innocence didst lead a life so austere and mortified, grant that I who am a miserable sinner may expiate my sins by the salutary rigours of Christian penance.
 Pater. Ave. Gloria.

FOURTH PRAYER.

 O worthy servant of the humble Handmaid of the Lord! who can fittingly extol thine heroic humility? It was not enough to have trodden underfoot the riches and honours of thine illustrious and wealthy family in order to assume the poor habit of the Servite Order which thou didst found in thy city of Florence; but how greatly and with what studied methods didst thou seek to despise thyself with that contempt wherein true humility consists! Mistress and Mother of all, thou wouldst have thy nuns behold thee on thy knees before them, supplicating to be received as a servant into their holy company. Thou didst love to call thyself the vilest and poorest of all, and as such didst exercise thyself in the most menial and fatiguing offices of the monastery. Ah, I feel how far I am from imitating thee! Oh by thy powerful intercession extinguish in me the spirit of pride, the sad source of all my failings, and grant that becoming meek and humble of heart I may be an imitator of thy rare virtues and worthy of the grace of my God.
 Pater. Ave. Gloria.

FIFTH PRAYER.

 O Lady, strong and prudent, who in faith and constancy of purpose didst undertake honourable and sublime enterprises, and with admirable discretion conduct them to a glorious end; to thy zeal and ardent charity the Third Order of the Servites of Mary owes its birth. To thy cares Florence in great measure owed its freedom from internal feuds and scandals, and the peace which flourished there for many a year. I pray thee grant that I too, according to my station, may seek as far as possible to imitate thee in the exercise of these holy virtues, and that by the aid of Divine grace I may resist my evil passions, and in all my undertakings keep in view the maxims of Christian wisdom.

SIXTH PRAYER.

O Seraphim of love, who didst live for no other end than to love thy God! on Him wert thou continually thinking, for Him wert thou languishing, and with Him didst thou pass entire days in sweet and loving ecstasy. "Ah, let no one take my Crucified Love out of my heart," were words which thou wert often heard impetuously to utter from thy burning charity. Oh what a motive of confusion and of grief for me, who have so little love for my God, my Creator, my most amiable Redeemer! Ah, my heavenly advocate, obtain for me this holy love, detach my heart from earth, that all its affections may turn to heaven for evermore.

Pater. Ave. Gloria.

SEVENTH PRAYER

O S. Juliana, how beautiful was the death that thou didst die! At the news that thou wert to leave this world, thou wert filled with an unwonted mirth, and all joyous and jubilant thou didst hasten by thy desires the longed-for moment of passing to the sweet embraces of thy Divine Spouse. Hindered by the excessive weakness of thy stomach from receiving Him in the Holy Viaticum, thou wert penetrated with extreme sorrow, and weeping and sighing didst entreat at least to adore Him in the Sacred Host, and, still not content, thou didst implore to have Him laid upon thy breast, that by the nearness of Jesus, thy heart, all on fire with love, might be consoled. God, who willed the miracle, inspired His priest to second thy desires, and

scarcely had the Holy Host touched thy virginal breast when It disappeared, and sweetly smiling thou didst breathe out thy soul in the kiss of the Lord. O great Saint, my special protectress, obtain for me, I beseech thee, the grace of a happy death. Assist me in life that I may not sin; and assist me in the hour of my death that I may end my days holily fortified by the blessed Sacraments of the Church, and so may die in the grace of God and be preserved from death eternal.
Pater. Ave. Gloria.

HYMN.

Coelestis Agni nuptias
O Juliana dum petis,
Domum paternam deseris,
Chorumque ducis Virginum.

Sponsumque suffixum Cruci
Noctes, diesque dum gemis
Doloris icta cuspide
Sponsi refers imaginem.

Quin septiformi vulnere
Fles ad genu Deiparae
Sed crescit infusa fletu
Flammasque tollit charitas

Hinc morte fessam proxima
Non usitato te modo
Solatur, et nutrit Deus,
Dapem supernam porrigens.

Aeterne rerum Conditor
Aeterne Fili par Patri

Et par utrique Spiritus
Soli tibi sit gloria. Amen.

V Ora pro nobis Beata Juliana.
R. Ut digni efficiamur promissionibus Christi.

OREMUS.

Deus qui Beatam Julianam Virginem tuam extremo morbo laborantem, pretioso Filii tui Corpora mirabiliter recreare dignatus es; concede quaesumus, ut ejus intercedentibus meritis, nos quoque eodem in mortis agone refecti ac roborati, ad caelestem Patriam perducamur. Per Dominum nostrum Jesum Christum Filium tuum, qui tecum vivit et regnat in unitate Spiritus Sancti Deus per omnia saecula saeculorum. Amen.

V. Nos cum prole pis.
R. Benedicat Virgo Maria.

HYMN:

O JULIANA, thou dost claim
The nuptials of the heavenly Lamb,
Whilst thou thy fathers house forsake,
And care of virgins undertake.

And whilst with deepest sorrows pierc'd
By day nor night thy groans ne'er ceas'd
For thy dear Spouse nail'd on a tree,
His sacred image was in thee.

But wounded seven-fold thou dost weep,
And at God's mother's feet doth keep;
Whilst tears thy ardent love proclaim'd,
Thy tender heart is all inflam'd.

And hence when painful death drew near,
God took of thee unusual care;
His sacred body he bestows,
And puts an end to all thy woes.

To God the Father and the Son,
And holy Spirit, three in one,
Be endless glory as before
The world began, so evermore. Amen.

V. In thy comeliness and beauty.
R Go on, proceed prosperously, and reign.

V. Grace is spread upon thy lips.
R. Therefore hath God blessed thee for ever.

Come, spouse of Christ, receive the eternal crown, which the Lord hath prepared for thee.

O GOD, who didst wonderfully refresh Blessed Juliana, thy Virgin in her last moments, with thy Son's precious body, mercifully grant, through her merits, that we also, at the hour of death, may be so refreshed and strengthened therewith, as to be brought to our heavenly country.

THE END.

*In religious life
a man lives more purely.
Falls more rarely.
Rises more promptly,
Walks more circumspectly,
Receives the waters of grace
more frequently
Reposes more securely,
Dies more confidently,
Is cleansed from his faults
more quickly,
And in Heaven receives
a more magnificent reward.
—St. Bernard of Clairvaux*

IMAGE INDEX

I. THE LIFE OF S. ROSE BY FEUILLET

In the image citations for *The Life of St. Rose* by Feuillet the Arca listing refers to "Arte Colonial Americano- Universidad de los Andes. Proyeto ARCA Cultura visual de las Americas http://artecolonialamericano.az.uniandes.edu.co:8080/." Searching "Santa Rosa de Lima" on that site will bring up 280 images of S. Rose which is a large proportion but by no means all of the art which her life inspired in the 17th and 18th c. She evidently had as great an impact on that era as S. Therese on ours. She is patroness of the Americas, and one could fairly say, too, our S. Catherine of Siena.

Page II. St Catherine of Siena, "According to Augusta Drane, in *The History of St. Catherine of Siena and Her Companions* (1899), vol. 1, p. 184: "'Two likenesses exist of St. Catherine of Siena: one is the celebrated painting by Andrea di Vanni . . . the other is the almost equally celebrated marble bust which claims to be the work of Jacobo della Quercia, and to have been carved by him from a cast taken after her death.' The bust is on display in the church of San Domenico, Siena. (photo by Fra Mario Di Marco, OP)" http://50.63.119.146/Bust.htm

Page XIII. La Merced. Michael A. Fuentes, *Lima, Sketches of the Capital of Peru* (Paris: Firmin, 1866). The church and convent of La Merced were built in 1534 by Hernando Pizarro, brother to the Conqueror, and cost 700,000 piastres. The church has twenty-three altars." Fuentes, *Sketches,*24. The other churches of Lima were similarly furnished with many altars, no doubt to accomodate the private Masses of the many priests who resided n Lima. S. Rose frequented these and other churches of the city.

Page XIV. Dominican shield: in Domingo Augulo, O. P., del Instituto histórico del Peru. *Santa Rosa de Santa Maria, Estudio bibliográfico* (Lima: Sanmarti y cia, 1917), title page.

Page XIX. Harquebusier."The harquebusier was the most common form of cavalry found throughout Western Europe during the early and mid 17th century. Early harquebusiers were characterised by

IMAGE INDEX

the use of a form of carbine, called a "harquebus." Image and text from Wikipedia.

Page XXI. Decorative title page: Fuentes, *Lima,*

Page XXII. Nacimiento de la Santa Rosa de Lima, Basilio Pacheco, Actividad1738 - 1752

Page 3. The Baptism of St. Rose. The ARCA listing: "Bautizo de Santa Rosa de LimaAnónimo, Fecha: 1700-1799"; http://52.183.37.55/artworks/2654

Page 6. Cathedral, Fuentes, *Sketches,* 16.

Page 13. Church of San Sebastian. "Built in 1544, its construction is attributed to Francisco Becerra, was the first parish of Lima, and here saints and illustrious Peruvians were baptized as was Santa Rosa de Lima, San Martin de Porres, José Santos Chocano. Francisco Bolognesi, among others. "(https://www.go2peru.com/peru_guide/lima/religious_monuments.htm) The photo is from https://jpelsous.tumblr.com/post/168044205413/iglesia-parroquial-de-san-sebasti%C3%A1n-ss.

Page 15. St. Rose refuses a suitor: ARCA listing: "Santa Rosa de Lima rechaza un pretendiente; Anónimo, Fecha: 1700-1799."http://artecolonialamericano.az.uniandes.edu.co:8080/artworks/7540.

Page 17. S. Turibius, Wikimedia Commons.

Page 19. St. Rose takes the habit: ARCA listing: "Serie de la Vida de Santa Rosa de Lima, S. Rosa toma el hábito de terciaria; Anónimo, Fecha: 1600-1699."

Page 20. Dominic in Penitence, by Luis Tristán c. 1610-1624: Santo Domingo penitente https://commons.wikimedia.org/wiki/File:Luis_Trist%C3%A1n_-_St_Dominic_in_Penitence_-_Google_Art_Project.jpg.

Page 24. Church of St. Augustine, Fuentes, Sketches, 24. Fuentes writes: "San Agustin. — This church was built in 1554. Archbishop Loaiza laid the first stone, and the whole of the cost was defrayed by Hernan Gonzales de la Torre and his wife Donna Juana Cepeda. The church has sixteen altars."

Page 26. An indian woman. Fuentes, Sketches, ,202.

Page 28. S. Rose Takes the Discipline: "Santa Rosa en actitud penitente" in Carlos Page, "La vida de Santa Rosa de Lima en los lienzos del convento de Santa Catalina de Córdoba (Argentina)." https://www.academia.edu/22876718/La_vida_de_Santa_Rosa_de_Lima_en_los_lienzos_del_convento_de_Santa_Catalina_de_C%C3%B3rdoba_Argentina.

Page 31. Indian with bundles, *Sketches,* 95.

Page 33. Apotheosis of St. Rose.

Page 35. Horse drawn carriage, *Sketches, 1*50

Page 36. Bridge over the Rimac, the river that divides Lima. Fuentes, *Sketches*, 10.

Page 39. Indian woman with baby, Fuentes, *Sketches,* 172.

Page 40. St. Rose sewing; ARCA lisitng: "Santa Rosa de Lima bordando; Anónimo,Fecha: 1700-1799." http://52.183.37.55/artworks/7824.

Page 43. A pescadora (fish monger), Fuentes, *Sketches*, 155.

Page 45. Rose with hair nailed to wall: "*Santa Rosa de Lima penitente*; Autoría desconocida." http://artecolonialamericano.az.uniandes.edu.co:8080/artworks/2656.

Page 47. Map of Lima: Carolina Salazar Marulanda, *Plaza Fundacional En El Siglo xx* (Bogotá, Colombia: Universidad Nacional de Colombia, 2012), 177.

Page 51. S. Rose 's friendship with mosquitos: Page, *La Vida*. "*La amistad de Santa Rosa con los mosquitos.* Monasterio de Santa Catalina de Siena en Córdoba, Argentina" in Carlos Page, *La Vida*.

Page 52. *The Espousal*: Nicolás Correa (ca. 1660 - ca. 1720) - The Mystic Betrothal of Saint Rose of Lima. https://commons.wikimedia.org/wiki/File:Nicol%C3%A1s_Correa_-_The_Mystic_Betrothal_of_Saint_Rose_of_Lima_-_Google_Art_Project.jpg

Page 54. St. Rose's Vision of Paradise: ARCA listing: "Vision del paraiso de Santa Rosa de Lima, Anonimo, Fecha 1700-1799; artecolonialamericano.az.uniandes.edu.co:8080/artworks/2640"

Page 56. Dominican Tryptch by Gregorio De Ferrari, with S. Rose, S. Vincent Ferrer, and S. Louis Beltran, in the Convento di San Domenico (Taggia). Foto by Carlo Dell'Orto at https://commons.wikimedia.org/wiki/File:Gregorio_de_ferrari,_i_ss._rosa_da_lima,_vincenzo_ferrer_e_luigi_bertr%C3%A0n,_San_Domenico_(Taggia).jpg.

Page 58. A Franciscan. Fuentes, *Sketches*, p. 26.

Page 63. The Virgin with S. Rose and S. Dominic: La vierge avec l'enfant remettant un rosaire à saint Dominique en présence de saint Rose de Lima, patronne des Amériques by Onorio Marinari. https://commons.wikimedia.org/wiki/File:Onorio_Marinari_La_Vierge_avec_l%27Enfant.jpg

Page 64. S. Rose collects water from a fountain; Santa Rosa recoge agua de una fuente. Monasterio de Santa Catalina de Siena en Córdoba, Argentina in Carlos Page, "La Vida."

Page 69. Rose before the Inquisitors; ARCA listing: Santa Rosa de

Lima ante los inquisidores. Laureano Dávila, Fecha: 1700-1799, http://52.183.37.55/artworks/388

Page 70. A nun. Fuentes, *Sketches*, p. 31.

Page 72. Noble lady. Fuentes, Sketches, 103

Page 75. S. Rose drinks from the side of Christ: Cristo le da de beber a Rosa sangre de su costado abierto. Lienzo de Cristóbal de Villalpando en el retablo de Santa Rosa de Lima, ca. 1702. Parroquia de los Santos Apóstoles Felipe y Santiago, Azcapotzalco, Ciudad de México. http://books.openedition.org/cemca/docannexe/image/2318/img-8.jpg

Page 79. S. Rose with infant by Bartolomé Esteban Murillo 1617-1682. https://www.wikiart.org/en/bartolome-esteban-murillo/st-rose-of-lima

Page 82. S. Catherine of Siena; Robert Staes, O.P. http://www.domcentral.org/library/BobStaes/index.html

Page 85. Figure from Fuentes, *Sketches*

Page 88. Holy card.

Page 91. Lady cooking, "Indian picantera": Fuentes, *Sketches*, 126.

Page 92. A mansion in Lima, Fuentes, *Sketches*, 9.

Page 95. Woman on horse, Sketches, 151.

Page 97. ARCA listing: Serie de la Vida de Santa Rosa de Lima, S. Rosa envía un ángel de la guarda; Anónimo, Fecha: 1600-1699.

Page 99. ARCA listing: Defensa de la Eucaristía con Santa Rosa de Lima, 01 Anónimo,Fecha: 1650-1699

Page 104. A priest. Fuentes, *Sketches,* 32.

Page 106. ARCA listing: Bodas místicas de Santa Rosa de Lima, Juan-Tinoco, Fecha: 1680

Page 111. The Viceroy.Luis de Velasco, 1st Marquess of Salinas (known as Luis de Velasco, hijo to distinguish him from his father) (c. 1534, Carrión de los Condes, Spain – September 7, 1617, Seville), was a Spanish nobleman, son of the second viceroy of New Spain, and himself the eighth viceroy. He governed from January 27, 1590 to November 4, 1595, and again from July 2, 1607, to June 10, 1611. In between he was viceroy of Peru for eight years (July 24, 1596, to January 18, 1604).

Page 112. S. Catherine:"The famous fresco of Catherine of Siena by Andrea di Vanni, one of her many disciples. Vanni, besides being a well-known painter, was also a politician. According to tradition, he painted the fresco on one of the pillars in the Capella delle Volte ("Chapel of the Veils"), where Catherine and the other Mantellate prayed in the church of San Domenico in Siena. Later, the fresco was placed above the altar in the same chapel where it can be seen today." From www.drawnbylove.com http://www.drawnbylove.com/Vanni%20portrait%20of%20Catherine.htm

Page 114. Bunuelera (fritter-woman). Fuentes, *Sketches,*

Page 115. Indian woman with pots, Fuentes, *Sketches*, 199

Page 116. Woman with vase. Fuentes, *Sketches,198*

Page 117. Mulatress, Fuentes, Sketches, 81

Page 118. Servant woman praying, Fuentes, *Sketches*, 78

Page 119. Indian woman with braided hair, Fuentes, *Sketches*, 92

Page 122. S. Rose as nurse; ARCA listing: Santa Rosa de Lima enfermera, Anónimo, Fecha: 1700-1799.

Page 124. Misturera (flower-girl) of the Arcades. Fuentes, *Sketches*, 219.

Page 127. Saint Rose of Lima praying in the Hermitage: ARCA listing: Santa Rosa de Lima rezando en la Ermita, Francisco Martínez, Fecha: 1740-1770.

Page 129. Melon hawker of Lima. Fuentes, *Sketches,*201.

Page 130. Kneeling nun, Fuentes, *Sketches*, 33.

Page 133. S. Rose with noble lady in garden: ARCA listing: Los árboles se inclinan ante Santa Rosa de Lima, Laureano Dávila, Fecha: 1700-1799. http://52.183.37.55/artworks/386.

Page 135. A nun. Fuentes, Sketches, 34.

Page 136. The Acho Promenade, Fuentes, Sketches, 71.

Page 139. Death bed scene: Muerte de Santa Rosa de Lima. Lienzo atribuido a Angelino Medoro. Basílica Santuario de Santa Rosa, Lima.http://books.openedition.org/cemca/docannexe/image/2318/img-14.jpg.

Page 145. "Retrato auténtico de Sta Rosa de Lima, original de Angellno Medoro.—1617. (Santuario de Sta. Rosa)" in Augulo, *Estudio*, 11. Given that S. Rose died in 1617, that her eyes are closed, and that she would have been resistant to portaits, presumably this portrait was done post-mortem.Page 148. Sculpture: Tránsito de Santa Rosa. Escultura en mármol de Melchor Caffá, 1665. Iglesia de Santo Domingo, Lima. http://books.openedition.org/cemca/docannexe/image/2318/img-17.jpg.

Page 151. Dominicans carry her body; ARCA listing: Serie de la Vida de Santa Rosa de Lima, Funerales de S. Rosa, Anónimo, Fecha: 1600-1699. http://artecolonialamericano.az.uniandes.edu.co:8080/artworks/4694.

Page 155. Entierro de Rosa. Grabado de Cornelis Galle. En Juan del Valle, Vita et historia S. Rosae As. Maria, Amberes, primera mitad del s. xvii.http://books.openedition.org/cemca/docannexe/image/2318/img-15.jpg.
Page 158. Rose gazing upward at infant. Claudio Coello (1642–1693).
Page 161. French holy card.
Page 164. ARCA listing: Santo Domingo por intermedio de la Virgen presenta a Santa Rosa de Lima ante la corte celestial, Angelino Medoro, Fecha: 1700-1799
http://52.183.37.55/artworks/2643.
Page 172. Rose of Lima and Pope Pius V by Giovanni Ceffi - Mazzoleni Altar - Sant'Anastasia - Verona.
Page 178. ARCA listing: Santa Rosa de Lima coronada por el niño Jesús, Gregorio Vásquez de Arce y Ceballos, Fecha: 1650-1700. http://artecolonialamericano.az.uniandes.edu.co:8080/artworks/16156.
Page 182. ARCA listing: Santa Rosa de Lima y el milagro de los claveles, Anónimo, Fecha: 1700-1799. http://artecolonialamericano.az.uniandes.edu.co:8080/artworks/7658.
Page 189. S. Rose holy card.
Page 191. S. Rose holy card.
Page 194-195. Popes from Wikipedia.
Page 196. Holy card with dates.
Page 197. "Fin," Fuentes, *Sketches*, 220.

II. THE LIFE OF BLESSED COLOMBA BY DEGLI ANGELI

Page 198. Holy Card.
Page 199 Dominican Shield.
Page 200. Holy Card.
Page 206. Ornament.
Page 212. Ornament.
Page 220. Painting. Colomba holding lily. "Da un quadro del Perugino, esistente in S. Domenico di Perugia."
Page 226. Holy Card.
Page 231. Painting. S. Colomba. Before altar w/ skull . Artist:Workshop of the Cabrera brothers, with the cooperation of Antonio and Manuel Palacios. Title:Saint Columba of Rieti, Date 1837-1841.
Page 234. painting.

Page 238. Dove ornament. Miller & Richard (Firm). *Printing Type Specimens: Comprising a Large Variety of Book And Jobbing Faces, Borders And Ornaments* (Edinburgh, 1921), 474.

Page 248. Ornament.   Miller, *Printing.*

Page 253. Painting. S. Colomba holding dove.

Page 261. Ornament., Miller, *Printing.*

Page 268. Ornament, Miller, *Printing..*

Page 273. Ornament, Miller, *Printing.*

Page 274. Charles VIII. Wikipedia

Page 275. Alexander VI. Wikipedia

Page 276. Cesare Borgia. Wikipedia

Page 277. Pius III. Wikipedia

Page 279. Painting of Christ carrying cross, taken from her cell. "Un giorno la B. Colomba desiderava di vedere il ruo Sposo celeste. Ge*ù le apparve su di una tela, incamminato al Calvario. Cosi rimase impresso su quella tela, ehe ancora si conserva dalle sne figlie a Perugia." *Il Rosario.* Vol 18. (Ferrara: San Domenico) 275. " One day the B. Colomba wished to see her celestial Spouse. Jesus appeared to her on a canvas, on his way to Calvary. Thus it remained imprinted on that canvas, which is still preserved by its daughters in Perugia,.."

Page 285 Fish Ornament: George Bickham , The Universal Penman, (London: Robert Sayer, 1760), 111.

Page 288. Lucreza Borgia. Wikipedia.

Page 291. Dom. Orn. Bickham, Penman, 111.

Page 299. Ornament. Miller, Printing.

Page 306. Dove ornament. Miller, Printing.

Page 309. Ornament. Miller, Printing.

Page 310. Ercole d'Este. Wikipedia.

Page 311. Bl. Osanna. Wikipedia.

Page 313. S. Pius V. Wikipedia.

Page 316. Painting Colomba kneeling. *Comunione mistica della beata Colomba* from Il Monastero delle Domenicane di Sant'Agnese a Rieti

Page 318. Historical marker.

Page 319. Colomba's monastery.

La Cella della Beata Colomba si trova all'interno del Monastero della Beata Colomba. Esso si trova nell'edificio dell'ex Conservatorio della Carità in zona Porta Sant'Angelo a Perugia.

Il monastero ospita la ricostruzione dell'originaria cella della Beata Colomba come si trovava nell'antico monastero accanto alla chiesa di San Domenico, dove visse e morì. L'interno della cella è completamente in legno, con suppellettili e reliquie originali.

Al suo interno vengono conservati svariati oggetti sacri e non tra cui: il dipinto con il Cristo "portacroce" di autore sconosciuto, una tavola con l'immagine della Beata, ex voto sulle pareti, un Monte Calvario in cartapesta, degli oggetti appartenuti alla Beata Colomba come un asciugamano, un tovagliolo, una mantello, una camicia e altro, e il reliquiario contenente la parte superiore del cranio della Beata conservato su un piccolo altare. http://www.viaggispirituali.it/2011/07/cella-della-beata-colomba-perugia/

The Cell of the Beata Colomba is located inside the Monastery of the Beata Colomba. It is located in the building of the former Conservatory of Charity in the Porta Sant'Angelo area of Perugia.

The monastery houses the reconstruction of the original cell of the Blessed Colomba as it was in the ancient monastery next to the church of San Domenico, where she lived and died. The interior of the cell is completely made of wood, with original furnishings and relics.

Inside are preserved various sacred and non-sacred objects including: the painting with the Christ carrying the cross by an unknown author, a table with the image of the Blessed, ex voto on the walls, a Monte Calvario in papier-mâché, some objects that belonged to the Blessed Dove as a towel, a napkin, a cloak, a shirt and more, and the reliquary containing the upper part of the skull of the Blessed preserved on a small altar.

Page 325. Cosimo Ulivelli. Beata Colomba da Rieti, Florence, San Marco. From the site ICONOGRAPHIE CHRÉTIENNE, http://har22201.blogspot.com/2015/05/blog-post.html

Page 331. Dove flourish. Bickham, Penman, 111.

III. THE LIFE OF S. JULIANA BY LORENZINI

Page 332 Frontispiece: Francesco Lorenzini, Vita di S. Giuliana Falconieri fiorentina, fondatrice del Terz'ordine de' servi detto delle Mantellate. (Roma : Stamperia del Komarek, 1738).

Page 333. Servite Shield

Page 334. Painting The Seven Holy Founders, from Servidimaria, http://servidimaria.net/sitoosm/it/storia.html

Page 337. Bl. Alessio, from Servidimaria, http://servidimaria.net/sitoosm/it/storia.html

Page 338. Santissima Annunziata, Florence.

Page 341. S. Philip Benizi: Santa Maria dei Servi (Padua) - Altare dell'Addolorata - Philip Benizi de Damiani sculpted by Giovanni Bonazza.

Page 343. Death of Blessed Alessio:Bernardino Poccetti, A Monk on His Deathbed;Alternative title:Study for the Blessed Alessio Falconieri, The Death of Saint Alexis Falconieri at Monte Senari, Preparatory drawing for the Blessed Alessio Falconieri painted in fresco in a lunette of the Chiostro Grande (Chiostro dei Morti) at SS Annunziata, Florence (1604–1612). https://collectiononline.fondationcustodia.fr/bronnen/drawings/detail/380e92f4-4cff-6ae9-9a4a-1c5cac3a1dcf

Page 344. Our Lady of Sorrows.

Page 346. S. Giuliana in Santa Maria dei Servi (Padua) with S. Philip flanking the Altare dell'Addolorata, sculpted by Giovanni Bonazza.

Page 349. Holy Card

Page 351. Holy card. The papal tiara to one side is a symbol of S. Philip having refused the papacy..

Page 352. Another vestizione.

Page 355. Benedict XIV. Ritratto di Benedetto XIV - Papa Lambertini, Fondazione Cassa di Risparmio in Bologna, Genus bononiae, Musei di Citta:BRI 00431; BRI 00644. (1675-758)https://collezioni.genusbononiae.it/products/dettaglio/804

Page 359 Holy Card

Page 363. Holy Card.

Page 366. Holy Card

Page 368.. Holy Card.

Page 371. Paintng, Anonimo romano sec. XVIII, Morte di santa Giuliana. Fondazione Federico Zeri. Universita di Bologna. Entry 61912 Falconieri. http://catalogo.fondazionezeri.unibo.it/ricerca.v2.jsp?locale=en&decorator=layout_resp&apply=true&percorso_ricerca=OA&filtroaat_OA=8049&sortby=LOCALIZZAZIONE&batch=10

Page 372. Juliana in state. "L'altare con le spoglie di Giuliana Falconieri nella Santissima Annunziata di Firenze" https://it.m.wikipedia.org/wiki/Giuliana_Falconieri.

Page 374. Holy card.

Page 386. Holy card.

Page 388. Gonzaga. Wikipedia.

Page 391. Clement XI. Wikipedia.
Page 391. Benedict XIII. Wikipedia.
Page 392. Clement XII. Wikipedia.
Page 393. From the Facebook page of St. Peregrine Laziosi Parish & Diocesan Shrine https://www.facebook.com/stperegrine.ph/posts/2170903249595953
Page 411. By Robert Staes, O.P. http://www.domcentral.org/library/BobStaes/index.html

Saints Rose, Martin and Turibius

Convinced that we Catholics of the 21st century are losing contact with the glories of our past, Arthur M. Gilbert and Son is dedicated to re-covering, re-typesetting and re-issuing classic books in an affordable and beautiful format. So much saintly literature and lives of the saints are in fact in print, but machine read, speed copied and priced outrageously. We, on the other hand, are producing high quality books copiously illustrated and eminently affordable.

THE REAL DE RANCÉ

ILLUSTRIOUS PENITENT AND REFORMER OF NOTRE DAME DE LA TRAPPE

AILBE LUDDY

Penitent Priest

The Abbè de Rancè was a penitent priest and saintly founder of the Trappists (reformed Cistercians) in late 17th c. France. His strict interpretation of the Rule of St. Benedict re-invigorated the Cistercian order of his day, an order which in its time had been salt and light for all of Christendom. Founded in 1098, within decades the Cistercian order had populated all of Europe with hundreds of fervent monasteries, but by Rance's time had fallen into mediocrity and disorder. While his reforms restored his abbey and attracted ardent candidates from all over France, his interpretation of the Rule of St. Benedict was very controversial in his time and in ours as well. By now practically all that the Cistercians keep of the Trappist charism is the name, and both de Rancè and his writings are hardly known among them.

Surely this is due in part to the odium that Henri Bremond, S.J. poured on him in his book *Tempetè* (published as *The Thundering Abbot* by Sheed and Ward in 1930). In *The Real de Rancè* Fr. Ailbe Luddy, a Trappist of Mount Melleray Abbey in Cappoquin, Ireland, responds to Bremond and thoroughly rehabilitates the reputation of this saintly abbot. He supplies abundant motives for both religious and lay to hearken once again to the wisdom of de Rancè

Order on Amazon!

Again we have RANCÉ in print:

DE LA SAINTETÉ ET DES DEVOIRS DE LA VIE MONASTIQUE

by the **Abbé Armand-Jean de Rancé** was translated and titled

ON THE SANCTITY AND THE DUTIES OF THE MONASTIC STATE

by Dom Vincent Ryan of Mount Melleray Abbey in **1830**.

NOW AS

BACK TO ACETICISM: THE TRAPPIST OPTION

An edition of 650 pages in two volumes, Dom Ryan's translation, has been **re-typeset, re-titled, edited, updated, annotated, and its many citations corrected and amplified.** Also, we have supplied it with **52 illustrations** together with an **Image Index** and an **Index of Scriptural Citations.**

To foster its wide circulation and **the speedy recovery of monasticism** it is **currently** available to you on **Amazon** at **far less cost** than comparable books.

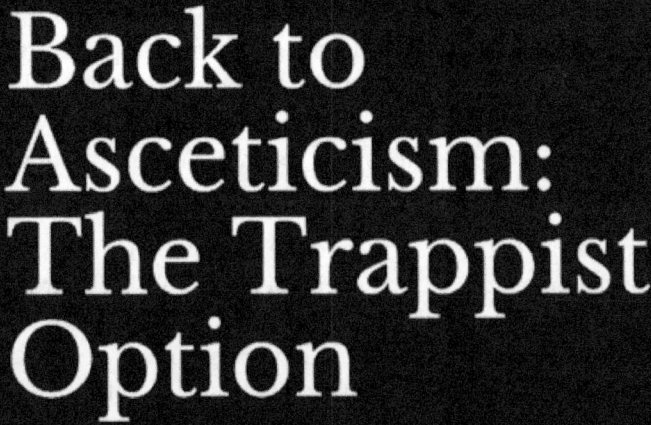

Order your copy today!

Praise for Rancé's *De la Saintete*

"His *De la Saintete* is unquestionably one of the most important works of post-medieval Cistercian writing and occupies a major place in the history of spirituality."
DAVID N. BELL, author of *Everyday Life at La Trappe Under Armand-Jean Rancé, Understanding Rancé*

"This work, treating of the sanctity and the duties of the monastic life, contains a doctrine accurately derived from Holy Scripture and the tradition of saints. The reading of it will discover to monks the obligations and the perfection of the angelic state to which they have been called. It will prove not less profitable to people in the world by making them understand, from the austerities and the humiliations practiced in the cloister, how great is the corruption in which we live, how deeply the poison has penetrated our hearts, and how violent and incessant must be our efforts against ourselves if we hope not merely to prevent the growth of vicious habits but to pluck them up by the roots."
JACQUES-BÉNIGNE LIGNEL BOSSUET, Bishop of Meaux (1681-1704

It used to be said formerly that one should have lived like St. John Climachus so as to be able to compose his divine *Ladder of Perfection*. The same can be said of the author of this book. Five years ago I had the consolation both to hear from his lips and to see put in practice the grand and holy maxims which are contained in his volume, so that what is written in these pages is but the expression of his thoughts and actions. I have read the work attentively. Everything in it, as far as I can judge, is calculated to edify, and full of the Spirit of God. The sentiments are noble and elevated, and on the whole, gives one a sublime conception of the religious life."
ETIENNE LE CAMUS, The Bishop of Grenoble (1681-1707) and Cardinal

No book within the memory of man has won for itself greater esteem at court, amongst the people, in the upper circles of society. But that would be little, if it had not at the same time produced inestimable fruits of virtue whereof I am myself a witness."
OLIVIER LEFÈVRE D'ORMESSON: magistrate and associate of Madame de Sévigné , Racine , Boileau , La Fontaine , Bossuet , Bourdaloue.

As to the results of its publication Bossuet wrote to de Rancé "The book has produced all the good effects I had anticipated. It has done great good everywhere. You ought to give thanks to God for giving you so happy an inspiration."
"

www.ingramcontent.com/pod-product-compliance
Lightning Source LLC
Chambersburg PA
CBHW071223230426
43668CB00011B/1281